ART DOCUMENTS 01

VASUDHA THOZHUR

Diaries, Projects, Pedagogy

1998–2018

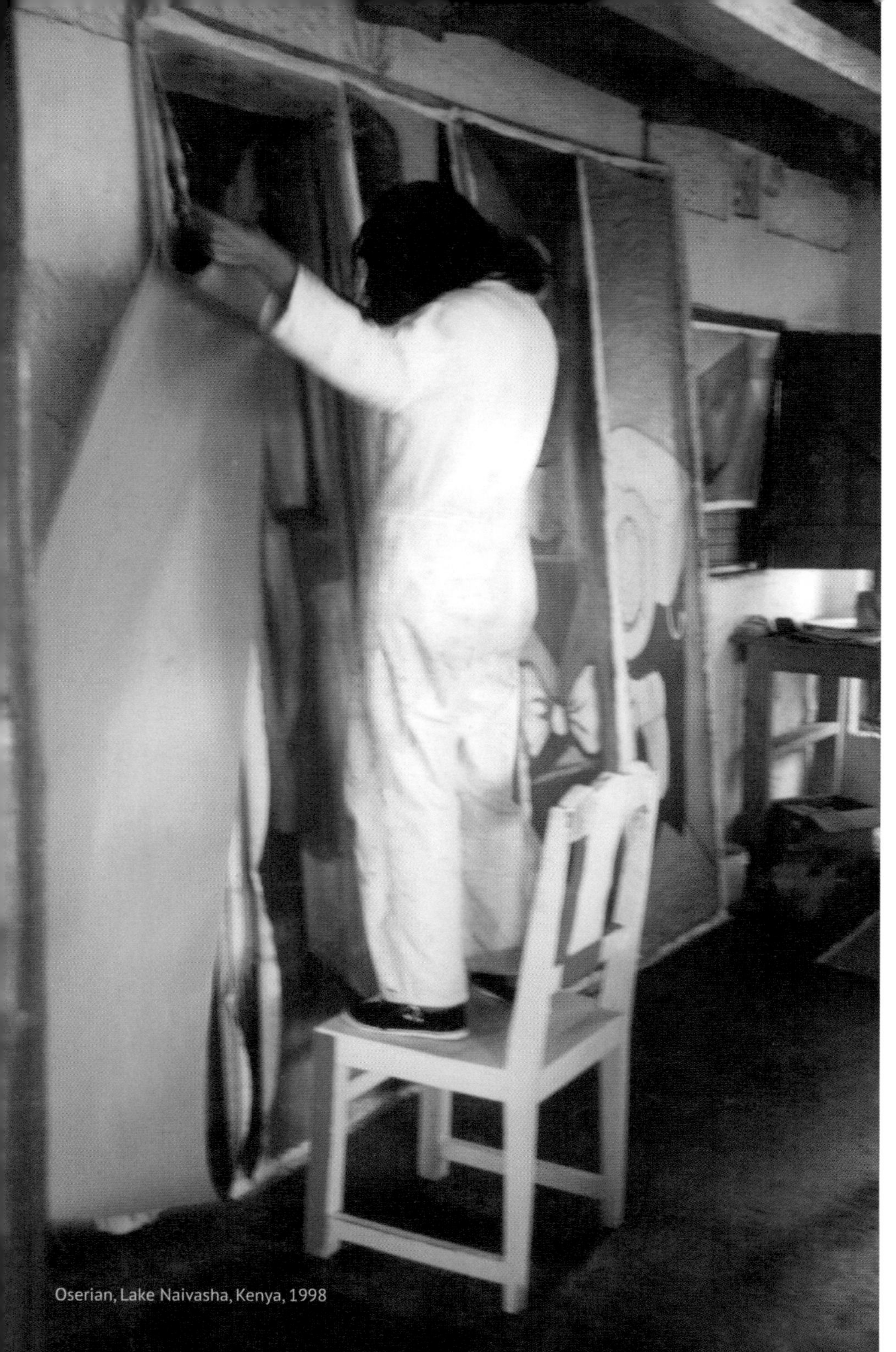

Oserian, Lake Naivasha, Kenya, 1998

VASUDHA THOZHUR

Diaries, Projects, Pedagogy
1998–2018

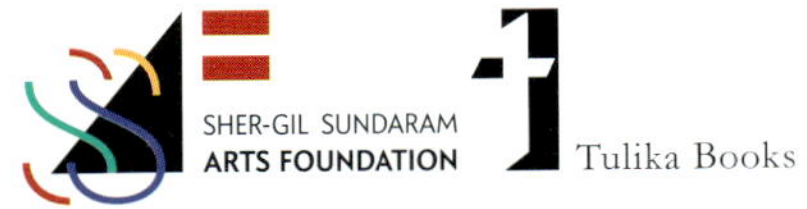

Art Documents, under the SSAF–Tulika Books imprint, is conceived as a series of montaged text and image documents, at once archival, contemporary and contextual. Creatively introduced and edited, these books seek to present multivalent forms of discourse where there is no single thesis, and no necessary convergence of the vectors released in the process of inquiry.

The series, as contemplated and set apace, includes a book based on an artist's self-reflexive journals and pedagogical texts. And another on an artist's interventionist projects that take wing across myriad terrains: from political activism to perilous journeys. A further two books signal the imminent threat artists perceive in present-day India: one performing the corporeal anguish of an indefatigable dissenter; another indicting through raging forms the violence perpetrated by the state.

The series will engage with filmmakers' incursions into history: their processing of the narrative form through an archival dig, and of the *mise-en-scène* as locus for uncanny renderings of the contemporary. There will be books that are specific to the art object: say, a bare apparatus installed to give pause to techno escalations – an anachronism within lens-based practice that offers the poignancy of a perceptual blur.

The series will also traverse recurring sites of struggles: the activism of feminist collectives that have generated theatrical forms and radical iconographies; the contours of student protests within and beyond institutional mandates; artists' research on soil, environment and sustenance framed by struggles within India's rural economy. It will investigate the ethics of representation in cultural manifestations of caste and labour, and address issues of social justice articulated through art practice, critical inquiry and forms of resistance.

These are some ideas in process; others will unfold over the years.

Geeta Kapur
Series Editor, Art Documents

CONTENTS

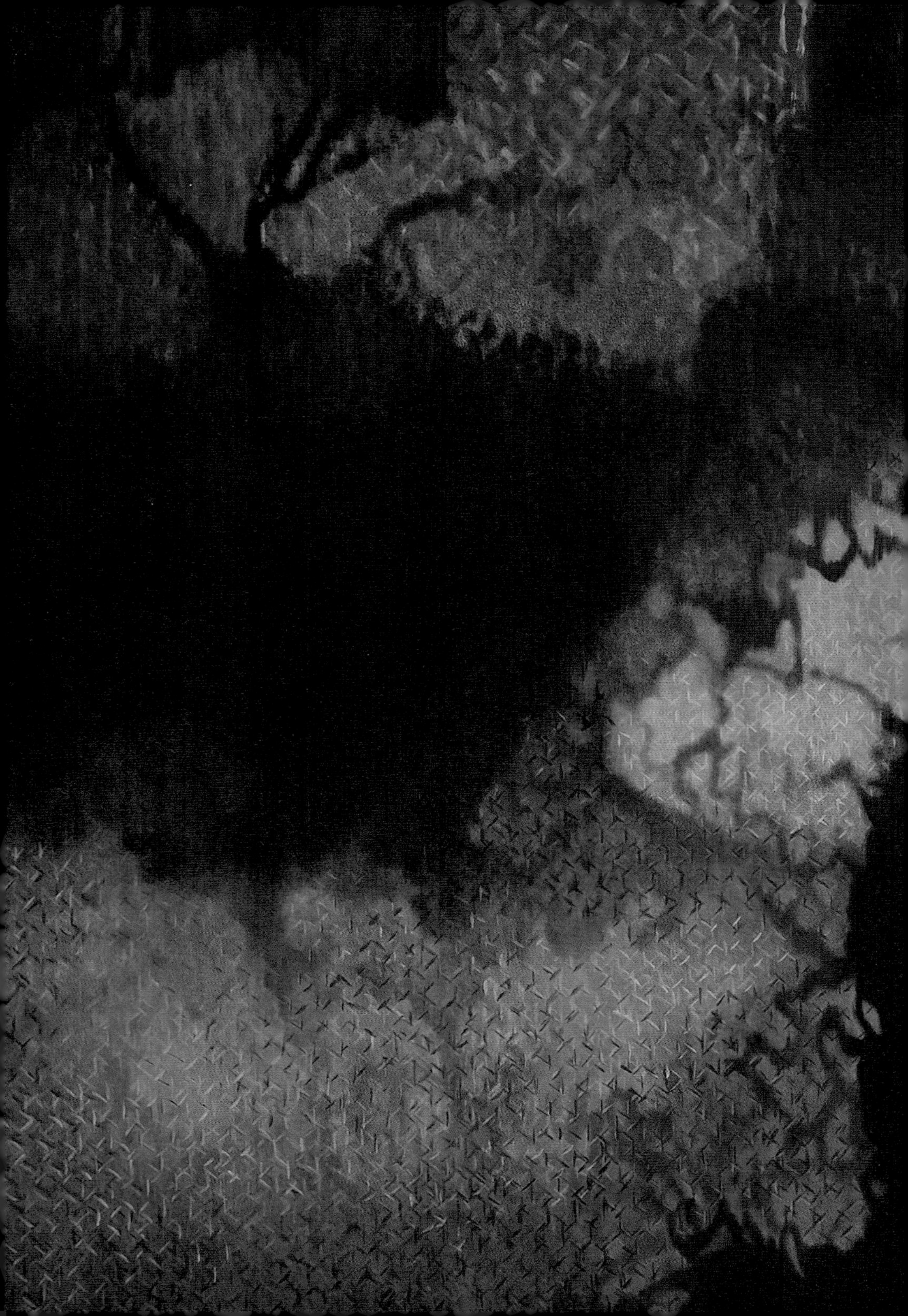

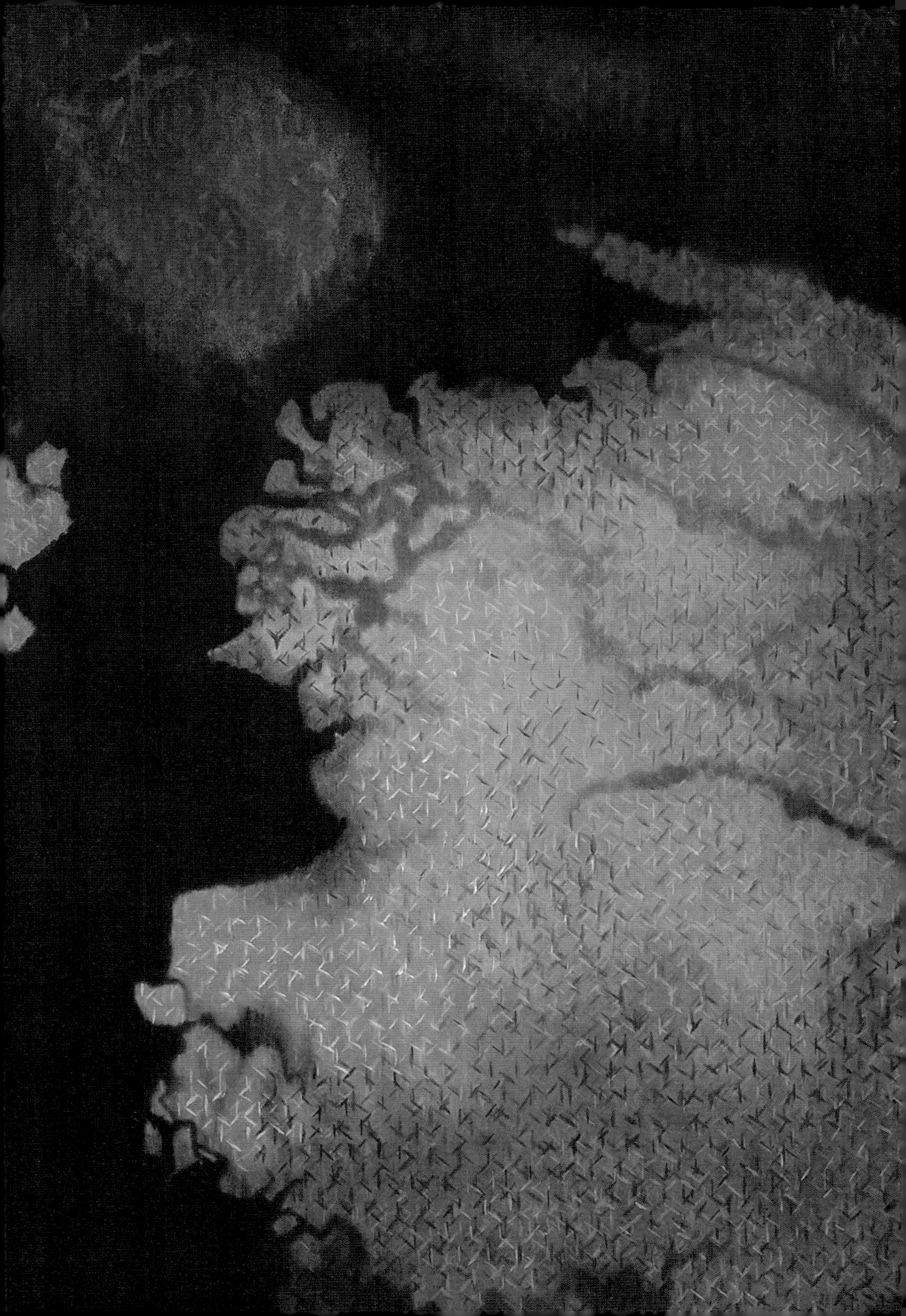

SECTION ONE

pages 6–7
Landscape I (detail), 2008

THE VOICE PROJECT: AN AUTOBIOGRAPHY IN FRAGMENTS

My first entry this year, Brecht on acting.

So you should simply make the instant
Stand out, without in the process hiding What you are making it stand out from.
Give your acting
That progression of one-thing-after-another,
That attitude of Working up what you have taken on. In this way You will show
the flow of events and also the course

Of your work, permitting the spectator

To experience this Now on many levels, coming from Previously and Merging into
Afterwards, also having much else Now alongside it. He is sitting not only
In your theatre but also
In the world.

17. 2. 1998 / Baroda

Things already envisioned die before conception, physically, that is.

Something commonly discussed; the seeking of an 'accident'.
A further insight for those of us who work in such a manner –
Something as physical as a painting can only be realized in execution;
the actual act is indispensable to its conception, without it, it remains in a
different realm and there is no crossing over.

In the realm of visions?

What can be conceived with the brush/tool is inconceivable as a vision –
Could be transcribed into text?

A painting is a vision, never fully realized; it can only fire your senses.
A painting-vision occurs with the act
A thought-vision with thinking
A thought-vision is, in fact, incapable of equalling a painting-vision,
which as a life world, exceeds it

I make studies of spaces that I have lived and worked in during the course
of my travels as an artist, and attempt to bring them all under one roof; to
sustain continuity in the manner of living one's life, doing one's work and
conceiving of situations worth sharing with a larger audience. Built into the
colours and objects that I use are the experiences that these spaces have
housed and sometimes engendered. The structure has therefore evolved
from personal circumstances, but the events that animate it encompass
the internal and extend beyond it into the realm of common concerns, the
emphases shifting with the passage of time.

The idea of the 'interior' could be translated in several ways; at the most
basic level as different kinds of physical and metaphorical spaces. As
dislocation becomes a way of life, and limits on mobility and transgression
become less and less perceivable, the idea of fitting these spaces into the
format of a house intrigues me; that speed and mobility need not always
create distance but could actually be one more way home.

A different kind of an interior – *The Journey* – was a painting in memory of
other paintings made before leaving Paris in 1996, to describe that sense
of retreating from a reality that I had lived with for so many months. There
was a necessary withdrawal into the intra-venous, the sub-terrestrial, into
the body with its proliferating cells, its network of nerves and blood vessels,
its intestinal plumbing. I worked with transparent washes of colour in
vermilion, burnt sienna, black and white: watered blood and body fluids.

28.5.1999 / Paris

My House
That amorphous state which shimmers
Between the places I inhabit

The blood that I shed

In strange places
at unexpected times

amongst people I love
so limitlessly

Interior (detail), 2008–10

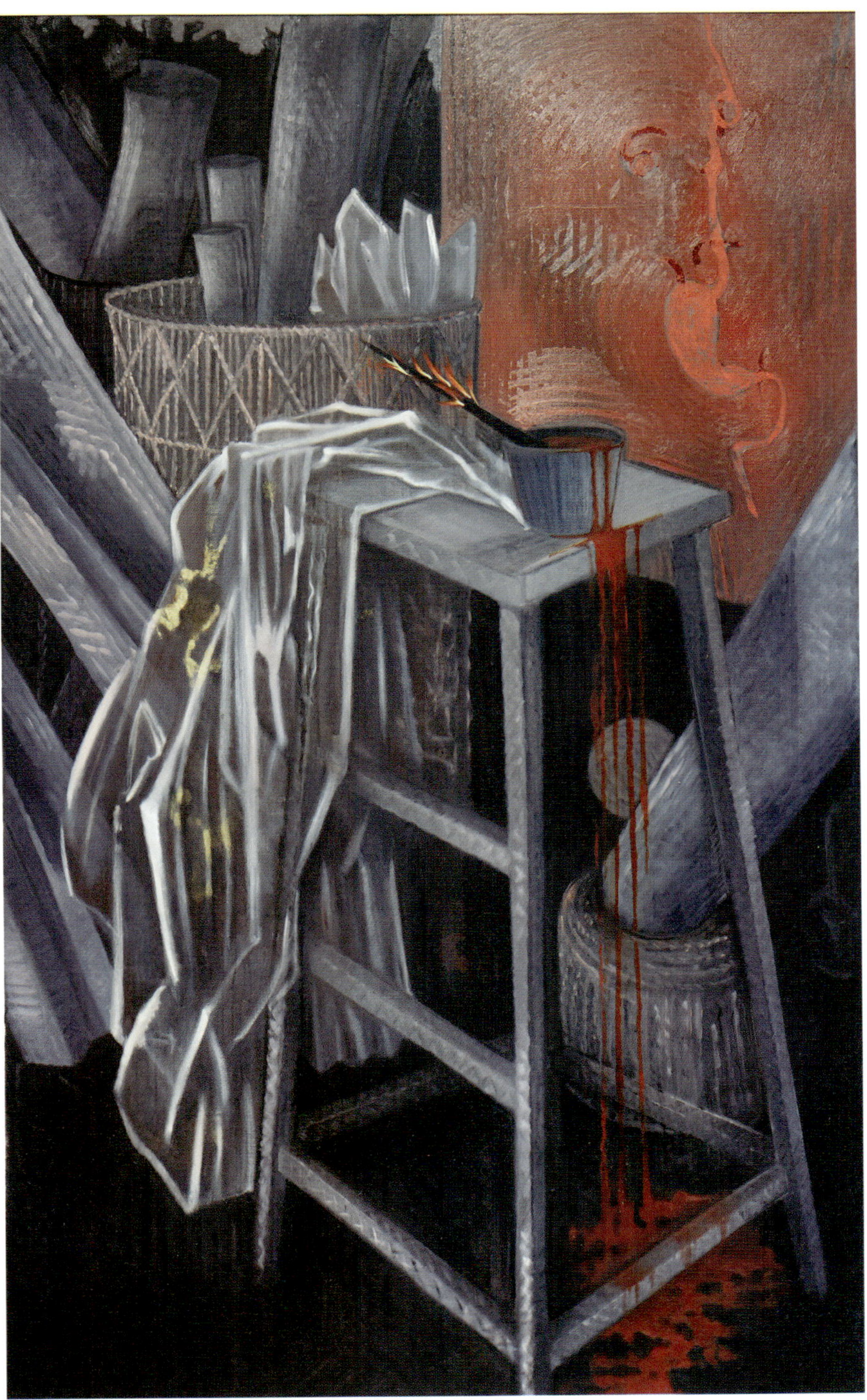

THE SECRET LIFE OF OBJECTS

Space as more than pictorial space
Time as spreading beyond the phenomenon of a single painting
Methodology as inseparable from its result
Adherence to a certain methodology
Ways of seeing as integral to processes of working, for the artist
Ways of seeing as integral to seeing, for the viewer.
Ways of seeing are ways of working
Ways of seeing are the artwork

not

the artwork itself

The rose as a wound
Multi-scabbed rose

Work as inseparable from methodology

Associations are random to start with, and therefore formally less related –
But as an intention is born, they begin to acquire greater physicality/bloom
with greater physicality/define themselves with greater clarity/lucidity
and I begin to lend myself to the intention and subscribe to its dictates

This does not make the earlier uncertainty any less capable of
making propositions which tantalize for their very lack of definition.

And all this a part of formulation; therefore, something which must be
shared, as much as a resolution.

An earlier idea that I had played with/touched upon/was one of passage
through a house/my house, from the bedroom to the studio

as a ritual which preceded, in fact held, those hours given to painting –
within a practical/physical framework

This passage divided itself into areas of experience which were rooted in
the mundane but contained an element of the surreal – not purely in terms
of fantasy but as encompassing all those vast spaces encountered
at different times in life

uncharted

in terms of their relationship to those vast expanses of private experience
which form the hidden core of our lives

the hidden undertow which directs our lives
(undercurrent?)

those secret streams of experience

Literally, this translates itself into paintings in different sizes and formats
treated/formally/in different ways; the transitions as small fractures rather
than a smooth passage

Between, there is complete silence.

/No Bridges/

The bridge, being a conceptual area, which grapples with impressions of
what is left behind, engenders a distancing and an abrupt entry into another
world.

In preparation of silence.
A mind well-primed in preparation for silence.
A glut of imagery
And impossible chasms between
The fall and the silence so severe as to warrant an equal and opposite
reaction –

The way we live is not gentle or homogeneous in any way. The way we
travel is a multi-pronged path with few comforts or interconnecting lanes.

catalogue / 1998

My teacher tells me that in a sequence of musical notes, a fracture presents
a problem.

When there are multiple fractures, the frame is shattered and can never be
whole again. Such violence pre-supposes the birth of a new structure.

7.7.1998

We no longer live in gentle homogeneity. We travel, crossing worlds and
lifetimes.
To travel is to put one's past at stake.

7.8.1998

Around '95–'96 the painting as a restricted time–space phenomenon ceased
to exist for me. I saw resolution and continuity come together as one more
dual entity. I could not predict what would happen where – a lack of short-
term commitment perhaps. Like grappling with several pieces of a puzzle
at the same time; certain omissions prominent by their absence. Sometimes,
impossible to resolve their disparities on a single surface; and, therefore, I
began to cut them out, leave them aside for a time while other resolutions
took place.

Knowledge is sometimes formidable; it assumes a physicality which doesn't
dissolve around the edges to accommodate other forms.

Indeed, it repels them, leaning towards the exclusion of other things,
therefore incomplete and in being incomplete,

untruthful,

or misleading

or incapable of entirety

This entirety I find in absence, in the chasm between polarities.

Relationships are as much to do with affinities as with distances.

A hall has to be acoustically treated to support silence, and this is more difficult than the support of sound.

To change a form from within

the distinction between that and experiments which take place on the fringe. Easier in a sense because one unburdens oneself of the past, its traditions and patterns. One shrugs off the known, and in the lightness of that freedom, creates propositions which go beyond the pale of responsibility or criticism. It is something else altogether to take on the monster in its fullness and to alter its form, it is possible to perish in the process, to fail and to risk everything.

9th Aug 1998

- - - - - - - - - - - - - - -

... Eight categories of nature, sixteen accidental properties; the soul; five vital airs; the three-fold qualities; mind; evolution and re-absorption ...

From The Farce of the Saint-Courtesan these rather magical words –

These rather nonsensical words –

An extract, in essence; a list of ingredients, in words; to find their replicates in my personal dictionary of strange forms.

For all this to exist in unity, there is the daily transit from the bath through the bedroom into the studio every morning, and the creation of a deviant history.

I do not think of painting as something that grows within a frame, the frame comes later. I do not think of painting as existing within a frame but as a fragment torn from the body of life.

Where is the divide?

I begin working with the cloth/canvas on the floor because as a presence
it occupies my space – it is not something that hangs conveniently on the
wall/I need to recognize the intrusion/disruption, its presence within my
space – if this is not conceded it cannot materialize.

A coming to grips with its entry – working in various positions on and
around the field, to gain complete access –

Interactive dynamics, movement, dance –
In a sense a victim to the same limitations of space and time.

A thing is defined by its limitations. It also defies its limitations.

At all times what I guard with all my life is the spirit which moves me to
expressions more real than the surfaces of things.

1st Sept 1997

- - - - - - - - - - - - - - - -

In a previous text, I spoke of passage, rooted in actual geographies of living
and working spaces, of cities and countries visited. It is implicit that such
physical transmutations should correspond with those streams of private
experience – that hidden undertow which erases and re-formulates patterns
for our lives.

As a recurrent preoccupation, this has led to the evolution of a format for
painting that most resembles montage, as a living, occurring sequence
exceeding the confines of a single spatial or temporal frame. Equally
symptomatic is the progressive collision of miscellaneous phenomena, the
emphasis shifting between linkage and polarity, existing in mutually exclusive
units, incapable of entirety: which I find in absence, in the chasms between.

What do I contain? I wouldn't know unless I emptied myself, let it all spill
out, examined the contents. Years later, I try to lay it all out in some kind of
order with a greater exercise of will.

An organism of doubtful affinity
the title of a painting that I made in 1979 in England.

What do I contain? I wouldn't know unless I emptied myself. Therefore, I let spill, examine the contents; lay them in some kind of order. I am conscious of the present as a tool for demarcation. Beyond it lie the terrors of infinite growth.

The present is invaluable in that it demarcates; beyond it lie the terrors of infinite growth.

Excerpt from text for catalogue '98

About linkage: to attempt linkages with other entities it is necessary to dissolve a little around the edges.

Organisms of doubtful affinities prefer to co-exist. Or pose a contradiction so complete as to create a mutual dependence between affirmation and negation, and set it in motion – as the revolution of the earth unifies night and day?

to root myself in every moment and thereby hope to cross each day

Or halt this relentless progression of days and nights, this meaningless repetition of actions devoid of joy.

Yellow and Black, which I work with now
Life and Death
Light and Dark
and I poised on the margin between

I, poised on the margin between
try for a dark gold

Let me try this again.

Yellow and Black
Life and Death

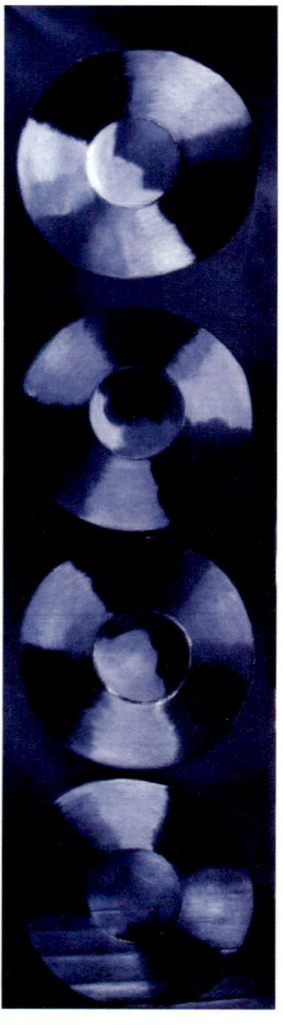 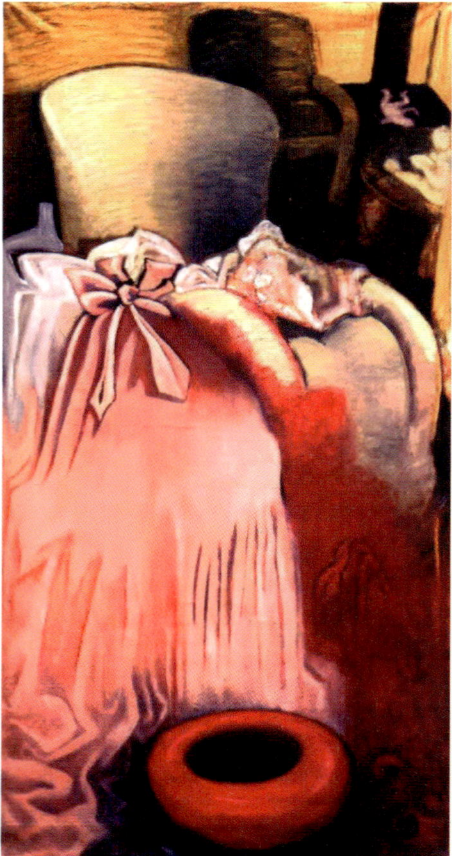 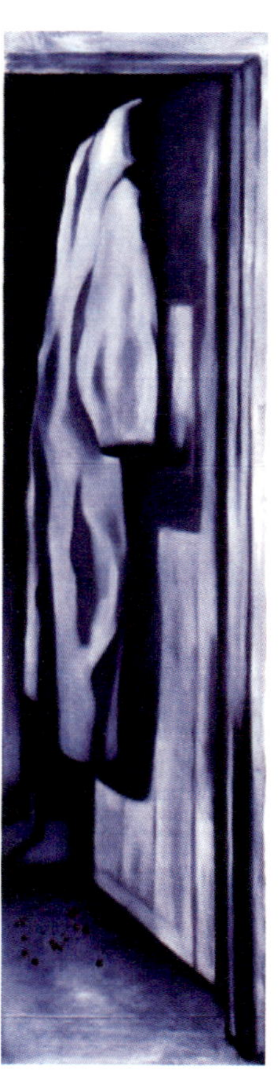

Secret Life, 1998

both young in stance
limited in expectation

I,
neither young nor dead
limitless in expectation
try for a dark gold

April 1998

- - - - - - - - - - - - - - -

I present work in different ways in different situations
Some, I hesitate to frame for fear that it would hamper the fluidity with
which one set of imagery flows into the other
The work at this point is still in transit from one venue of display to the
other
If it finds a permanent resting place, I could conceive of it as something
framed –
Like a trophy which one preserves –

A trophy is a mere memory of the act that wins/warrants it

So too the painting-at-rest.

Working around a canvas – somehow a feeling of being intimately
connected with it, being caught up in a sort of coordinated movement which
calls forth varied mutual responses

The studio becomes a stage/podium where this is performed

Dance?
Theatre?
Performance?
Or the record of a performance?

August 2001

A recent painting, *Secret Life* is a portrait of myself seated in my studio at the Cite des Arts, with a tiger at my feet. The idea of a tiger in Paris is of course incongruous, and at a superficial level touches upon the notion of the 'exotic' and the 'native goddess' among other things; so too the jewels on the right.

It is also a story of loss and enrichment.

To use melodrama to trivialize –

To make palatable real suffering –
Strange –
why?

being an indulgence, it brings relief
it eroticizes to the pitch of fantasy
something orgasmic and therefore a release?

September 2000

In a sequence of musical notes, my teacher tells me, a fracture presents a problem, a space that has to be bridged.

If there are multiple fractures, would the frame be shattered?
Would it never be whole again?
Does such violence pre-suppose the birth of a new structure?
Could a sequence of fractures be a structure, the chasms constituting an invisible body, infinite in magnitude?

An invisible body alongside the visible, taking shape/form or defying both?

January 2001

- - - - - - - - - - - - - - - -

To create a comprehensive body – composed of thought, sound, appearance
– something you can see/hear/touch/smell/taste?
To find ways of incorporating text into image

Text into sound, through speech and music – the idea in itself is not new, but it grips
me because I have found a new path
A real connection with myself
Another way home

January 2001, Baroda

I have not mentioned the earthquake, on the 26th of January. I was in Bombay.

February 2001

– – – – – – – – – – – – – – – –

A poem from Stephen Spender, which I found inscribed on a sketch in Meera's home – with a slight modification –

– Of what use is my weeping?
It does not carry a surgeon's knife
To cut the wrongly multiplying cells
At the root of my life
It can only prove
That extremes of love stretch beyond the flesh to hideous bone
Howling in hyena dark alone.

April, Bombay

– – – – – – – – – – – – – – –

In Bangalore now, since mid-April.

If there are real wounds, they are naturally visible.

They do not have to be created. Bruises and marks on the surface of the canvas are in fact hard to erase. An artificial scar, hard to create. Why try? It happens naturally, if you are indeed wounded.

The way I work – impatient sometimes, careless, not quite in control at all times, and therefore prone to making wrong decisions – all this goes into making a painting and it shows – a reflection?

June

- - - - - - - - - - - - - - - -

on a writing assignment for a website featuring profiles and essays on artists. In the meantime, a piece of text for the Khoj catalogue.

One of my projects for Khoj was to have been the making of a Khoj diary from the *taqtis* that I found in the market. I did not get beyond the fourth or fifth page.

Mail from Subba reminding me about the catalogue piece
 I now try to recall what I did –
The bamboo pieces –
The newspaper/fabric pieces
The painting, of myself painting
The discovery of how to set a process in motion, in a situation resembling a vacuum –

To discover the raison d'être of an artwork/the methodology which needs to be formulated for the purpose

The methodology is to set in motion the cycle of cause and effect, in the creation of a phenomenal reality governed by a given set of variables/a given set of concrete elements peculiar to the situation on hand – the people, the available material, the house, the environment –

What I enjoyed most were the patterns made by the tiles on the floor, a different one for each room. The desire to preserve these as memories – I spent the first couple of days tracing them out on paper, which I wanted to colour – still have a roll of these tracings, as yet unused, awaiting their moment.

Catalogues since the last few days, and writing almost ceaselessly.

The wheel begins to turn again.

I had dinner with friends last night – I was wearing red glass beads, and one of them said – you are wearing a necklace of *anardana* –

We were talking about someone in his family, a woman with two grown children, who had killed herself with an overdose of sleeping tablets. She had been suffering from a neurological problem – constant pain in the region of her cheekbones – I imagined two warmly glowing points of light, like *anardana*, never diminishing. Specialists diagnosed the ailment but gave her no hope, there was no cure.

She left behind a note for her son – I could not bear the pain any longer.

About Khoj, again: what I had at the end of it all were a set of questions: displaced from one's community of origin or choice, we still perform as is expected of us – but who are we looking at? What is the quality of the attention that we command, if at all? Are we forced to tailor our performance to catch rather than expand the quality of attention? Do we lose eye contact?

An unfocused gaze, one that looks into the far distance –

I realize that I actually seek to return somewhere, off stage; to allow things to sink deep.

I read Rilke on the train back to Bangalore – some breathtaking passages, and among them, this:

Books are empty … it is blood that matters, it is blood that we must learn to read.

6th July, Bombay

a workshop on drawing at the National Institute of Design
I looked at myself in the mirror in the bathroom:
where have you been all these years?

Materials required for tomorrow
charcoal – soft sticks
rags
mugs/glasses for water
pins
easels and sticks
tracing paper/black paper
mirror
magnifying glass

The system that I follow: touch upon various things, come back to them periodically with the knowledge gained in movement from one to the other

I enjoy evolving the progression of exercises as we go along, putting down thoughts as the sessions progress, working out things as they begin to happen.

This seems to me a more disciplined existence than the one I normally lead – endless cups of tea and coffee and the blaze within me setting everything on fire. This is quieter, more peaceful, more quenching.

Like a vision, every day, around noon, a rainbow forms over the pool below – between water and light.

29 July, Ahmedabad

- - - - - - - - - - - - - - -

A minor storm, and heavy rain early in the morning – I ran nonetheless.

Evening now and a little darker.
Always the storm and always a raft

What if I no longer want to stay afloat? Too much agony, the effort to ride the waves, and always into

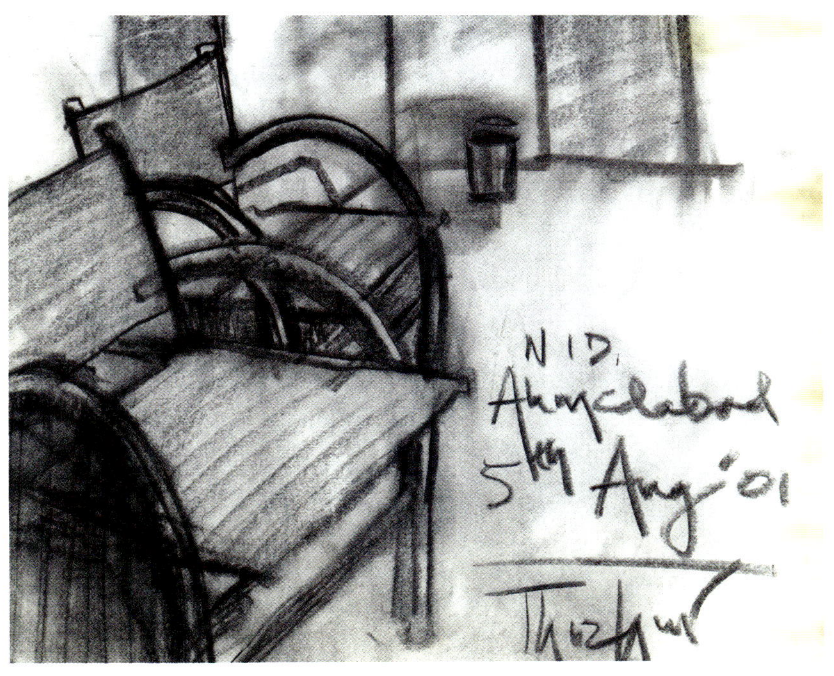

The eye of the storm, the black hole determining the dynamics of my life –

When I come to you, I do not bring with me the comfort of hope or the joy
of expectation
I come to meet my death
in a suspension of active desire
With a sense of the inevitable,
the sense of a reality I cannot escape.
A death-wish.

4th August

One more day to go – this session of two weeks has gone well, much energy and a lot of work done.

Maintaining a certain variety, as a challenge – when the mind settles into a groove, to unsettle it again –

9th Aug 2001

- - - - - - - - - - - - - - -

Preparing for the course on colour

Synaesthesia
Fragrances
Textures
Qualities
Henna, tea and coffee – natural substances
Structure adds its own possibilities to colour
Slides

Called Suresh Emmanuel who tells me the session is between the 3rd and 14th
In the meantime I will continue with my writing – and re-working the bedroom
I want to put slides together for a presentation in the faculty

Recent work
Links with earlier work
In segments
Black and white
Old prints
Black-and-white paintings (England)
Where would I fit that in?
They are minimal
Key paintings – *Rites of Passage*
My City on its Sandy Shore

The early heads/England
Which ones to scan and clean?
Secret Life of Objects
Set of works on paper in acrylic
Hyderabad/Africa
Works on newspaper – how do I budget for it?
Prioritize.
Should you rush into it between assignments/give it more time?

15th Aug, Baroda

- - - - - - - - - - - - - - -

Colour and Meaning, John Gage

In statements of medieval aesthetics –

*It is a language full of terms for radiance, brilliance, sparkle, and it reinforces
the imagery of light. ...*

*... It is as if one had entered heaven itself with no one barring the way from
any side, and was illuminated by the beauty in all forms shining all around like
so many stars, so one is utterly amazed. Thenceforth, it seems that everything
is in ecstatic motion, and the church itself is circling round. For the spectator,
through his whirling about in all directions and being constantly astir, which he
is forced to experience by the variegated spectacle on all sides, imagines that
his personal condition is transferred to the object.*

Lorenzo Ghiberti

On light-giving opaque and translucent bodies

*The first is the sun and fire and some precious stones, the second ... is that
which is of earth or other hard or dark (tenebrosa) material. The third is the
translucent (diafono) body: air, water, glass, crystal, chalcedony, beryl. ...*

As exercises:
Kandinsky and blue: Annie Besant and Theosophy and Blue
Read text

Exercises in blue –
Magazines – interiors?
+white
+black
coloured texts –
colour and language
colour stories
Base all exercises on your own practice?
Drawings, in black and white
The symbolism of red
Symbolic use of colour
Local colour as opposed to unifying colour
Slippage into black and white again – but qualified by the journey through
colour.
Colour as light
Illumination
Many ideas, yes.
But back to the same question
How do I structure the exercises?

Breath.
In everything that you do.
A structure for life.

Structure in movement
A rhythm for life.

30th Aug 2001

Colours for Blood

...ce invited for Buddhist ...rs, 153 cm. girl, MBBS ...l officer, working in Bo- ...Municipal Corporation ...MS/MD IRS/IAS/CA/ ...t/executive /engineers/ ...B.Tech no bar, Write ...o. C-4826, The Indian ...s, Express Towers, Nari- ...oint, Mumbai-21.
L/I ACB-31199

...ce for good looking Jat ...girl, 28, 5'3", MBBS. ...ng in private hospital. ...professionals. Write Box ...-4923, The Indian Ex- ...Express Towers, Nari- ...oint, Mumbai-21.
ACB-5007

GENERAL

...y girl 24 PG. 160 beauti- ...nployed, wanted emplo- ...groom. Write with self ...Box No. C-597, The In- ...Express, Nagarwada, Va- ...
AI LM (B) ACB 5560

...ce invited for an Anglo- ...girl 28/158 B.Sc., ...PGDCA from parents ...l employed boys. Box ...5, The Indian Express, ...drum 695 010.
7 TVM 1265 GNL G

...a Iyengar 33/4'8", ...ed seeks professionals ...laced boys sub-sect no ...ox 8048, The Indian Ex- ...Chennai - 2.
7 56101 GNL G

...Indian, Indian Christian ...seek Christian preferab- ...helor late forties for ...er teacher Gulf 43/5' ...Box 0222, The Indian ...s, Madurai 625 009.
7 MDU 979 GNL G

...girl 24 PG 160 beauti- ...ployed wanted emplo- ...oom. Write with self ...Box No. C-597, The In- ...press, Nagarwada, Bar-
AI-LM(B) ACB-5560

...e sought for a Jaipur ...convent educated Nair ...Sc., MBA, employed ...Rajasthan. 24/5'5", ...i. Write details to Box ...406, The Indian Ex- ...w Delhi-110002.

002.
14 56136 GNL G

Alliance invited for Brahmin + SC only daughter M.Sc., M.Phil, 24/5'6", Lecturer from Engineer / doctor goodlooking Brahmins only. Brahmin mixed Hindus may also apply Box No. 8089, The Indian Express, Chennai 600 002.
14 56138 GNL G

Mukherjee girl 27/5'2", B.Com. B.Ed., teacher 3000 p.m. fair, slim, Govt. employee or Bank employee Bengali Brahmin need apply. Write Box No. 4233, The Indian Express, Hyderab...
14 ... GNL G

Dheevara B... M.Ed., 25/165/5,000... Chithira Aleppy. Write... oscope Box No. 423... Indian Express, Hyderab... 29
14 H... GNL G

GUJARATI

Suitable groom 25 years pretty Gujarati Vaishnav beautician 5' F.Y.B.Com. wheatish complexion, Gujarati Box No. C-5040, The Indian Express, Express Towers, Nariman Point, Mumbai-21.
LMS/ACB-32728

HINDU

Alliance invited from employed boy for Manglik Saxena girl 26, M.S. (Human Development). Send bio-data & horoscope to Box ... 1361, The Indian Express, Ravinagar, Nagpur.
(G-Hindu/7/12)

Officer boy for Yadav girl 21, tall, homely, beautiful, BA. Write to Box No. C-4917, The Indian Express, Express Towers, Nariman Point, Mumbai-21.
LMS ACB-31835

Wanted two grooms (two real brother twins) for two Hindu twin sisters (dentists) age 23, sweet, beautiful, well-mannered. Apply with photograph, caste no bar. Doctor, engineer or other professional preferred. Ad for better choice only. Apply : Dr. Ketan Vakil, Vakil House, 11/181...

dowry write Box ALM-6422, The Indian Express, New Delhi-110002.
D-1899/97

KHATRI

Engineer/well settled tall handsome below 28 yrs match for slim beautiful Convent educated post-graduate 24/163/... Delhi based Khatri girl Box ALM-6413, The Indian Express, New Delhi-110002.
D-1888/97

MUSLIM

Alliance invited for a smart looking MCS lecturer Muslim girl 25 years 5'3" doing ... through startful and also a beautiful Muslim ... doing B.C.S. 22 yrs 5'1" for Muslim boys of 30 & 26 years respectively well settled, post graduate, computer engineers ...s or boys having sound business background send bio-data with photograph at S. M. Iqbal, 981, Bhavani Peth, IIIrd Floor, Pune-411042.
ACB-041823

Suitable match for Muslim Sunni Pathan fair girl 25/5'2", studying B.A. Box ALM-6426, The Indian Express, New Delhi 110 002.
D-1908 97

MARATHI/KONKANI

Alliance invited from qualified, established young bright groom for a good looking Maharashtrian Hindu Teli girl practicing law, earning Rs. 10,000/- a month. Height 5'3", age 27-1/2. Apply Post Box 7990 - P, Mumbai - 400 034.
SB 32226

Settled in England, Deshastha Brahmin, widow, one daughter, 47, 5'4" graduate service. Expectations - Brahmin, widower O... desire to settle ... Write with photograph, Box No. C-4924, The Indian Express, Nariman Point, Mumbai-21.
VL 31857

Alliance invited for Baroda based post-graduate smart girl 24/157 working in reputed concern. Caste no bar. Apply with

Bombay based Kerala parents invites proposal for their daughter 31/150/6500 Central Govt. from parents of employed boys. Send bio-data and horoscope, caste no bar. Write to Box No. C-4963, The Indian Express, Express Towers, Nariman Point, Mumbai - 21.
LMS ACB 32126

Proposals from well placed professionals under 28 preferably engineering management accountancy for well employed very affluent Nair girl entrance 23/166, slight Uvshajathakam. Write to Box C-4900, The Indian Express, Nariman Point, Mumbai-21.
SB 31722

Dhivya girl Age 22, height 160 cm. final MBBS a good looking, parents both post graduate doctors only brother engineer financially sound. MS, MD, DM or medical post graduate student preferred. Reply with horoscope, P. B. No. 731, Vivahaveedi, Calicut-673003.
14 ... KER G

Proposals invited by UK Physician for beautiful RC graduate girl 23, 161 cm. fair professionals based outside Kerala, preferably doctors with FLAB. Write with details plus photo. Box No. 278, The Indian Express, Kochi 682 0...
14-KQ 975 KER G

Brother invites correspondence from widower/divorcee for smart, accomplished, beautiful, divorcee Nair girl, own business, 37 years old with one child. Write Box No. 605, The Indian Express, Chennai-600 002.
14-BO 2624 KER G

Proposals invited for accomplished well to do Samantha girl of excellent disposition law graduate apprentice at law star Makeeryam age 23 daughter of retired senior revenue service officer now in legal profession from well educated young men of character in profession or Management etc. belonging to good Samantha, Nair, Menon, etc. families preferably from North Central Kerala. Write Box ALM-6415, The Indian Express, New Delhi...

(Kshatriya) parents ...iance for their beautiful ...r 26/5'6", M.S.W. ...g as executive in lead-ing business house from prefer-...hilla / Tank / Kshatriya ...stha, well qualified, pro-...al / post...ate de-...employed...octors ...neers / MBA write to ...o. C-599, The Indian ...s. Nagarwada, Baroda.

AI LM (B) ACB 5572

...als invited for protest-...vidow, 40/5'2"/slim/...heatish (looks ...r). PGT senior teacher ...vo independent sons, ...ll settled sober wido-...rcee. Correspond ...otograph & full details ...Jackson, The Indian ..., 186-B, Industrial ...andigarh.

LMI 662

...s B.Sc. (Maths) help-...hers in coaching clas-...comes officers MNC, ...irways, Navy, Defen-...t. officers, no bar, pre-...Christians, Telugu, ...Box No. C-4646, The Express, Express To-...Nariman Point, Mu-...

SB-29684

...affectionate Japanese ..., seeks humble, gener-...ing husband. Respond ...otograph Box No. 267, ...Indian Express, Kochi

14 KO 969 CNB G

...te, employed Bangalo-...d cultured girl, Hindu, ...", seeks alliance from ...tled presons at India / ...no bars. Box No. ...C/o The Indian Express, ...ore - 1.

14 BG 583 CNB G

...in Mumbai widow, 52, ...beautiful, unencumb-...financially independent ...established alliance. ...o Box No. C-4891, The Express, Express To-...Nariman Point, Mu-...21.

LMS ACB-31680

...ce invited for intercaste ...age girl 30/5'/ (B.Com, ...DIP. Computer) Bro-...4/5'6"/ B.Com / 7000 / ...ouse Mutual alliance pre-...caste no bar. To Box ...117, C/o The Inian Ex-...Bangalore 560 001.

7 BG 447 CNB B&G

DOCTOR

son 16 years requires good partner Indians foreigners good positions. Reply to Myers 14/5, 4th N'Block Raja-ji Nagar, Bangalore-560 010.

21 BG 668-GNL G

For Iyengar girl Srivatsa Rev-athi 32/150 H1 visa post-doc-toral, fellow, USA horoscope, bio-data, Iyengar 66 2nd Cross, Gokul 1st Phase, 1st Stage, Bangalore-54. Phone 91 080-3378394, Bangalore.

21 BG 659-GNL G

Alliance invited for RC girl 36 convent educated Tamil grad-uate teacher. Write Box NO. 1092, C/o The Indian Express, Belgaum-590 001.

21 BEL 1018-GNL G

Kamma Naidu B.A.M.S. doc-tor 29/5'6" slim beautiful good natured seeks tall smart qualified professionals from same/sub-caste. No hroscope. Reply with details Box No. 0227, The Indian Express, Madurai-625 009.

21 2926-GNL G

Alliance invited from indepen-dent, well-placed groom for 29/157, attractive converted, M.A., B.Ed., M.Phil., well-pla-ced daughter of retired Central Govt. officer. preference Bihar, UP, MP, caste immter-ial. Box No. 162, C/o The In-dian Express, Bhubaneswar.

21 3924-GNL G

Syrian Christian professional Priest, Missionary, for M.S Home Science Marthomite 5'1", 23 years God fearing set-tled in Gujarat, highly efficient and talented. Reply Box No. 620, The Indian Express, Chen-nai-600 002.

7N 3934 -GNL G

Graduate Tamil Brahmin 29/164 widow son 4-3/4 daughter 9 months. Broad minded afflu-ent professionals Hindu veget-arian non-smoker teetotaller, below 36 may only apply. Those working abroad prefer-red. Contact Box No. 2280, The Indian Express, Coimbato-re - 45, or (0422) 436480.

14 CBE 783 GNL G

Roman Catholic Vellalar MS computer 27/164 girl fair US employed seeks professionally employed. Box No. 2279, The Indian Express, Coimbatore - 45.

14 CBE 781 GNL G

Senghunthar bride 23/159, B.Ed., Chennai employed seeks employed grooms wan-ted. Reply Box No. 8087, The Indian Express, Chennai 600

JAT

Alliance invited for Jat-Sikh B.P.Ed., studying M.P.Ed. 24/5'3" smart sweet natured hom-ely girl. Write Box No. 1359, The Indian Express, Ravina-gar, Nagpur.

ACB-3291-7-12

KAYASTHA

Suitable groom for Kayastha graduate girl 25/151 fair slim, beautiful, convent educated. Box No. 160, The Indian Ex-press, Bhubaneswar 751 001.

14 3794 Kayastha G

KANNADIGA

For Madhwa Shivali Brahmin girl, 25/160, B.Com., appea-red final C.A., fair, Mumbai-based, Jamadagni Gotra. Reply Box No. C-5100, The Indian Express, Express To-wers, Nariman Point, Mu-mbai-21.

LMS ACB-33168

Suitable match for goodlook-ing Billawa girl, 26, 5'4", B.A. Computer diploma. Fa-ther Suvarna, mother Salian. Write Box No. C-4864, The Indian Express, Express To-wers, Nariman Point, Mu-mbai-21.

ACB-31453

KHATRI/ARORA

Alliance invited for well man-nered, beautiful, fair, graduate Punjabi Arora girl 25/164, done advanced computer co-urse from leading institute, currently employed with Aptech as faculty, earning des-cent salary, Hindu Punjabi professional match preferred, boys merit and family main consideration. Contact: Mr S.P. Malick, Flat 101, 35 B Shreenath Appt's Kailash Park near Geetha Bhawan, Indore 452001.

D 1903 97

Gursikh Khatri/Arora boy Khatri girl 23/160 graduate diploma fashion designing fa-...defence officer posted Ba-...re settled in Jalandhar no ...Box No. 1208, The In-...Express, Bangalore-560

21-BG 647 Khari/Arora-G

Arora Accounts Assistant M.Com. girl 28/5' no Narang...

ACB 31413

Father Maratha, business mot-her Gujarati Patel only daugh-ter 23, 5'4" B.Sc. diploma in dress designing, convent, hob-bies : Swimming, Tennis, weat-ish complexion, beautiful, slim, expects Maratha or inter-caste married, Maratha grad-uate suitable ready to go abroad. Contact alongwith horoscope or bio-data to Mr Sudhakar Dhandhere 1/2 Shukarwar, Peth Pune-411 001 Ph 457203.

Ganesh-043253

MALAYALI/KERALITE

Alliance invited from decently employed Bombay / Bangalo-re based Nambiar / Nair / Menon boys of respectable family background preferably from North Malabar for fair, employed Nambiar girl 30/170. Reply with details horo-scope and recent full size photo (returnable) to Box No. C-4853, The Indian Express, Nariman Point, Mumbai - 21.

ACB 31324

Menon girl Pooyam slight do-sham 25/1/3 - 5'2", M.Com., ICWA (Inter) officer PSU Bo-mbay. Respond with bio-data / horoscope to Box No. C-5017, The Indian Express, Express Towers, Nariman Point, Mu-mbai- 21.

ACB 32560

Nair girl 24/160, smart cultu-red post-graduate officer in public sector, Oil Corp., well placed. Chowa Dosha Jatakam seeks alliance from well set-tled boys. Write to Box No. C-5018, The Indian Express, Nariman Point, Mumbai - 21.

LMS ACB 32563

Nashik based Ezhava parents want well employed boy for daughter 22, 5'2", Uthiritathi, post-graduate. Write Box No. C-5004, The Indian Express, Nariman Point, Mumbai - 21.

LMS ACB 32464

South Kerala Saiva Vellala girl 22/155, Punartham, Chowa 7th House M.Sc. Elec-tronics, Lecturer, Goa medium complexion, Naval officer's daughter seeks alliance from educated employed youths. Apply with horoscope to Box No. C-5003, The Indian Ex-press, Nariman Point, Mumbai - 21.

LMS ACB 32461

I am impatient to begin, as usual.
Impatient to grasp the thing in its entirety
Exhausting, dealing with a larger number of students –

I just wonder if I should start tomorrow's session with a talk on gold/the
use of gold.
In religion:
Gold – jewellery for deities –
the sacred – light, the sun, the heavens
stained glass.

3rd Sept

The session seems to have gained momentum – why is it so exhausting?
Different from the drawing session – colour is difficult in more ways than
one – in the use of it, in the teaching of it – to get the students to loosen up,
to make decisions/choices, take risks –

The way I sometimes construct a text in my notebooks

The sense is not linear – connecting segments in the adjoining page, the
connection indicated by arrows
boxes
I had a vision of text like a whirlpool, being sucked into a centre
Many layers of texts each one reading into and out of the other.
being pulled into a centre

And so I come to the end of this notebook, a significant moment. I will go
back to the one I started in Baroda, in '97.
Regress in time, pull it into the present, as I do my painting.

A whirlpool of text/words.
Will I actually be able to pick up the threads where I left off?
Will the story continue from that point where it broke off? Will I be able to will
it to happen? Will it happen anyway as part of a natural flow, a natural logic?

Evening, at 7

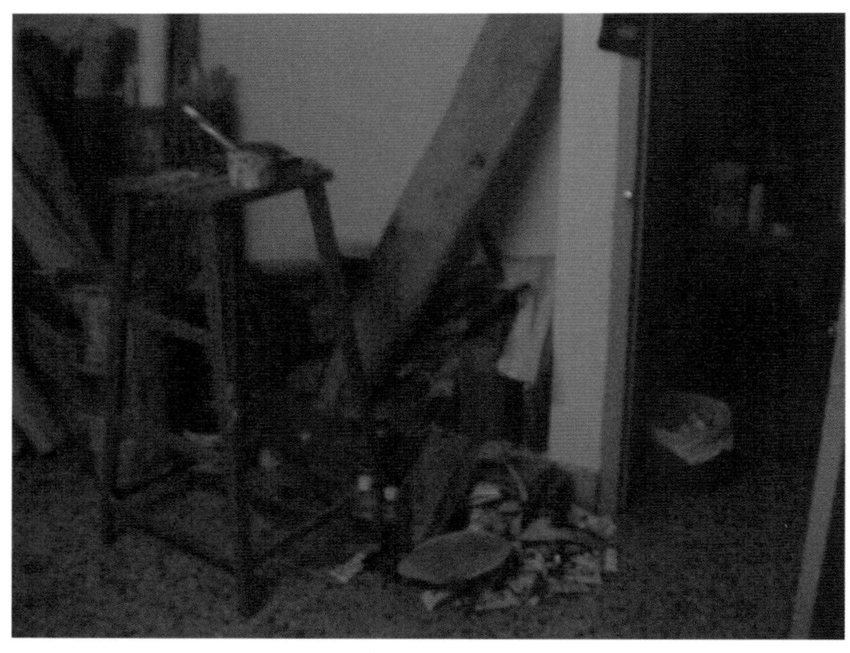

Godhra, and now Ayodhya.....curfew in the city, an eerie quiet. Will continue with the paper anyway, and the painting.
Afternoon, the deathly silence continues.

March 1, 2002
Baroda

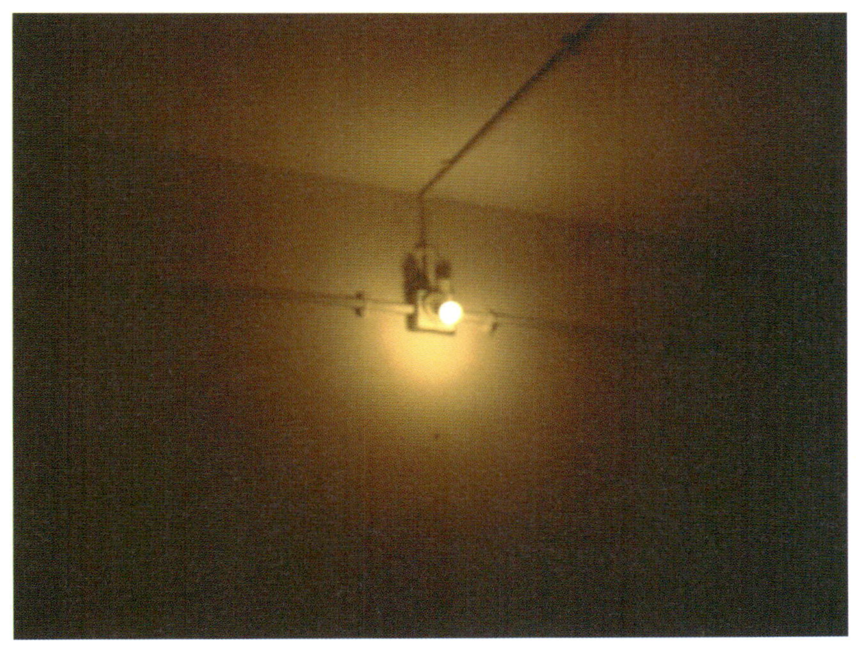

March 6, 2002
Baroda

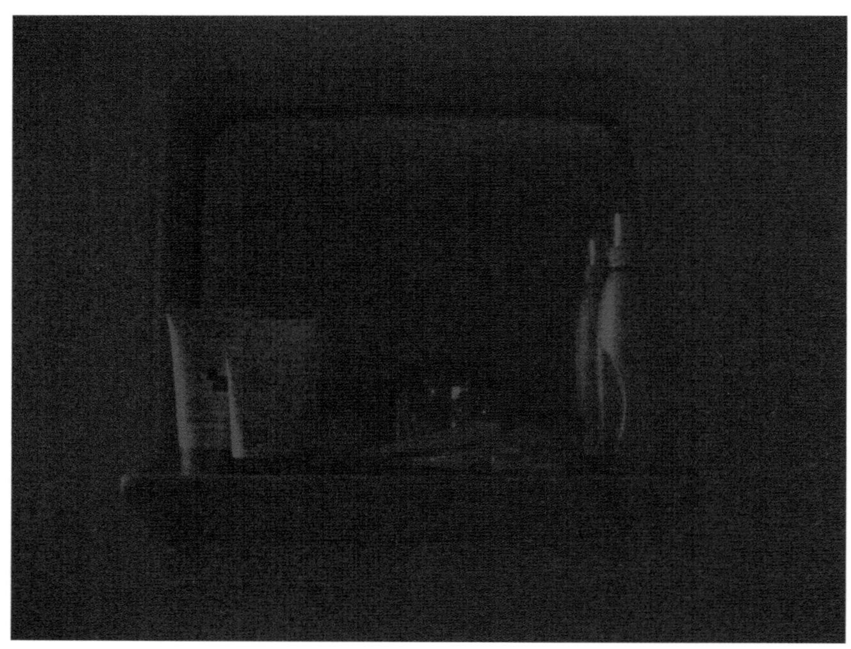

There has to be a Dawn,
it happens after every night.

When there are nights
without stars

There are days
Forever bright

March, 2002
Baroda

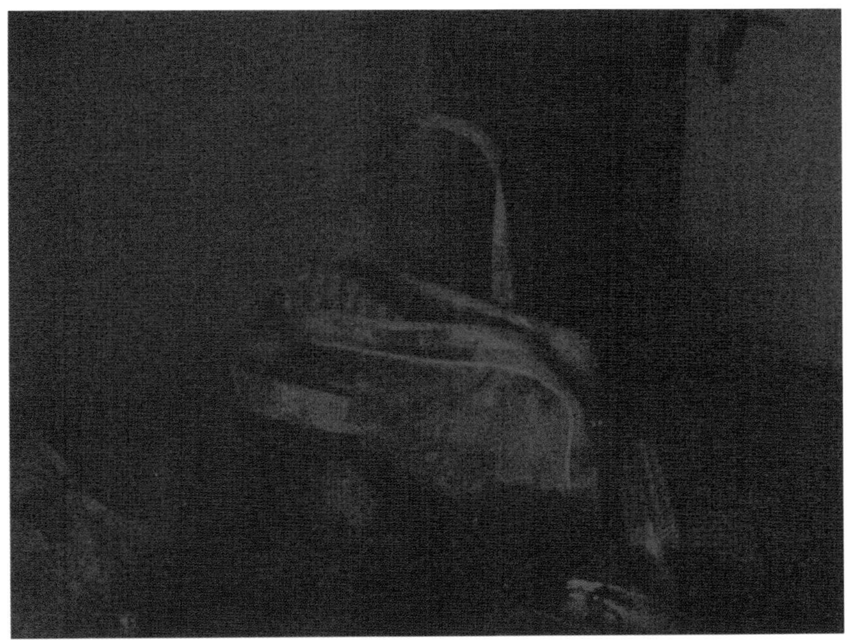

My thoughts turn increasingly to God, as this seems to be the crux of every issue. After fifteen years of practice, I realize that the most fascinating and indeed most miraculous discovery is the underlying unity of all things, and more important, to be able to perceive this unity. It is something I try to impart to students, through talks and studio sessions. To conceive of a matrix large enough to hold all systems of thought and practice, their contradictions seen in terms of an interdependent dynamics rather than as mutually intolerant and therefore self - nullifying entities. I see this matrix as God, and I experience it in varying degrees everyday and in every act of my life. It is in fact the basis of my practice, as it is basis of all creation.

Strangely enough, it seems necessary to articulate the obvious, centuries down the path of human evolution....

March 27, 2002
Baroda

Communal violence – curfew in the city, an eerie silence. The slide talk
tomorrow is obviously cancelled; the storytelling conference/workshop in
Ahmedabad mid-month will also probably not take place. One is left with
a vacuum – apart from distress over the political situation in the state.

Will continue with the paper anyway, and maybe start painting too.
Afternoon, the deathly silence continues.

1st March 2002

Curfew continues, but the violence has abated. The army is on patrol.
Vishnu sent me a photograph of a peacock. Facing away from the viewer,
profile, beautiful feathers on display. Manisha finally located yet another
photograph of one – perfect front view: now I have all that I need. The
moment has finally arrived.

2nd

Gathering for peace at Sayajigunj around the statue

5th

My writing is suspended for the time being – bad news first thing in the
morning. Maybe this is good after all, it makes me go out and look for
other options.

6th

so decided to start the peacock painting, as a challenge.
Why do I use black and white?
It is once removed from what it represents/narrates/talks about.
– a feeling of distance – like a memory.

7th

Benoy and some other students went around collecting responses to the riots from artists to put on the net – here is mine:

Following so soon after the earthquake, one marvels that we have not yet had our fill of suffering. I remember my reactions after 11 September, too. In the midst of the oppressive aftermath, the imminence of war, I walked into a shop selling musical instruments, to buy one for my *riyaz*. As an artist, one went through years of life feeling guilty for playing a comparatively passive role in what one imagined were things that really mattered. For the first and last time, this myth was shattered – I actually felt a sense of pride – to be seeking instruments of peace and beauty in the face of such devastation, to be working in contradiction to systems based on technologies that manifest themselves as war against the dreaded or despised other, technologies that are indeed dependent on destruction.

Art, at least the way I wish to practise it, implies non-cooperation with such systems.

I think of Gandhi, and the gruesome irony of the present situation.

My thoughts also turn increasingly towards god, as this seems to be the crux of every issue. After twenty years of practice, what I now begin to experience is the connectivity of all things: when I design projects for students, it usually comprises seemingly different modules and exercises; when I make a painting, it is composed of disparate segments. I realize that the most fascinating and indeed miraculous discovery is the unity of all things, and more important, to be able to perceive this unity. It is something that I try to impart, in talks and studio sessions. To conceive of a matrix large and complex enough to hold all systems of thought and practice, their contradictions seen in terms of interdependent dynamics rather than as mutually intolerant and therefore self-nullifying entities. I see this matrix as god, and I experience it in varying degrees every day and in every act of my life. It is in fact the basis of my practice, as it is the basis of all creation. Strangely enough, it seems necessary to articulate the obvious, centuries down the path of human evolution and so-called 'progress'.

27th

Bangalore –
Have been to the IFA to check out possibilities for funding. I would like to work with an activist/organization –
base myself in Baroda, travel, document through various means.

5th April

Yesterday, a thought or a sequence of thoughts –
The One Truth
how it comes to you in the form of love, or hate or god. Excluding/obliterating all else.
The object of its focus immaterial in fact – or mistaken/illusory: a poor substitute.

May 29th

the peacock is the antithesis of light, of my other painting. If darkness were to shine, it would glow like a peacock.

31st May

- - - - - - - - - - - - - - - - -

When I paint, all the joys and sorrows of the world are confined to the one act: a perfect state, one that I can control.

Every painting tells me how it should be painted
each layer is a study, an effort to break the code, arrive at the structure. The final layer is sight – knowledge: still, comparative.

I will now start with the diamonds.

God is something that you work up to a kind of perfect pitch.
A rhythm that unifies all detail.

4th June

Emptiness teaches you patience. In the infinitude of no hope, every moment rests in peace.

9th

so many palettes for the peacock.

14th

Completed the painting. Plan to return to Baroda.

17th August

- - - - - - - - - - - - - - -

The way it is currently practised throws up many questions, but to me, art is life/an alternative to death/violence – and a way of functioning, something which infuses every act. A painting/piece of music manifests it in a concentrated form – a form that might not be possible in situations of deprivation (war, need). The complexity of an art form is dependent on the measure of peace that we have attained – if we are then dissatisfied with it, maybe we earned it by dishonest (metaphorically speaking) means? Or in ignorance? Redressal could take various forms as well.

When one is worn out in spirit, it passes beyond one's capacity to be able to achieve art – that can happen at any time. One continues out of habit – but does not achieve it. It is not a given, but is the closest to divinity that we can ever get.

letter to a friend

Picking up the threads – several things in the offing – a trip to Jaipur on a teaching assignment.

12th Sept

As if pain has its own landscape, its own history; existing independent of all earthly desire or longing, complete, multifarious, multifaceted. No longer connected to anything. Just a blazing, simmering, wasted, wasting landscape.

3rd Oct, Jaipur

All feeling suspended, all history forgotten. A new city does that to you, before you start repeating the pattern all over again –
regularly hammering away at the keyboard, but 'writing' less and less. It's all about proposals/statements. Finally accountable to the world for the life I lead –

9th Oct

ARTIST/ACTIVIST COLLABORATIVE

Conscience has been a troublesome companion, but I could never fool myself into thinking that I would, by consciously adopting a prescribed process, make socially relevant art, nor do I feel compelled to do so within the context of painting, the limited reach – or what is perceived as such – of which is obvious to me. I have no quarrel with this limitation, it is an area of research to which one brings to bear time, experience and discipline; it would require a complementary engagement in the area of reading or interpretation to be fully communicable. It forms the bulk of my output and is in fact a political act in that it implies non-cooperation with systems driven by linear notions of progress or direct material gain. I would hope that when it is accessed, it would have the power to move, without posing threat as an incentive.

But what does it mean to engage with something like this?

As the months pass, what becomes as disturbing as the violence itself, is the shutting off – by the public and administrative spheres – of what is happening. If this were accompanied by adequate redress, it could be called resilience. But it seems more of a muffling of reality, and I begin to wonder if this muffling pervades every sphere; I begin to understand the oft-repeated statement that every system has failed. Maybe it surfaces because systems that one thought were adequate have proved tragically ineffective – but this does not apply to political systems alone.

As artists, there are choices that we can make – if we are comfortable with these systems, let us not then speak of change or revolution or subversion – it becomes a ritualized enactment of a role we no longer desire. We see our purpose as fulfilling a demand that is shaped and channelized through them.

If, however, the nature of art as we understand it seems to seriously doubt this comfort?

In that case, why is there such a limited scope for an artist to articulate or effect a different world-view? Reflections of this sort are part of the processes which prompt us to create art – their articulation however

has become a regulated affair, monitored and kept in place – we titillate
ourselves with notions of radicalism, while our space shrinks further – we
are as much a marginalized or a minority community as any other though
we are better equipped to pull ourselves out of such a position. Why do we
not do it? Because we have been provided comfortable spaces wherein we
are allowed to indulge ourselves, and are content to stay there by virtue of
the carrots that are being dangled before us? These spaces serve a purpose
no doubt; the problem is the confinement. Dissent has been suitably dealt
with, voices silenced. We are all culpable, myself included. The degree
varies. There is very little that we do, apart from teaching, which has a direct
bearing on 'necessity', as defined by the existing consensus. We are therefore
compelled to continue being 'artists' within the very limited connotations
that the term now assumes, in the limited way in which possibilities
present themselves to us. We fulfil a purpose, no doubt – the problem is
the confinement, and the difficulty of being unable to make a living in any
other way, other than to stop practising art as we understand it. A cycle
of shrinking applicability. Why do we then teach at all? To perpetuate this
cycle? Rebellion is comfortably accommodated within it, yet another gilded
carrot representing free speech and self-expression.

If earlier we were convinced that art in relationship to faith was an
outdated phenomenon, we have seen what that kind of thinking has
resulted in. Art assumes various roles at different times, there are times
when a clearer articulation of these roles, or a wider application, becomes
possible through a process of re-prioritization. Maybe we are in a sense
fortunate in being provided with such an opportunity.

From a paper for the IFA / October 2003

The cheque from the IFA arrived on the 9th. I have yet to deposit it in the
bank – have decided to use my almost defunct bank account.
A meeting with Bina: discussed the budget, a trip to Ahmedabad together,
a workshop with the women in Vatva – she tells me this will have to
happen minus infrastructural support as the elections are on the 12th, and

obviously, it becomes everyone's main concern. Would be foolish to let this pass without having done anything about it. Picked up a CD from Raj Kumar – Gujarat Carnage – INSAF.

13th November 2002

On the 15th: met Ilesh to fix up a schedule – picked up some magazines, photographs from him; he suggested the writer Aziz Kadri as someone who could help with the text/slogans.

On the 14th: met up with Bina, went over to her place to look at posters etc. in her collection, and then on to a round of NGOs – Shishu Milap, OLakh; finally a peace demonstration against the impending US attack on Iraq, minus Bina.

In between, however, many doubts and insecurities. Feeling out of my element, taking so much time away from work, painting, myself. Can I sustain it? Bina felt the same, and we discussed it in the auto on the way home – that maybe we would be glad to have done it in the end – if there is an end.

How do I fight this emotional numbness, born of extended trauma? A deadening of passion, dormant, accepting, wanting to be taken away, dear god, I don't belong here, I am so ill at ease in the world. No choice but to stay. Nothing seems to matter: Gujarat, violence, the end of the world, all so superficial.

This morning, at the multimedia class, a digital prayer, with the Image Map exercise: create a slice, give it a name, an alternative name, god. Click on it and open up a cloudburst, a rainbow. At the door to the temple again, god. Dear god, a cyber-prayer, but you don't need to be e-mailed.

Picked up a compilation of articles/talks around the current threat of fascism: *A Cannibal Time*, published by Seagull, Calcutta. It helps me to focus.

My thoughts turn to something I told Ranjit: Places are states of mind. Baroda represents for me that state of mind with which I left Madras: now in a sort of time-warp. Bangalore, something I cannot come to grips with. Not quite sure where to go from here, from Baroda.

About the project: Important, always, to bear in mind the despair of summer 2002 – no future, find a door or create one, to break out of the isolation of my studio, my life emptied of all desire, my empty life. To link with an area where the despair takes a physical aspect, a far more intense one – more warranted, I, actually have no reason to despair. Therefore – Despair (within myself) – find the reasons for it (outside of myself). The personal finds legitimacy in collective trauma, I take up despair as my cause.

A meeting with Bina in the evening, a good discussion.

16th Nov

Size of the poster – 18" by 23" – ideal for offset 20" by 30"/15" by 20".
At Axis Designers, having the photographs of the earthquake scanned.

There will be those among you who will not be able to look
At a woman again,
the mere look of the wound, the smell
If you survive it at all, will be enough, …

Zsuzsa Takacs, 'The Perennial Lament', in *The Colonnade of the Teeth*

18th Nov

– – – – – – – – – – – – – – – –

Text for the posters:
sleeping very badly. Very tired today, but a productive week, without doubt – met Aziz Kadri yesterday.

Printed on the eve of the Gujarat State Assembly Elections 2002 by Artist/ Activist Collaborative: The Right to Life – size – 23" by 36"

Met Kadri in his home again, but with Bina this time. He showed/recited his work in his study. I was of course handicapped by the language factor – Hindi – Gujarati – Urdu – as in Paris, as in Germany – very disturbed, but full of light too – a sense of a new life beginning. A very intense week, the images were finalized today, to our satisfaction.

23rd

The final work on the posters scheduled for today.
Concept and Design: Vasudha Thozhur in collaboration with Bina Srinivasan,
Printed at Lalita

An argument with Ilesh: he thinks the posters are elitist and inaccessible to
the 'masses'. It put me in a defensive position for a while.
I had imagined they were too obvious.

25th

– – – – – – – – – – – – – – –

Yet another poster, with an inscription by Kadri – the translation, from Urdu:
Who could foresee such a time, when innocence is punished
When doors of homes are shattered and the living consumed in flames!

26th

Working on the last poster in the set of four. Should be ready in the
afternoon or tomorrow at the latest.

Last evening, a call from Bina – the Election Commission has banned the
use of posters – should we go ahead and print it? We decide to go ahead –
change the text a little, to avoid mention of the elections. Mass distribution,
as far as the project is concerned, is vital.

29th

Completed work on posters/decision to print all four – no more 'production'
after this, so I suppose it's all right.

30th

Call Bina to discuss:
1. The price of the posters — take orders in Ahmedabad
2. handbills and translite?
Display at Convention?

1st Dec

THE STORY OF FIVE POSTERS

I was impatient to start work on the project. It seemed a huge responsibility.
The elections were coming up on the 12th. Many meetings of various
groups, to discuss pre/post-election strategies – mostly in the form of
demonstrations, with posters/pamphlets. One meeting that we attended had
members from different groups – some NGOs, some representatives from
left-wing parties, from the PUCL, from Shanti Abhiyan. We decided that yet
another umbrella organization was necessary within the context of a need
to voice peoples' concerns: Lok Avaaz, the voice of the people. The concerns
were around good governance and the preservation of basic human rights,
all of which were disregarded with such impunity. I offered to make posters,
something that Bina and I had decided upon as the only possible course
of action in the circumstances. Some people evinced interest: a few phone
calls, and then no follow up. We decided to go ahead with the work.

I remembered a visit to SPRAT in Ahmedabad in September, speaking with J
in his office. Displayed on the shelf behind him was a bangle in a glass case.
He pointed to it and said – That belonged to a girl who was raped.

The image stayed with me, more haunting than many others more gruesome
– the papers, magazines, were full of them. Charred bodies, slit open, innards
exposed. Young children, babies, unnamed adults.

In Baroda, on the way to my multimedia class, a bangle-seller passed by,
pushing his *lari*. I chose different shades of red, my favourite colour, and put
them on, enjoying the jingle – a sound that I did not normally wear. There
was the comforting feeling of subscribing to given notions of femininity, one
way less that I stood apart. I asked Ilesh if they could be scanned, he said
yes; we scanned them, they were beautiful images.

George, when he visited us, felt that we had used them irresponsibly. As
a 'popular' symbol, the bangle was problematic in terms of the history of
its usage: in films, where it represented a patriarchal view of femininity;
in popular sayings and custom, which linked it with male cowardice. Bina
too felt that these connotations had not been unpacked enough. I did not

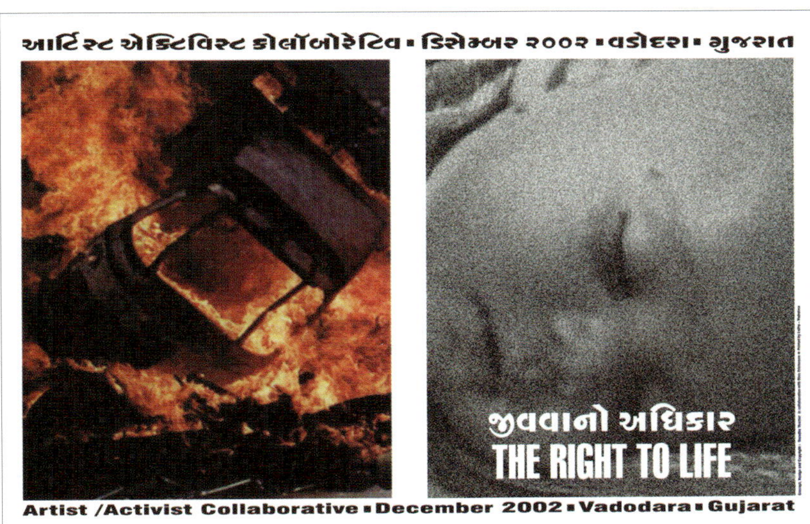

agree with them – the upfront view that we had used seemed to tie up with neither. To me it spoke of sisterhood, with an identifiable symbol rooted in the collective consciousness. I had used the vermilion circle innumerable times in my own paintings, long before I thought of it as a bangle. I broke one and scanned it, pasting the pieces on a card with glue. In the scanned image, the glue looked like dried blood.

We scanned one of Ilesh's photographs as well – one that he had taken in Kutch after the quake – of a house in ruins, and juxtaposed it with the image of a bangle – so easy to break trust, so hard to rebuild. I hoped to create an area where images of the quake and of the riots would overlap in a complex message, which would speak against violence/destruction in all forms, natural or human-made.

For The Right to Life, we used a photograph of a baby from the INSAF CD, juxtaposed with an image of a burning autorickshaw from an old issue of *India Today*. I wanted to use the caption *'Hindutva ya Manavta?'*, but Bina thought it provocative in the circumstances.

Ilesh wanted to know why we did not use the image of the burning train in Godhra, I replied that it was already the election symbol of the BJP.

A sleeping child, a baby: Why a sleeping child? – as between life and death, an ambiguous image. Also the story of Kausar.

Burning was so much a part of the mode of destruction/delivering death during the riots. Following the Godhra model. Death delivered at your doorstep, your home in flames, courtesy the custodians of god – god as defined by a package spelling violation, rape, loot, torture, fire, death.

In Ahmedabad, which had seen the worst, my friend Nina and I showed the posters to her *safaiwali*. She identified the rubble as an image from the quake immediately, but did not expand the context. I was disappointed.

The earthquake occurred in 2001. The woman remembered it.
As for The Right to Life, the baby, in her reading, had died in an accident.

The riots had barely ceased. The elections were a week away. If there was one thing that marked the riots, it was the burning; in one instance, a foetus was ripped from its mother's womb and thrown into the bonfire.

She did not make the connection. Amnesia? Ignorance? I still think about it.

For Kadri, we made one more poster, converting the red bangles to grey scale, multiplying the images like so many more voices. Circles on ashes. How could one foresee such a time, when innocence is punished, when the doors of homes are shattered and the living consumed in flames? We scanned his verse, written in Urdu, but Bina and Renu of Sahaj felt that no one would understand Urdu in Gujarat. It would, in fact, be misunderstood in Gujarat. Perhaps we could use it in Kashmir? It was a collaboration after all, the collective will prevailed. As one passer-by had shouted at us as we stood in a human chain around Sayaji Circle during a demonstration for peace, early in March, soon after the initial outbreaks – Why don't you take your demonstration to Kashmir?

I wanted to use it as a visual element, as a tribute and an apology. We finally had it transcribed in Hindi. It lost much of its impact. We stored the image on the hard disk, ready to use it on demand.

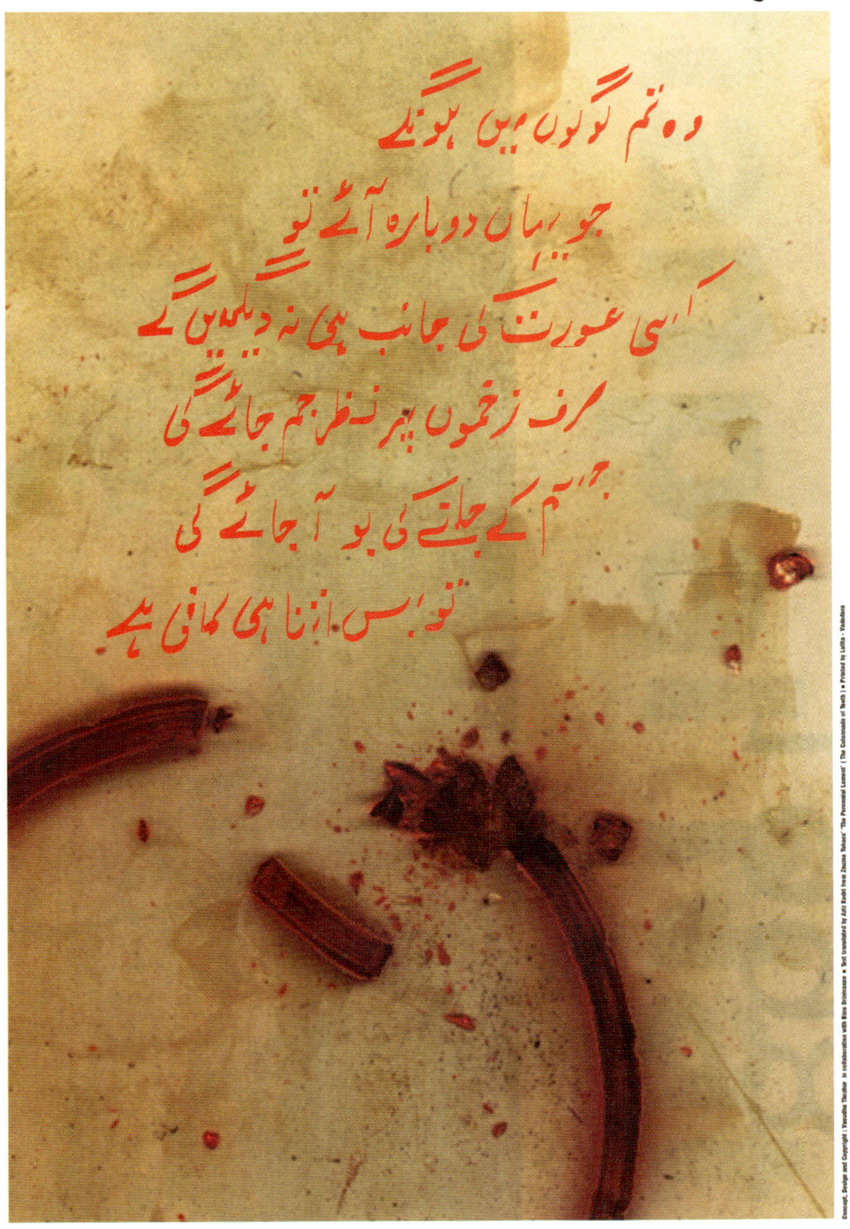

Artist /Activist Collaborative ▪ December 2002 ▪ Vadodara ▪ Gujarat

Similarly with one more image, a close-up of a broken bangle with Takacs translated into Urdu. Purely visual, no attempt at a readable script.

No takers. Awaiting one, on the CD.

The last poster focused on Articles 14 and 15 of our Constitution.
I wanted straightforward images of a man, woman and child, and identified those that we might use from the INSAF CD. The man wore a charm around his neck that identified him as Muslim. Yet another, an elderly man in a cap. The latter was immediately rejected – there should be no overt signs of bias towards one community as against the other. The woman, trauma writ large on her face.

It would, in addition, be better if they were not recognizable.

I blurred, skewed and scaled the images to universalize them, all signs of the charm, of identity, were effaced.

Written in Chennai/30th Dec 2002

THE PROJECT

I returned home to my mother in Bangalore in April 2002, after a month of political turbulence in Gujarat.

Baroda, where I lived, was dysfunctional, one could plan nothing – or plan with the knowledge that it might not happen at all, which took the motivation away. Outbreaks of violence everywhere, looting, burning, killing. It felt like a civil war. No time yet to take in the ghastly details, we were in the midst of it. Financial transactions went haywire – many parts of the city under curfew, especially the old city and the area where most head offices were situated.

The first two weeks in Bangalore, I caught up on my sleep. Therapeutic, but many nightmares.

I was walking along a street, I did not feel at all well, and could not open my eyes, they felt gummy and encrusted. I was dressed like a beggar. I was a beggar, I certainly was not myself. I sensed a blinding heat and light around me, the heat of the approaching summer in Gujarat.

Someone, a vendor, walked across the pavement towards me and alongside, insistent, repeating – *Pudi! Pudi!* – Hold this! Hold this! In Tamil. I couldn't see what it was that he wanted me to hold, and did not want to anyway, I could not – I screamed at him in frustration. A burden whose contents and sense were unknown to me.

Days later, another nightmare. A community situation, labyrinthine buildings where many artists, friends and acquaintances were working or just moving around.

I wandered on, belonging nowhere; moving upwards till I was walking on the branches of a metal arabesque – the sky behind me, chambers at different levels, which I entered and left, finding comfort in none. The pattern grew finer, the branches tapered into further intricacies. I was hopelessly enmeshed, I could not proceed, nor go back that impossibly complicated path – I looked at the beautiful, shining, curling metal, incapable of supporting my weight. I heard someone say – Let go, Vasudha!

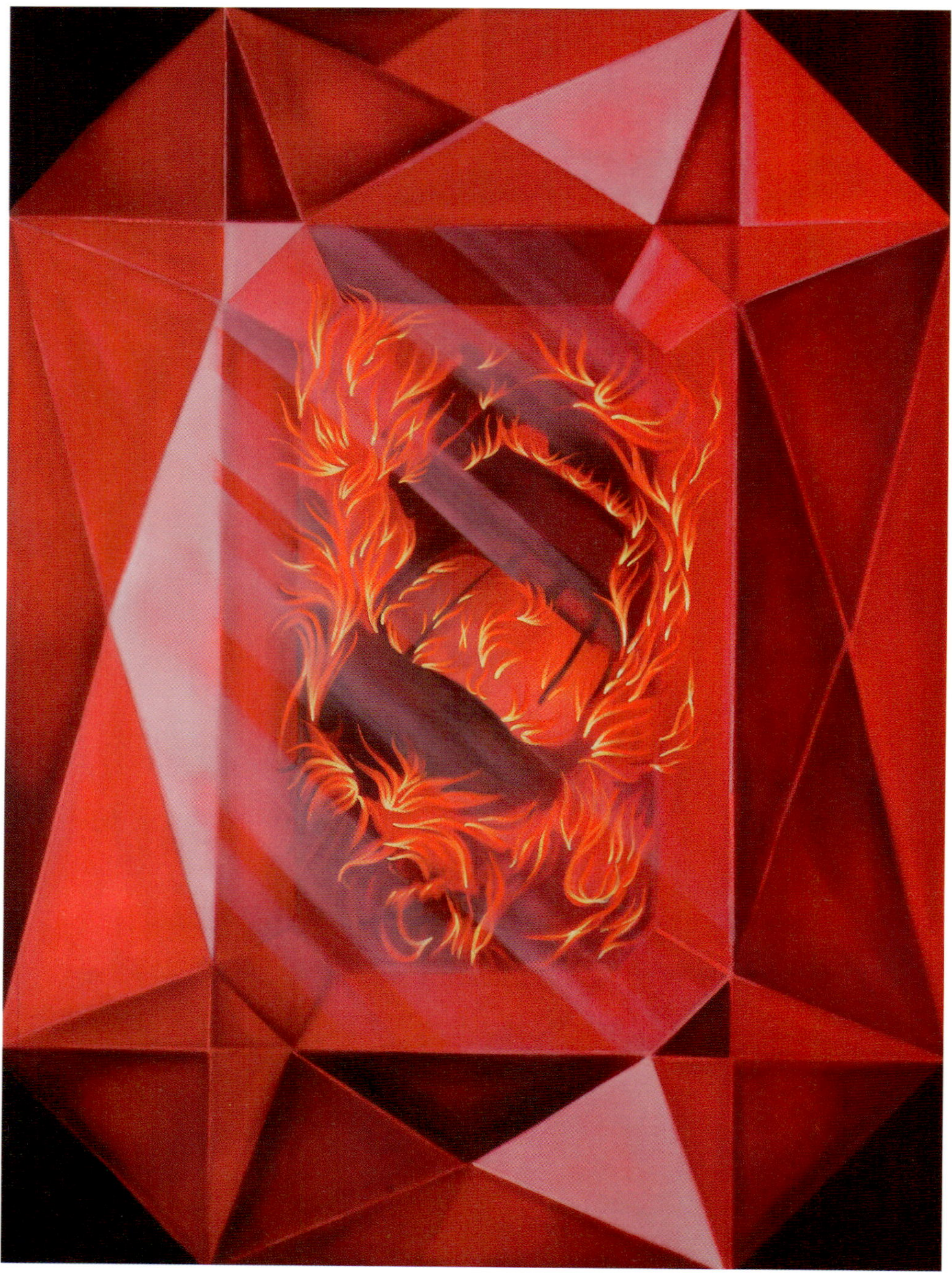

It was certain death, I was high up with nothing but emptiness around me, but I remember that decisive instant – I let go, falling a long way. Weightless, blissful in the knowledge that I had no choice.

A few weeks later, Pushpa invited me to participate in a raffle that was being organized as a fundraiser for the victims of the ongoing carnage in Gujarat. My paintings were in Baroda, I had nothing with me in Bangalore. I thought about them very often, I had started one around a self-portrait: my hair was being shaved off by a barber, who held me with indifferent tenderness as the blood streamed down my shoulders. I hoped it would be safe, with the city in such turmoil.

By chance, I had discovered a few days earlier that I was carrying a floppy with some images that I had shot in my studio and living space in Baroda, in the dark, at night. In Praise of Shadows.

A friend had visited me mid-February and had brought along with her a digital camera that I tried out. When I looked at the images on the computer in Bangalore, I found them beautiful, like paintings; my son Vishnu thought they were photographs of my paintings. And here was Pushpa asking me for a piece of work. I decided to combine the images with entries from my journal, entries made at the time of the initial outbreak of rioting. I took great care to frame them, and was happy with the result.

When I drew up the project proposal, I decided to extend, during the course of my work, the same idea into a longer narrative, in a similar format.

When asked, in Baroda, to contribute a piece of work for 'Voices Against Violence', to be held at the Faculty of Fine Art in October that year, I reproduced the same set of prints; the opening was very well attended, a charged emotional energy pervaded the gallery – humid, palpable. I left for Jaipur the same evening, on a two-week teaching stint at the Indian Institute of Crafts and Design.

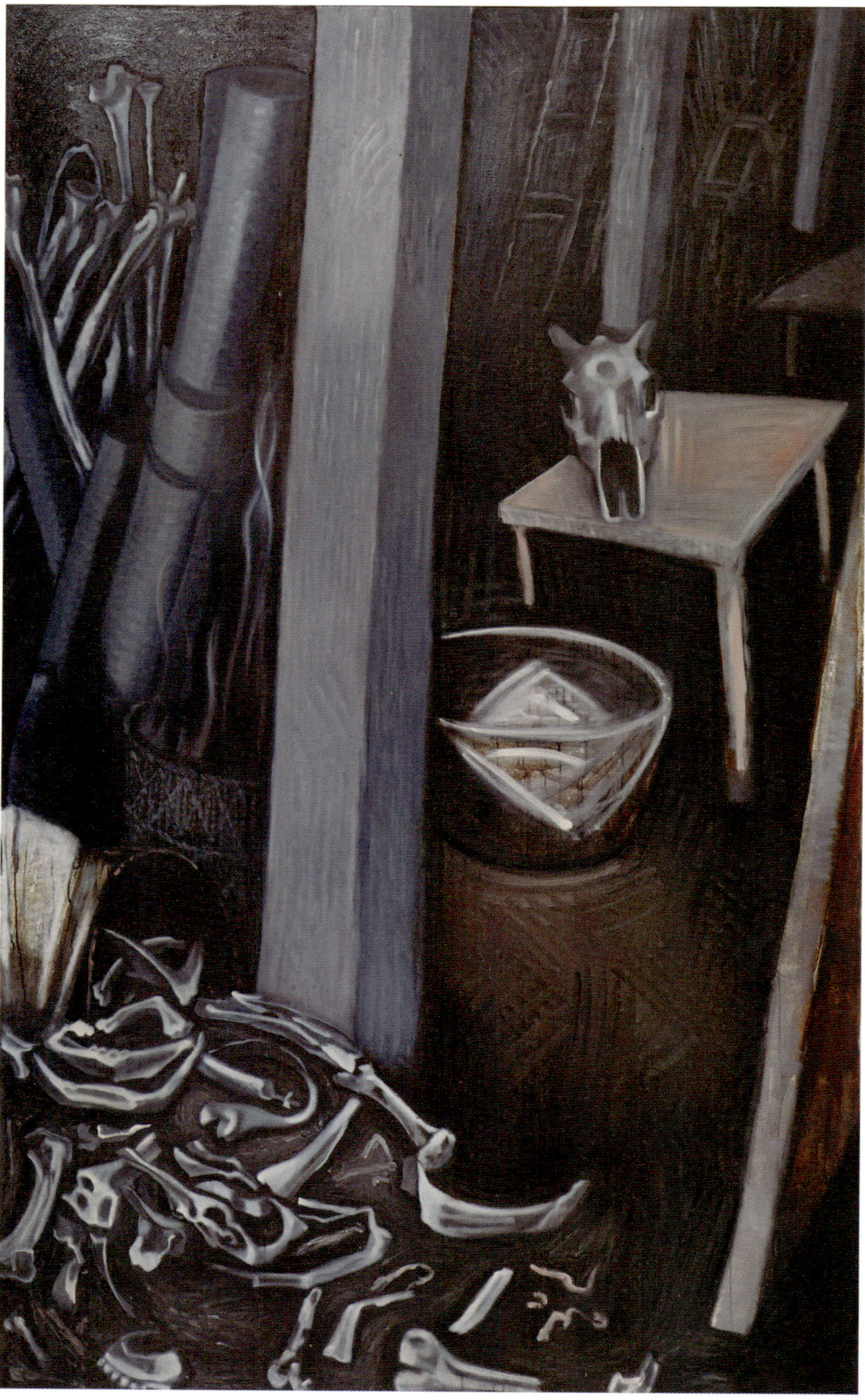

We are now in the second week of January. Almost a year after Godhra, and about a month after the State Assembly elections which have returned the BJP and Narendra Modi to power with an overwhelming majority.

Bina and I began working on our project during the third week of November. We had earlier scheduled an art workshop in Vatva with the women that she had worked with, but things were gearing up for the elections and the infrastructural support from the concerned NGOs was unavailable at the time.

Further, a major convention involving 2,000 women from all over the state and from outside of it took place on the 8th of December; public testimonies by victims were heard by the huge gathering.

Bina was assigned the task of writing up the report:

A note about the testimonies. I have retained the flow of the narratives of the women, with very little editing. This is deliberate. I think it is important to represent it as it was said.

Report of the Women's Convention
9th Dec 2002, Tagore Hall, Ahmedabad

The Women's Convention was held under the banner of the Mahila Ekta Manch, a network of organizations in Gujarat. It was attended by more than seventeen organizations from all over Gujarat. More than 1,500 women from Ahmedabad, Baroda, Sabarkantha, Kutch, Chota Udepur, Banaskantha and Panchmahals took part in the programme. Several organizations and individuals from Delhi, Mumbai, Pune, Bangalore and Lucknow attended the convention to express the solidarity of women from all over the country. In addition, women's groups from Calcutta, Hyderabad, Mumbai and other cities had expressed their heartfelt solidarity and support for the convention, despite their inability to attend it.

Sheba George introduced the three main speakers, Kamla Bhasin, Syeda Hamid and Ruth Manorama
Kamla Bhasin, a well-known Delhi-based women's rights activist, has long worked on women's issues in India and within South Asia. She is associated with Jagori, a Delhi-based women's group and SANGAT, a South Asian network of women's groups and movements. She has conducted many training programmes

all over the country and in South Asia and has produced a large amount of literature on women's issues. Known all over South Asia, Kamla Bhasin has been an inspiring personality within the women's movement in India and South Asia. We are happy to have her at the convention to help strengthen our struggle.

Dr Syeda Hamid, also based in Delhi, is both a writer and advocate of women's rights. In particular Dr Hamid is also part of the Forum for Muslim Women, which is a network very actively promoting social and legal reform within religion. The Forum also seeks to protect women's rights and has organized large programmes that have brought Muslim women from all parts of the country together. Dr Hamid has been a member of the National Commission for Women and through the NCW has initiated several inquiries into instances of violence against women. Dr Hamid is also a writer and the focus of her work has been on women's issues.

Ruth Manorama is a Bangalore-based Dalit leader and activist, known for her passion and commitment to the struggle for the rights of Dalit and Muslim women. Very significantly, her vision includes women of all marginalized communities. She works on many issues both nationally and internationally. Dalit and Muslim women, in her perspective, are not merely to be included in terms of their numbers, but also within decision-making structures.

Overview of the violence in the state: as collated by Sheba George
The death toll in the riots was reportedly 3,000–5,000. Ahmedabad and Panchmahals were the worst affected. Three hundred and fifty masjids and dargahs were destroyed. The total economic loss reportedly amounted to Rs 4,000 crores. Police atrocities have been recorded in report after report. More than a lakh of people were forced to seek refuge in camps. The state has a responsibility towards protecting its citizens, in this the state machinery is profoundly guilty.

Overview of the legal steps: as narrated by Bhushan Oza of the Legal Cell of Citizens' Initiative
With regard to relief, no complaints had been filed by the police. People asked us what they could do. We went to different relief camps, the police were not ready to take note of the names of the accused. So we helped to write the complaints and sent it off by registered post.

We had a meeting with the judges. It must be remembered that High Court judges also had to vacate their houses and move to safer locations. In this context, how do we file a case? The Mallika Sarabhai petition was filed. The police machinery had broken down, the constitutional machinery had collapsed, the rule of law had collapsed.

Three to four petitions were filed. These were admitted. The main demands were: a CBI enquiry, implementation of NHRC recommendations. However no stay was granted. With regard to rehabilitation, the main question was where to send the displaced people. A writ was filed. Again, no stay was granted. The cash dole was raised from Rs 5 to Rs 7 after a petition. Right now, there are cases in the Supreme Court. It is very important that witnesses give proper statements. If all that we heard today in this hall is sent to the Court, the Court will be forced to give a proper judgement.

Testimonies

Women from areas like Naroda Patiya, Vatva, Gomtipur, Chamanpura in Ahmedabad and from Panchmahals, Sabarkantha, Palanpur and Pandarva spoke in this session.

Naroda Patiya

R.

On 28th Feb there was police firing in Patiya. A mob of 5,000 people got in. We started running, the police started a lathi charge on us. They used hockey sticks. Many were injured. The people in the mobs wore kesri *(saffron) bands and khakhi shorts. They used petrol and chemicals.*

My child was stripped and burnt. My son told me to run. My daughter was also burnt. My son was so severely burnt. When I tried to lift him, his body fell to pieces in my hands.

B.

Seven people in my family were killed. We ran to Gangotri society. The Hindus came in the mobs to kill us. Why can't Muslims live in India? Is it only for Hindus? We were forced to say Jai Sri Ram.

V.

In the violence, my entire family was scattered in different places. I could meet them only after one month. My daughter was set on fire.

L.

*My husband died, we were married for twelve years. I am alone now. I live with
my in-laws.*

C.

*My husband was burnt and killed. My daughter was set on fire. I saw what the
mob did. I saw them kill a disabled boy, a woman raped.*

Vatva

E.

*The mobs came in the morning. The police did not do anything. On the 20th, we
saw a column of smoke emerging from an area that had been completely burnt
down. So, we gathered to look at it. The police came and fired. They approached
us as though they were going to talk to us. Then they fired on us. Two women
were injured. One died. I tried to help the other woman. My clothes were soaked
in blood. The police would have fired at me too, but they thought that I was
already injured, that is how I escaped. It was like a war. Why are women always
victims? The guilty should be punished, only then something will happen.*

M.

*I was sitting in the masjid. I was injured by a police bullet. I have polio in one
leg. Later, I was arrested by the police and released after two days.*

Gomtipur

M.

*My husband is a carpenter. After the violence, Muslim women whose houses had
been destroyed came to me and asked me if my husband would work for them.
I immediately agreed. Why not? I said. I told my husband – you have to go and
work for them. We have to be together. After all, we all face unemployment.*

C.

*There has been so much violence. I feel very bad to see this. We are Dalits, no
Patel ever comes to help us. Women from the Dalit community in Gomtipur have
decided that we will never allow our men to participate in violence. We have
decided to use Jai Bhim as a greeting. I am part of Mahila Shakti.*

S.

I have become homeless today. I used to live in Gulbarg Society. I have been dispossessed. I lost my 24-year-old son. On that day, from the morning itself there was tension. Ehsan Jafri lives there. We rushed to his house. He called the police. The police inspector came. My son then told me that there was nothing to worry, there would be police bandobast. *It will control the situation. But nothing of the sort happened. Instead the mobs came. They started burning shops, pelting stones. It went on for a long time. They had filled nailpolish bottles with some chemicals. They exploded the walls of our homes with gas cylinders; all the vehicles parked there were destroyed.*

Jafri was a good man. He worked for everybody, regardless of religion. Anybody could go to him. Social relations between Hindus and Muslims were good in our area. But everybody was involved in the violence. My bhabhi *also lost three children. Whose fault is it? Our lives have been destroyed. We cannot eat, or sleep. It is a living death. Everybody had* trishuls. *See our house now. If they can do this to a building, you can imagine what they can do to human beings.*

Lots of phone calls were made. They did not do anything. We have no orders, said the police. Nothing is left of our homes. All our houses were burnt. The society was engulfed in flames. There was a heap of dead bodies. Jafri's house was looted. They asked me and my bhabhi *for the key of one of his cupboards. They hit us. A disabled woman was beaten up.*

Twenty-nine people died in our family. The tailor's daughter was raped after being hit by a sword. I saw it myself. They got hold of me and said, hoist her on the table and strip her. I pleaded. They put me on the table. One boy from the mob took pity on me. He recognized me, and said you live here, don't you. He took pity on me. They let us go then. My son was killed in front of my own eyes.

B.
Why should anybody suffer in Ahmedabad for what happened in Godhra? Dalit and Muslim women should get together. That is the only way ahead. We should defeat the BJP.

Sabarkantha

V.

In Sabarkantha there was a lot of tension. Thousands of lives have been destroyed. Himmatnagar was badly affected. For three days the police was inactive. The BJP has done a lot of bad things. I have seen how people have suffered. We protected some families for a few days. Then we were forced to tell them that we cannot protect you any more. Mobs came from all directions – they were collecting the local boys. They had a plan to destroy the masjid. How can anyone go on like this? This government must go.

Pandarwad

L.

My son hid in a field. He was hit eight times. My grandson and I are the only ones left alive now. My son was killed. They hid in a sack of grain. He was hit. I threw water on him, the water rolled off. My blood ran cold when I saw that. My daughter-in-law was scared. I took her away. People were fleeing into the forest. I went to the sarpanch *for a vehicle to take my injured son. My son was still alive then. Jaswantbhai told me, the adivasis will kill you. I went back to my son. He was dead by then. We went to Lunawada. There my daughter-in-law gave birth to a boy.*

Fatehpura

A.

On 2nd March they came, they destroyed the masjid. I went out to check. I saw 15–20,000 people. They kept breaking the walls of one room after another in our house. We ran from one room to another. I had a young daughter. She was stripped in front of me. My daughter hit them, a Hindu woman helped us. She gave my daughter a shawl to cover herself. We were taken to the police station. We stayed there for three days. We went to Rajasthan. Our children now get terrified when they hear drums. I did not see my husband for thirteen days. He had died in the violence.

In Fatehpura, they still taunt us, threaten us. They could have taken whatever they wanted, why did they have to kill my husband?

C.

We have always lived peacefully in Fatehpura. When the tension spread, we got together and decided to stop the violence. Hindu families helped us, but after some time they told us to go.

The mob burnt everything. I had seven daughters. My husband pleaded with them. We gave them Rs 70,000 worth of gold. We will give everything, my daughter said. They took everything. They came in with petrol. My brother was killed. I told the police. The police told me, why did you do this in Godhra? Haven't you read the pamphlets? We are not going to save you.

Godhra

L.

Many families from Fatehpura had to flee to Rajasthan. The Hindus of Rajasthan were not angry. Why did the Hindus in Gujarat become like this? There was no plan in Rajasthan. For twelve days, the Hindus of Rajasthan kept people from Fatehpura. Why are Muslims disliked in Gujarat?

B of Randhikpur fled with seventeen members of her family, but she came to the Godhra camp alone. Everybody else was dead. She was raped with all the other women in the family. She has a daughter today. She cries every day, and wants to kill her daughter. Who will look after her, she says, what if the same thing happens to her?

As we discussed the ethics of such testimonies, my friend and painter, GR, who was sitting beside me said – you want 2,000 women weeping – you have it.

We had sat away from others in our group, among them, the painter NS, as we wanted to mingle. I was overwhelmed by the size of the gathering, felt unease at the rhetoric and rousing tone of some of the speeches, though in agreement with much of what was said. I had a headache at the end of the day from the booming, echoing loudspeakers.

We had wanted to put up some posters, and to sell some of them, but I was unprepared for the carnival atmosphere and uncertain as to where they would fit in. We distributed the few that I had brought along with me from Baroda. Also shy of pushing them when more immediate concerns were being discussed – that familiar guilt that led me to take on the project in the first place.

A friend who had been conducting a series of workshops with schools in the affected areas in Baroda, felt uncomfortable with the 'class' divide, as we all did. Here we were, in solidarity with 2,000 women, still so set apart.

My first taste of what it meant to be outside the comforting walls of a gallery space. The white cube seemed like a womb in comparison. I had never thought of it in those terms before. The pleasures of insularity. Insularities breed polarities.

The convention went well in terms of participation, according to Kamla Bhasin and Syeda Hamid. We thought so too, the only jarring element being the young woman who presented the talks and testimonies in a tone and language of overdone sympathy, straight out of a B-grade soap opera. Wheedling, maudlin. A small enough detail, but it undermined the gravity of the whole event.

We attended a Citizens' Initiative meeting at the Institute of Behavioural Sciences at St Xavier's College the next day. The purpose of the gathering was for the local activists to meet Kamla Bhasin and Syeda Hamid, and also to discuss the Asia Social Forum in Hyderabad in January. It was a good meeting, among the things discussed were the arrests that had taken place subsequent to the riots to satisfy statistical requirements. Most of them, ironically enough, involved members of the minority community – some of them young men who were still in university, bright students who now languished behind bars or were out on bail, demoralized, their futures uncertain. There were lawyers in the meeting who were trying to have them freed. There were CPI (M) members there who were confident that the BJP would not be voted back to power. We were not so hopeful, but felt encouraged nonetheless.

The next day, we visited a Dalit Muslim/Hindu *basti* and a Muslim *mohalla* in Abad Nagar. Both had suffered damage during the riots. In SS, as the former was called, a small school was in progress. The children were beautiful.

The inhabitants of Abad Nagar gathered around us, showed us the wall that had been erected (for safety) between them and the adjacent locality. It had been painted a bright blue, and looked new. The sight of it chilled us. The women felt much safer with it in place; even before the riots, men from the neighbouring locality would come in and use the corner opposite the entry as a *pishapkhana*. The women deemed it unseemly in the presence of so many young women and children.

During the carnage, full bladders served a different purpose.

People groaning in pain due to burns were asking for water. Here is water, they said and urinated on them, and those who tried to help the people were set on fire, were beaten up and also set on fire. Urinating, they said, take water, you set fire to the train at Godhra, didn't you?

They burnt my father-in-law. He was 70 years old.

Now, there were no overt signs of damage, no injuries, physically, they had healed.

Bina spoke of the time during the riots, when terrible burns and wounds were everywhere in horrific evidence, along with corpses – the most difficult aspect of working in the field at the time.

In the *basti*, a woman invited me into her home. It was in perfect repair, gleaming vessels lining the walls. Above them were a series of circles. The rims were brushed with smoke/soot, leaving beautifully formed configurations, evidence of fire, and what she must have lived through. She wanted a sewing machine, so she could earn a living – I wondered, where does art fit into all this? I wanted to give her a machine, and wished that I had the resources to do so. Syeda was making a list of requirements, and we put down her name among others who had similar requests.

Back in Baroda, I asked Bina – where does art fit into all this? Does it have to be tied to material benefit, in terms of locating outlets/markets? How does one go about it?

She said – these are decisions that I made years ago – that there are things that one is unequipped to do. For instance, there is a woman who insists that I put the man who killed her family behind bars – I cannot do it.

It was hot and dry, as only Ahmedabad can be.

We drove around Mani Nagar, Modi's constituency. All I could see were
tin sheds and box-like constructions with heaps of rubble around them.
Symbolic. Not quite garbage; anonymous piles of cement, brick and
nondescript waste. It also left me mystified. One would have imagined that
more attention would be given to the developmental aspect of what was
after all his political base. Maybe there were other sections of the locality
that looked more like human habitation.

Election strategies were various, we attended several meetings where they
were discussed. As the elections were currently the primary, if not only
focus, Bina suggested that we make some posters in response to the views
expressed during these meetings. It was generally agreed that there should
be a positive reinforcement of the basic constitutional rights, as these were
openly violated, with impunity. It was also felt that an assertion of these
rights, even if appropriated, could not go wrong or be misused; the political
climate on the other hand would not respond favourably to provocative
slogans or imagery; these would be counter-productive.

During one such meeting, I offered to make posters according to given
requirements; I decided that I would make my own as well as offer my
services to those who had more experience. There was some interest, a
couple of phone calls, but no serious follow-up. We wanted to go ahead
with it anyway. We visited the offices of several NGOs/womens' groups,
and looked at their collection of posters. They seemed a bit lacklustre. We
decided that we would print and sell ours through these groups, use some
during demonstrations, paste some on the walls of the city, show them to
people and thereby raise funds for sponsorship.

Working on them certainly gave us a reason to connect with people whom
we might otherwise not have met. It was decided that they would go beyond
the immediate requirements of the elections, and could be used outside of
that particular spatial and temporal context. We wanted to print handbills
as well. And perhaps make, as a sample, a translite of one of the posters,
something which could be carried around and plugged in wherever possible.

A few people promised sponsorship, but this did not materialize. It seems
to need serious pursuit, which neither of us could undertake, considering
other commitments that required attention as well. A miscalculation. I, for

one, was busy throughout the day, working on the computer, composing the visuals and text.

Ilesh Vyas, who runs the design studio where I worked, suggested a writer (who wrote in Gujarati and Urdu) whom he knew – Aziz Kadri – who could perhaps help us translate some of the text into the appropriate languages.

Kadri lived in Madhuram, and we went to visit him there. Now in his 60s, he had been a trade union leader in his time. He had not been formally educated beyond the fourth grade, but was a scholar of Persian and Urdu, and a noted Gujarati writer.

He showed us sheets of text, on different kinds of paper – wrapping paper, butter paper, pieces of faded red fabric used to bind books – covered with the most exquisite calligraphy. He showed me how he sanded his nibs down to provide him with the desired flat tip. His convictions had taught him not to accumulate wealth, and he lived within the barest of needs; he still cycles several kilometres to the press where he works.

Bina wanted to do a biographical profile on him, and I gave him a scroll with the visuals that I was working on; we requested him to write down a few slogans/pieces of text around the images, provided they met with his approval. I had used some stills from the INSAF film, *Gujarat Carnage*, and some of Ilesh's photographs, taken on his trips to Kutch.

The latter were mostly of the earthquake – crevices and cracks that marked and split the earth. I wanted to combine the associations and the differences – some of them tragic – into a message that would underline fabricated disasters as redundant, to say the least.

Kadri's enthusiastic response encouraged us, he came back in a day with several sheets of butter paper covered with verses in Urdu, and with translations in Gujarati of some of the matter that we already had, including Articles 14 and 15 of the constitutional rights.

After three weeks of work, it was brought to our notice that posters were banned by the Election Commission headed by J. M. Lyngdoh, something we had read about but had not till then taken seriously. Putting them up on the city walls would involve courting arrest, for which we were not prepared;

combined with this was the respect that we felt for Lyngdoh, and our belief in his integrity.

In the meantime several possibilities for sponsorship had come up, and we decided to print the posters anyway – the sponsorship did not materialize.

I slept badly at nights, and had the most disturbed dreams. I remember one very distinctly, I was woken up early next morning by a phone call from Bina and was relieved to hear a familiar voice.

I recounted the dream to her. I was seated in an aircraft of some sort, completely exposed, no roof or sides. I don't remember the presence of anyone else around me. Maybe I was just airborne, and it wasn't a craft after all. I was hurtling at top speed towards a hill; the slope tilted up to my vision. Walking towards me in the distance were relatives that I hadn't met with in years, adults and children, my daughter among them. They were coming to welcome me. At the very last moment, the craft veered wildly away from the approaching figures, now receding rapidly, and we were again hurtling into infinity, this time towards certain death.

I felt resigned, but woke up in what seemed to me like an informal hospital-cum-dormitory, there were people I recognized, like Natraj and Gargi, painter friends of mine. Most were wounded; I was not sure if I was and did not want to know. I feared disfigurement, and evaded the confrontation, wandering from room to room. There was debris on the floor, organic debris, faces which had dried and crumbled, open like rib cages, ashen in colour and texture. I did not want to identify them as faces. I asked a friend if mine was intact, she replied with a half-smile, almost a smirk – it's all right. Much later, I gathered the courage to look into a mirror and found half my face disfigured and swollen, the other half unrecognizable. There had been a crude attempt at re-construction, eyebrows had been drawn in, very badly, with a black eye-pencil – and I thought to myself that I could have pitched in to give myself a better face, I certainly could draw better.

I wandered into the last room, a shabby room which served as a sort of transit lounge. There were others there, waiting without hope, and resigned to an indefinite stay.

I asked them where we were, as I was the most recent addition to the community, and someone replied – There is nowhere that we can go. We are here because we have lost our documents in the crash and must wait till we find them. I felt desperate – how could one recover documents from debris, from fragments scattered over god knows where? The question was left unanswered, hanging in the air.

We distributed some posters at the convention in Ahmedabad, sold some at a meeting in Baroda, and left batches of them with various organizations and individuals. Now that the urgency of the elections is past, we will find a way of distributing them in an organized manner. The process is going on, and we are learning and evaluating the outcome at every stage.

There are a few ways of carrying this forward:

1. To ask other artists to contribute their posters as well, put them all on a CD and distribute them to relevant organizations. This could be done over a period of time. The responsibility/costs for printing would then not be such a burden.

2. We could make some more during the art workshops in the field, and again, store the images for future use.

3. Continue to find outlets for their sale.

4. Maybe wait to collect more posters and paste them on the walls of the city now that there is no ban. It would be interesting to observe/record the reactions of passers-by.

5. Draft a letter explaining the project and mail it to interested organizations, so as to build up a sustained relationship.

The posters are just one more channel of collaboration, and interaction around them leads to different kinds of encounters.

Several festivals and concerts for peace were organized in Baroda, a memorable event was the staging of Soumya Joshi's play that was attended by a wide cross-section of people. Ranjit had made sure that some of the children from the city schools that she worked with were there.

There was a panel discussion, with Praful Bidwai, Sudhir Chandra, I.G. Patel, also at the Hansa Mehta auditorium. It was a working day at the university, students everywhere on campus, but not in the audience. Much of all this tended to be limited to a circle of regulars, and some of us wondered if it made any sense at all to invest precious resources on these events at a time like this. Maybe some of the effort should go towards gathering the right kind of people, those that needed to be informed, whose opinions would perhaps be formed by such exposure.

George's visit was something we had looked forward to. Bina was in Godhra with one of the observer groups, and I spent the major part of the day with him; took him around the studio, introduced him to Ilesh and Azra, and showed him the images on the hard disk and the posters.

His reaction was that they spoke of a very non-specific universality, verging on the banal, in the face of a very specific, complex threat. We discussed this when Bina returned. It seemed to me that there were two perspectives at war here – the panoramic as opposed to an attempt at location/ collaboration, operating from within the constraints of and in negotiation with a crisis-torn state. The discussion left me very troubled. It seemed that my artistry and intellect were in question, when I had wanted to focus on neither. Which is not to say that they were not exercised, they were, but towards negotiation rather than excellence per se. On the way to the bus station, we went past jeep-loads of armed soldiers – the elections had just been held, and there was no knowing what might happen.

On the 20th, I was in Ahmedabad again, at a conference entitled 'Story-Telling in the Digital Age', which was hosted by the New Media Department at NID. I had submitted a paper for the monograph that would be brought out, acceptance of which meant attendance minus registration fees. This was way back in March – I was hard at work on it the last days of February, during the initial outbreaks of violence. I had completed it on the 1st of March. At the time, we had no idea that there would be such a prolonged chain of events, the conference was, of course, postponed. I was surprised, and glad when in November I got to know that my paper had been accepted.

There were different kinds of presentations, and there were participants from all over the world: technocrats, puppeteers, folklorists, artists, cultural anthropologists. I was lucky to see two films – one made by tribals in South America and the other by villagers in Kutch. I had wanted to facilitate a similar activity in Vatva.

The eye, and its location, make all the difference. Apart from the lack of self-consciousness with which we face the camera when it is held by one of our own, our pre-occupations qualify the perspective and thereby the focus and the frames.

One was shot in a fishing boat on the river. The concentration on the face of the man seated opposite the camera – the frame and the river almost eclipsed by his bare torso, his limbs lengthened by the distorted close-up shot – as he assessed and negotiated the flowing sweep of the waters, was so intense as to create a sense of total identification – the viewer becomes as involved in what is happening.

In another film, the salt pan workers in Kutch focused the camera for several minutes, repeatedly, not on each other but on the seawater and the repetitive act of wielding their implements. Something soothing about it, and it reminded me of those Warli paintings in which every blade of grass is marked on the surface, every drop of rain.

I took down the e-mail IDs of the anthropologists who initiated their making.

I stayed in the empty apartment of a young friend who happened to be Muslim. When he moved back to Ahmedabad after a stint in Bombay, he had difficulty in finding accommodation – this was a few years ago. During the riots, however, the inmates of the other flats in the block assured him that he would be safe, and had nothing to fear. This was very much on my mind when I met the neighbours to sort out details regarding the water supply; it would have needed courage to have taken such a stand at a time like that.

My friend's flatmate was the son of yet another old friend, a noted architect, Neelkanth Chaya. Visiting him was a rewarding experience, and helped resolve certain nagging doubts. He had been involved, along with other architects, in a project in Kutch after the earthquake in 2001, re-building an entire village. I told him about my project, and he shared his experiences with me.

The work that I did in Kutch, he said, is not something that I can talk about to those who are familiar with my work, nothing that I can discuss with my colleagues. There were times when I wondered if architecture was at all relevant in that context, whether there was any need for architects to be there. The structures that we put up looked like *dubbas*. When the government agency that had commissioned us visited the village and saw them, they asked us – what are you architects doing here? And we replied – we don't know what we are doing here.

But the villagers have built around the core that we provided them with, each to suit his own needs, which might not have been possible with something prefabricated or resolved. That was encouraging. And at the end of it, I look back and feel a great sense of satisfaction, and you will feel the same.

The day after the conference closed, on the 23rd, I met Dr Ashok Chatterjee.

He had earlier been on the panel that scrutinized the IFA grant proposals, and was now invited to moderate the sessions that took place in the afternoons during the conference. I discussed with him some of the things that troubled me, given his many years of experience with the communal situation in Gujarat. I was struck by something that he said during the course of our conversation – the one common need that was felt during interactions with survivors and victims of the carnage was the overwhelming desire on their part to tell their own stories – a desire as strong as the necessity of rebuilding their lives.

He further felt that it was crucial to identify an NGO based in Ahmedabad which would provide us with a framework within which we could function.

During the earlier convention at Tagore Hall, we had debated the necessity of public testimonies, and had come to the same conclusion – the catharsis and the sense of self that they gave the narrators perhaps outweighed the trauma and the shame of standing, emotionally exposed, before an unknown audience.

More recently, I attended the Asia Social Forum at Hyderabad as an extension of my research/groundwork for the project. A local friend, art critic and curator, Rasna Bhushan, had organized an art event which included a poetry reading by M.F. Husain, the installation of a painting by him, and a possible act of solidarity by local and visiting artists in making a painting together. All this in an open tent that was one among those erected; it was obvious to us at the end of three days that an artist's intervention in such a situation needed to be re-formatted, more free-flowing.

The day before the opening, Rasna and Alex had boards put up, in readiness for the event. When we arrived, there was, on these very boards, in addition to a display of photographs by P. Sainath, some drawings on Hiroshima by a Japanese artist and a sale of posters by an unnamed organization. It was difficult explaining to them that the space had been set aside for the art event. The artists did not come at the appointed time, I in any case was more interested in hearing the talks – I could paint anytime, but it isn't every day that one hears Medha Patkar and Arundhati Roy speak. I put up my posters; Alex Mathew, sculptor, who is presently faculty at the SN School in Hyderabad, had contributed a drawing.

On the last day of the Forum, we arrived at the spot where the tent had stood – there was no sign of it, no sign of Alex's drawing, my posters, or Husain's painting. I left the same evening.

Today, on the 14th of January, I read about the 'theft', if it was indeed that, in the newspapers. It is as likely that it had all been dismantled and burnt as *raddi*, as is the practice after most melas.

Husain was surrounded by admirers and reporters the moment he alighted from his vehicle. They were scrambling over one another for his attention.

As far as I was concerned, a painting valued at several lakhs, as the newspapers had reported, had no place there. Assuming that it was more in the nature of a contributory gesture, I had earlier asked Rasna, would he mind if it were lost? And she had replied, 'Excuse me!'

Hierarchies remain *virgo intacta* when they are not tackled at the level of structure, despite forums and discussions.

This is where physicality comes in. Structure and physicality, method, a step-by-step progression, but start is at scratch. If already formed, unform yourself. Inform the circumstances at hand. What you seek to build is a new belief, with a knowledge of where and when the earlier rot set in.

A single faulty brick undermines the construction. Repairs are superficial and recurring. Words gallop ahead, if used indiscriminately. Experience lags behind, withers and dies. What you have left are empty formulations, which have superseded practice. If one paid more attention to the lived experiential, maybe this mad race towards destruction would slow down, and people would have the time to see life in all its beauty.

Art as concept in practice? Yes, if practised with conviction. As Ashok Chatterjee had said, get in there and do it. Take the consequences, expose yourself. Ask to be monitored. A crucifixion of sorts. Rasna in deep depression.

We left some posters for sale at the Orient Longman bookstall, but again, it was obvious that selling them required more of an input in terms of time and effort. Bina was there, of course, independently, and sent me information on the outcome of meetings which took place during the convention, including a series of events which were to happen around the 8th of March.

I would say that the past two months have been devoted to research, and on returning to Baroda on the 24th of this month, Bina and I will meet again to decide how we can further focus. Our work together on this project will happen at two levels: fieldwork, which will involve direct contact with persons and situations; documentation, in the form of text and images of a more private, subliminal nature. The former will bleed into the latter, and both would, together, inform my painting.

Bina's articles/excerpts from articles, e-mails and letters feed into a common pool of shared and forwarded e-mails between those of us who have collaborated in different ways during the past few months.

What we now have in mind are the workshops. The text/images that would articulate/document the experience. The smaller projects within the project – posters, etc. – would be embedded in the narrative. Facets revealed in different contexts. Like cut stone. I am now beginning to think in terms of an exhibit that will combine the different kinds of output that the project might give rise to.

Dr Ashok Chatterjee was concerned about the question of disseminating the work that we would do together.

The venues for the conventions that one has attended till now have specific parameters in terms of organization – a complex exhibit cannot be accommodated unless the organizers are contacted well in advance and possibilities are worked out together. We would prefer to think about this a little later on, when we have adequate material to work into shape.

Still, I ask myself – have these two months of my life made any difference to those who have suffered so terribly? Or, will these two months go towards preventing such suffering in future? And then the feeling that personal contact, just being there, is of utmost importance.

The fact that I spend so much time writing up proposals – if they did not speak the truth it would be valuable time wasted. They are part of my work, excerpts will be used in various ways. The project itself does not stand apart from life; at the time when I felt compelled to propose it, I was prompted as much by financial necessity as by a desperate need for belief, having lost one too many of those over the past few years.

The project is about process, and what attracts me about process is the transparency implicit in visibility. One has debated de-mystification. Much of the time, one has understood it in terms of subversion, implying a certain delight in destruction. I prefer to think of it in terms of exposure, of disarmament. The concept is still in place, as an aspiration; the process constantly questions and monitors it. Nonviolent, but still merciless. Truth anyway needs no support.

There is real anxiety that I haven't painted since October. Has this been imposed on me or is there a logic to it? The project is not a temporary distraction, it involves structural change, and therefore is demanding of time and effort. It arose out of various kinds of needs.

15th January 2002

Why did I undertake something like this at a time when I felt very sure about my ground as a painter? I could not bear the loneliness of working in isolation. Twenty years of studio practice.

I felt compelled by the recurrence of violence over the past three years. First the earthquake, then the bombing of the WTC and then this. Insanity on an unprecedented scale.

Do I feel anguish at all times? What is it that makes me go on? The commitment that I have made, the belief that people have in me, as an artist. The need to engage in something outside of myself.

Structural change involves major re-location. Some things have to be on hold in order to accommodate the changes. Even if I felt secure within myself as a painter, maybe, I could not have held out for very long if other needs were not met. Not just within, but also without, in the world. There is no difference – except that an individual functions at the microcosmic level – cosmic, nonetheless.

I feel unsure of my ground, I doubt everything. I feel exposed, accountable. Supported by taxpayers' money. There are copyrights on most things, ideas, symbols. Careful when you use them. The multiplicity of socio-cultural levels of understanding makes it so much more difficult. Differences in exposure to different things. Differences in levels of knowledge.

Whom are you speaking to? That is not such an easy question to answer in India. It could paralyse you. Be specific. Maybe it is this that paralyses us. Renders some of us dumb and others strident. These strictures are drawn from an alien vocabulary, of literalness, precision, linearity. This is all the more obvious on a shared platform, as in NID, when storytellers from other cultures presented their narrative/narrative structures alongside ours.

Ours has been a metanarrative, long before the word became fashionable. Meta to the extent of transcending time, space and logic as we are forced to understand it. The digital media has materialized these possibilities in ways comprehensible to logic, we found them instinctively. The structures of metanarrative as materialized by the digital media are structures we have used minus the digital media, for centuries. Doors within doors, windows within windows. Lifetimes within lifetimes, space/time warps. Lifetimes as finite entities within a nurturing infinity in dynamic doing and undoing, towards a centre, a black hole, a void. It is not this, nor this. It is but it is not. It is this and so much more besides and will not stay still.

Whatever you have to say, say it, in good faith. It has its place too, and from this multiplicity of voices speaking to multiplicities of audiences, the strands of true democracy will emerge.

I still have not come to grips with what I want to do. I will when I do the first workshop. Could it happen in April? Or after summer? One thing that seems obvious is that we will have to get some equipment.

There is a difference between the time when I first conceived this project, in April 2002, and now. There is so much material, in film, image, in words – all speaking about the same thing. There is now a risk of repetition. How does one overcome this, if one sees it as an impediment?

Go to the heart of it. In painting, it was the self. Now, there is the other, of equal significance. The heart is in the relationship between the two.

5th February 2003

The day I left Bangalore, I met Gopal Menon, who had made the first film on the carnage, released in March 2002. He suggested a few names of people in Ahmedabad who might help me to draw up a work plan for the project.

I showed Gopal photographs of my paintings. The spatial/temporal aspect intrigued him, the actual moving from one frame to another, the cinematic sequencing, the flashbacks, repetitions and quotes. He assumed that I would work in such a manner during the course of my project, and was disappointed when I told him that the accent would be more on facilitating expression through the visual media, in drawing it out from the community that I worked with.

You have a craft, and you should use it, he said. It's what you are best at – the other things have been done, are being done – but if you can work with it through your painting, it would really be something.

It was building into an argument, I decided it was time to leave, and I had a train to catch that very evening. But he had a point.

A couple of days later in Baroda, his film, *Hey Ram,* was screened at the apartment of a friend. A coincidence. I had not seen it earlier.

Before I left Ahmedabad, I had spoken with the administration at the Institute of Behavioural Sciences situated inside the St Xavier's College campus. The nature of the Institute creates a continuous flow of resident and visiting social workers and volunteers working around several issues. The director promised to put me in touch with those that I needed to meet. In addition, he suggested Monica Wahi, who was currently working with those survivors from Naroda Patiya who were relocated in Faizal Park, Vatva – her involvement, as far as my project was concerned, carried forward the work that Bina has done there.

We sat on the stone benches outside the building, while I outlined my project for her. She was negotiating with a UP-based NGO, Vanangana, to take on the rehabilitation work in Faizal Park on a long-term basis. All of us, as individuals, were from outside the state, and unlikely to remain indefinitely. She envisaged a centre with educational facilities, which would run five days in a week; she felt that I had come along at the right moment, and could work together with them. It was difficult to find fieldworkers who came in on a regular basis, say once in a week, who would actually spend quality time with the victims.

6th February

Monica took me to Vatva the very next day. On the way, she pointed out to me the remains of Ishanpur ni Masjid, a beautiful, historical monument, its curving stone dome rising above the ruins. A blackboard with white lettering proclaimed it a protected monument, so designated by the Archaeological Survey of India. A crane had been brought in to demolish it during the carnage, the destruction had continued for five hours. Massive, weathered stone pillars lying atop debris: no attempt made at reconstruction, people pass by indifferently.

We entered Shah Alam past the main *darwaza*, it was a long drive, a gradual transition from the relatively cheerful centre of the city towards bleak outer reaches. It gave me the opportunity to re-adjust my sense of time and place, to allow the oppressive memories of last year to re-surface. The relief camp had of course been dismantled. We visited the remnants of one in Jehangir Nagar, camp no. 9 – the canopy hanging in tatters, the bamboo poles awry. A few families, twenty in number, still left, waiting to be allocated homes to move into. The landlord who had offered the space for the makeshift structures was impatient, so were the inmates. Monica was greeted with much warmth. A mass wedding was to take place, and some of the families were involved. They were insistent that she should attend the *haldi* and then the *mehndi* ceremonies – wear old clothes, and you will see how it is done, they said. There was to be dancing, the inevitable *garba*.

One of the men had broken out in a rash, his face was pink and raw. He had made the mistake of applying, on his face, an ointment that had been prescribed to him for sores on his fingers. He showed it to Monica as a child would show his mother a scraped elbow – the man was in his fifties, his long, dishevelled grey hair dyed orange with henna, fading in streaks. We left him, belligerent, shouting at a female inmate who had, in his opinion, misled us with an irrelevant piece of information. Tempers were frayed, indeed.

All the while, disco music blared forth from a flashy new booth/shop opposite the camp, all shining aluminium and formica. We had to speak above the driving beat.

We went on to Faizal Park. A few rows of houses in the midst of a barren tract of land. I try to understand the way they were aligned, they seem to run parallel, but at an odd angle, set strangely askew. It was the 30th, and most of the families had gone to Naroda Patiya to attend the death ceremonies, which commence a month before the actual date. The 28th of February, 2002. Very few left in the settlement, for obvious reasons.

I had expressed my apprehensions about visiting the victims, but Monica had reassured me that things would seem almost normal on the surface. People were carrying on with their lives, they had no choice. Many, especially the men, had remarried. She especially wanted me to meet Shahjehan, a young girl of 17, who had saved herself and her younger brother from a fiery death by rolling over in the soil. She was illiterate, but keen to learn, anything – the SJ of Bina's report for Aman Samudaya, who had watched her older sister being raped and burnt. Monica was keen that I should work with her during the course of my project. She was undergoing, among other things, a series of surgeries for her burns, in Bombay. Monica gave me three photographs of the girl, I carry them with me in my purse. They keep me from growing complacent with delusions of normalcy.

The first house that we entered was where she lived, we met her aunt. Shahjehan had left for Patiya. Monica pointed out to me that the houses of those from Naroda Patiya were marked outside in stencilled, turquoise blue lettering: Faizal Park had been bought by the Citizens' Relief Committee, an Islamic organization, most of the relief camps had also been run by them.

From those whom we met that day, the stories were identical – loss of business, lack of work. Income is the main concern. Many of the women were proficient with the sewing machine, in making 'Chinese suits' (salwar suits) – their husbands would in normal circumstances find them custom. The husbands were now dead, and the women did not have a direct relationship with the client, who in turn did not know them, and was loath to give them business.

There was a terrible despondency about the place, lightened by the few children that were there. There had been a visit from the ice-cream vendor; they held in their hands multi-coloured iced lollies, frosted maroons and yellows, purples and greens. I asked a young girl – is this something that you eat every day? Her reply was a quick – no, on special days, he comes as you have come.

There is a light-eyed child of three with her, very active and bright – he had seen his mother set ablaze, and had repeated the story many times, to visitors and reporters, as he would describe a spectacle, a *tamasha*. The girl would prompt him – tell them what you saw.

It was difficult not to recall details and passages from the numerous reports that one had read. I remembered an excerpt from the account of a witness, Naeem Shaikh, and on my return to Baroda read it again.

Let me tell you about the pregnant woman they killed. She begged them to spare her, that she was pregnant. Everyone in her family was dead and her husband had run away. They said all right, come, we won't do anything to you. As soon as she walked towards them, they slashed her belly with a sword. She was pregnant – full-term. The baby, who fell out, was thrown into the fire; they tore her clothes and pushed her too into the fire. I saw all this with my own eyes. None of her relatives has survived, her brother, brother-in-law, mother, aunt – no one is alive except her father and a twelve to thirteen year old boy.

Still Life (detail), 2010–12

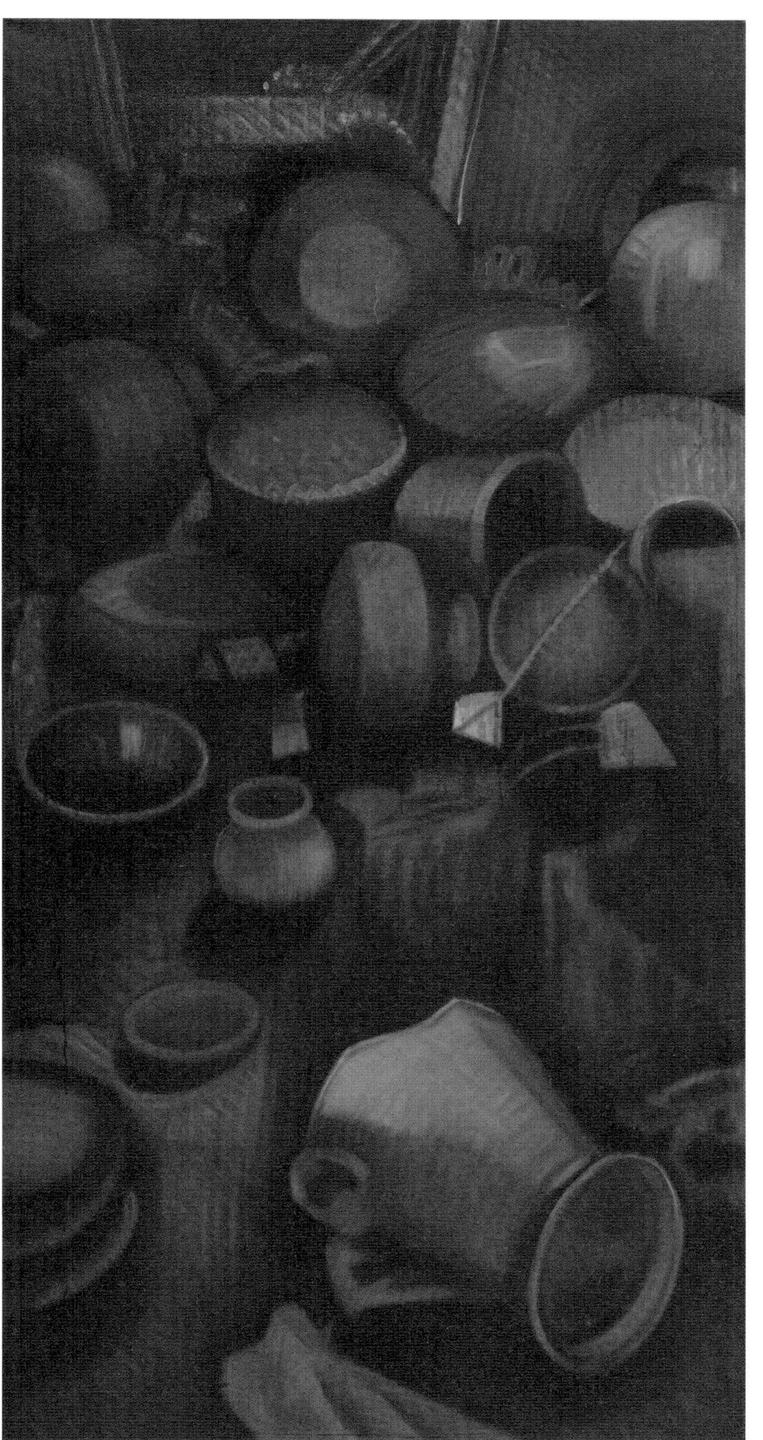

Her entire family is wiped out. They were the people who used to paint the flats in Gangotri and Gopinath during Diwali, yet they were not spared.

Kausar Banoo, as she was called, and her husband were from different sub-sects, and had faced much opposition to their marriage. Monica told me that the romance had extended over many years, but they had finally got married, and were expecting their first child. She had gone to stay with her mother for the baby's delivery.

Harsh Mander, who was working on deputation with a development organization, resigned from the IAS in horrified protest; his *Reflections on the Gujarat Massacre* was widely circulated through the internet. He had also written about her.

What can you say about a woman eight months pregnant who begged to be spared. Her assailants instead slit open her stomach, pulled out the foetus and slaughtered it before her eyes.

We met her father, who had been allotted a house along with Javed, the young boy. He showed us photographs of a young woman – this is Kausar – two boys, his wife, other relatives. They were misted over with the patina of death, except for Kausar, who was in sharp focus. The old man had married again, a young woman from Gulbarga, his hometown, to which he had returned for a while after the carnage. Javed had left, as he felt ill at ease with this new development. Monica described him as very disturbed, angry and aggressive, reckless in his newfound wealth – his share of the compensation for the loss of the entire family. It amounted to a few lakhs. Fourteen members of the family dead.

The old man, on the other hand, was very media-savvy, and repeated his own version of how he was 'being cheated' by Javed.

We visited Navapura village. Fieldwork had entered the rehabilitation phase. Residential schools had been located for the children, some good, some not so good. There is one in Raigarh in Maharashtra, which was set up by a well-known surgeon, Ungre by name, who practises in some of the best hospitals in Bombay. It is situated in beautiful surroundings, and is run by indulgent staff who pamper the children; they are fed fruit and milk apart from their normal diet, and receive excellent healthcare by virtue of the resident doctor. Monica is besieged by requests for admission into the school, her list grows longer, exceeding the available vacancies.

We accepted an invitation for a cup of hot coffee, and entered one of the houses: this one was owned by a woman, who had been a passport agent of some sort, and had travelled to Paris, Bonn, and to the Middle East.

The mosaic flooring was soot-stained, her television and other meagre luxuries had been burnt.

Chunaravas, the next village. The inhabitants belong to the OBC category, and are Hindus: the Chunaras, whose traditional occupation is the painting of houses and walls with *chuna* or lime. They brew illicit liquor among other things. When the mobs came, they had allowed them access to the dargah beyond, and some of them had joined in the fray. In retaliation, the local Muslims had attacked and destroyed most of the village, the rubble remains untouched. Local politics amongst those who were in charge of relief made sure that there was very little progress. Dishonesty amongst the populace added to the confusion, and things therefore remained as they were.

And then the Qutb-e-Alam dargah, which had provided shelter to those who ran in and shut the gates against the mobs. There are bullet marks on the walls. The village beyond the dargah is more affluent, and better equipped against attack, it was left largely undamaged. Schools had since re-opened in the locality, we met Munira, a student at the local college who teaches in one of them.

7th February

A meeting with Mira Rafiq that evening was postponed to the next day. I went alone, Monica was busy. A long drive again, past the signboard, Shah Alam in faded blue. I was growing familiar with the route. The Ishanpur masjid, or what remained of it. I waited for Mira at the Shah Alam Darwaza. Meher-un-nissa, one of her fieldworkers, came up to meet me and took me to the waiting two-wheeler.

We went up to her office, and I explained the project to her. The situation is now much worse, she said. The suicide rate has gone up, two more cases in the last couple of weeks. People are reluctant to give business to the Muslims, due to the uncertainty. The orders for kites for Uttarayan and *rakhis* for Raksha Bandhan had dwindled. Income generation was the central issue.

There was an economic boycott in force.

Mira was sceptical about those who had run workshops and then left, never to return.

The people would ask her every day – Where is so and so? Why don't they come back? What do we do with these things that we have made?
I wondered too.

The old question: Where does art fit into all this? Should one not locate markets before one goes into production of any sort? This was obviously not a situation where one could afford the luxury of experimentation. The walls of the office were lined with fabric-covered files, purses, handbags made by the women at the Centre for Development in Abad Nagar. We went there, two women were working, cutting fabric, running the machine. They were keen to learn some painting – What kind? I asked.

Flowers in vases, women carrying *matkas*.

I can work around preferences of that sort.

We visited a recreation centre for children at SS, or Sight and Service, as the *mohalla* is called. Mira had orders for greeting cards made by the children, and suggested that I work with them too. I recognized the centre from the last visit, with Kamla Bhasin and Syeda Hamid. It seemed like a long time ago.

I began to see that what Monica had suggested would be the best way to work, to supplement an income-generating activity with design inputs, recreation classes for the children, perhaps a small painting project that I could engage the women in, and a stipend, which could be paid to them every month for the collaboration. Initially, it would be vital to spend time and establish a rapport. On returning to Mira's office, I bought two files, one for Monica, one for the friend that I stayed with. I returned from Shah Alam with a much clearer and realistic picture of how I could contribute.

Monica was to attend a workshop the next day, but I went to the institute to meet her and Prasad for a final discussion before I left. The workshop was postponed; some participants were unable to attend due to a derailment on the Bombay–Ahmedabad sector.

Monica needed to visit Naroda Patiya, and offered to take me with her.

The horror story. The skin of normalcy grows over the most hideous of wounds. The Noorani Masjid, restored, fragile, freshly painted, almost festive. No peacock this time round – other motifs. Opposite, the narrow entrance lane adjoining a high wall – long, running along the whole length of the village, no avenues for escape. Leading straight to the infamous Gopinath and Gangotri Societies, in the far distance. The end of the road. Again, it was impossible not to remember.

I could not believe that all those people who ate my bread and biscuits could be so brutal.

The SRP lookout on the left, armed soldiers seated in the vicinity. It seemed unreal – how did these people regard them?

SRP men said, orders have come from above that today we should kill you.

On the other side of the village was the open maidan, where women were stripped, humiliated, raped and burnt. We walked across it, looking for the old well where the bodies were dumped. No one knew how many, it was believed that they were still there, and that the well had not been cleared since, nor the corpses dredged up. We did not find the well, and felt reluctant to continue the search, it seemed ghoulish to do so.

I had missed hearing Harsh Mander speak at the ASF, but I thought of him, striding up the incline towards the tents in Nizam's College in Hyderabad. I still have a fading printout of his mail.

I have never known a riot that has used the sexual subjugation of women so widely as an instrument of violence as in the recent mass barbarity in Gujarat. There are reports everywhere of gang rape, of young girls and women, often in the presence of members of their families, followed by their murder by burning alive, or by bludgeoning with a hammer and in one case with a screwdriver.

Beyond the maidan, the SRP quarters.

Women from the SRP families also said burn them, burn them … so that they also realize how those who were in that train felt.

The Institute of Behavioural Sciences has set up an office in Naroda Patiya, students work on their research there, a comforting presence. As we walk down the main lane, Monica is greeted by a bright young child, Saddam. We meet his mother, who is anxious about his welfare, his indifferent health. He was sent to the school in Raigarh, but his parents had him brought back; they were still undecided. The child wanted to be with Monica Didi, we went into his home for a cup of tea. Floor and walls stained black. The woman's elder daughter had three children, their father had been killed. The last she had seen of him was when he was being pushed by the mob towards a pile of burning bicycles. Much later, what was left of him was identified by his hand, which was found welded, by virtue of the ring that he wore, to the charred metal.

Monica tried to persuade her mother to have her married again, it was socially acceptable within the community, but with three children, who might not be welcome in the home of a stepfather? The girl would never even consider leaving them behind. The family was from Karnataka, and I spoke to the woman in Kannada – she held on to my hand as we prepared to leave.

Most of the families were from Kerala, Karnataka or Rajasthan, there were hardly any Gujarati Muslims there.

Two of the houses, where most of the family had perished, were vacant.

Why did they choose this village of all places, I asked.

It was part of an industrial belt, replied Monica, where most of the mills were situated, and most were shut down, leaving people unemployed, broken in spirit. The highway now ran past it, raising the price of the land – who knows?

Mayabehn Kodnani is the BJP MLA from our area. She was in the mob which attacked us, there were other women too (8 to 10). If she is brought before me today, I will tell her, we elected you to the assembly and you brought this on us.

Oasis, an NGO, has set up a recreation centre there for adults, and one for children; I met Ami, who is in charge, and very interested that I should work there. I took down the address of the office in Baroda, and will visit it soon.

We had lunch in a small restaurant by the highway, belonging to a young man who had lost eight members of his family. Monica said the attitude of Muslims in general had changed, they felt that they had not been 'good Muslims'; there could be no other explanation for the horror of it. They had begun talking about Iraq, Israel and Palestine, of a worldwide wave of hatred, a pattern. Perfect fodder for fanaticism, for further polarization.

That evening, I met Siddharth of the Shared Footage Group, late at night in his apartment near NID. The others had left, and he would too, soon; their work was done, the footage was in Bombay and could be accessed anytime.

We had earlier met Stalin, who had given us addresses of where we could hire cameras should we need them. In the space of those few days, most things seemed to fall into place.

SECTION TWO

THE HIMMAT WORKSHOPS

– imminent.

Thinking through what I should do.

Went round to the art shop to check out prices.

Poster colours.

Fevicryl, which can be used on fabric.

Powder colours.

Coloured inks. Colour pencils.

Oil paints – for marbling, which I tried out at home. Should try out a few more.

Handmade paper – for marbling and for the scrap books. Brown paper for the scrap books.

Should I have a set of six bound before the workshop commences? That would take two/three days – but might be just the thing to provide an impetus and a shape.

Thought I should start with colour/mixing of colour. Marbling might be a good way to start – requires very little effort. Go on to tie and dye, the powder colours might be useful here. Go on to mixing and the colour wheel?

Decide on the size, it can all go into the scrapbook.

Or just application? How to hold a brush/to mix paint? Fill in shapes in single colours?
Mix colours by overlapping shapes?

Organize trips to the Kanoria Centre, NID?

Each session could go on for five hours. We could have two breaks in between.
Collect newspapers and magazines for collage. There are bits of fabric at the centre. Look for a backing for a fabric collage, in khadi.

Work towards a fabric collage. The screen at Monica's?

Showing slides – where and how? At the centre. Hire a projector. Can work that out on arrival in Ahmedabad. Not urgent, still open to question.

First day – marbling: can use up a whole sketchbook; but we need six trays, oil paints and kerosene. String and clips for drying. Start with the scrapbooks immediately – samples of what they have done, feelings about what they do. At the centre, and at home.

Give them marker pens for drawing? Maybe, to start with. And to write with? Micro tips? Or just ink pens?

To introduce composition – what objects to use? About the workshops? Yes, with material from the scrapbooks. Can go on to fabric collage – white on white – the screen as something to work towards.

For the first workshop: Budget
Draw from the bank – 15,000 ?
Monica: 2,000
Girls: 500 x 6 = 3,000
Self: living expenses – 3,000
Art materials: 5,000

Need to buy in Ahmedabad:
Handmade paper for marbling
Glass paper for colour exercises
Pencils/erasers/rulers
Set of:
1. poster paints
2. oil colours (for marbling)
3. colour pencils?
4. kerosene
5. plastic cups for mixing paint/plastic mugs
6. brushes – for watercolours and oil colours (set of four per student?)

Should we just have a common pool of materials?
Still, set of four. All materials to be left behind at the centre.

7. scissors

8. cutters
9. string for drying
10. clothes clips
11. gum/Fevicol

Other materials
Newspapers
Magazines
Scraps of material, available at the centre.

27 December 2004, Baroda

- - - - - - - - - - - - - -

This is a day that cannot go unrecorded. I began the first session at Himmat in Vatva.
My students were Shahjehan, Rehana, Farzana, Tahera, Rabia and Tasleem.

I arrived yesterday by bus – staying at Monica's.

The workshops were to have started in December, but on the 7th of Dec., Bibi Banoo, one of the group, was set ablaze by her rickshaw-driver boyfriend. She had received a compensation of 3 lakhs (which she had invested in the bank) for the loss of six of her family, including her husband. She now lived with her two small children, a boy and a girl. She had recently befriended the man, but had come to realize that he was after her money and therefore refused to marry him – or would agree on the condition that he would not receive a paisa of her money in the event of an accident. He threatened her repeatedly, she filed a police complaint; he was arrested, but released on bail. He visited her again one afternoon at Faizal Park and, after an altercation, doused her with kerosene and set her on fire.

She was hospitalized for a month. Nothing could happen during that period – the community was very disturbed. I visited VS Hospital in Ahmedabad once during the time – she seemed cheerful and on the road to recovery; her mother and others from her family were visiting from Karnataka. The doctors had however warned Monica that things could very easily take a turn for the worse considering that she had suffered 60 per cent burns – the major organs were likely to have been been affected.

She passed away on the 7th of January. I had scheduled a visit on that day to start work, but Monica warned me that things were hanging in the balance. I decided to go anyway, as the responsibility of the grant was by then beginning to weigh very heavily on me – and also to hand over some money for the clothes that my friends had bought from Himmat. Monica had indicated that funds were needed for the medical treatment. She called before I left Baroda, to let me know that Bibi Banoo had passed away – I went straight to the hospital on arriving in Ahmedabad, and the money went towards funeral expenses.

Zaid came forward as I was leaving, and we fixed up a day that we could shop for basic materials, which we did. I also picked up some stuff from Baroda.

Anyway, I started the first workshop today. With some very simple exercises that I have categorized as colour mixing – some marbling, and some of those butterfly prints. The girls were in high spirits – Tahera a little cheeky.

Vatva itself so different now, more a part of the world that I am familiar with – unlike in 2002, when it felt like a distant nightmare – a nightmare in limbo – every time I visited it. Monica showed me around the centre at Mayur Park. There was a room in the corner of the open courtyard which we could use for art classes – there was the terrace as well, both without a roof. Another room inside with a little store attached to it, but it was small and used by the women. The terrace seemed spacious, so we decided to start there despite the sun – we had all prevaricated long enough.

Many thoughts and doubts cross my mind, of course. The session today was like one of those hobby classes for kids. I needed to find their level, yes.

Doubt – will we ever get around to making something more ambitious? This itsy-bitsy stuff bores me – but there is no other way to begin. Some of them haven't even held a pencil or a brush before, let alone drawn.

Almost three years now, since the riots. I go ahead very much on the strength of a commitment. This is something that has to be done. This is a group that I have a relationship with and therefore it is possible for something to be done.

Zaid will take Monica's place as a liaison person when she leaves.

I had some scrapbooks made in Baroda, bound in maroon. Three of the girls have taken them home. They have been instructed to fill them up.

24th Jan 2005

Session begins a little later today – at two instead of one. The girls had a wedding to attend. We made some bookmarks yesterday and today, hopefully, we will make some cards. And small drawings which I will frame to be sold at the next Himmat exhibition – Monica plans to hold one at JNU. Utility has to be kept in mind – among other things to validate the activity – drawings without a definable purpose would be hard to justify. Or even explain – so we keep the concept simple for the moment. I am here to teach them painting, as it might come in handy as a skill that they could put to use towards generating an income. This is something we discussed with their mothers.

We did a little field trip to the Kanoria Centre for the Arts. Shatrughan Thakur, an ex-student from the painting dept. in Baroda had a studio there – he paints with vegetable dyes, and explained the process to the girls. Kabirbhai, Shahjehan's father and a rickshaw driver, drove us around. We did not know till the last moment if he would come, he drinks and beats up his wife and children periodically. Thin to the point of emaciation, with a shock of hennaed hair and bloodshot eyes. But he was safe – and could be trusted upon to drive the girls back. We squeezed ourselves into the vehicle.

Met Sharmila Sagara, who runs the centre – she recognized me and was curious about the girls – I explained, and she invited us to attend the workshops that were scheduled as part of the yearly Arts Festival in February, free of cost.

Visited NID as well.

Every day is a challenge.

I plan to have Azra over to show them how to make stationery – envelopes? Bind books? Managed to do some *riyaz* in the evenings.

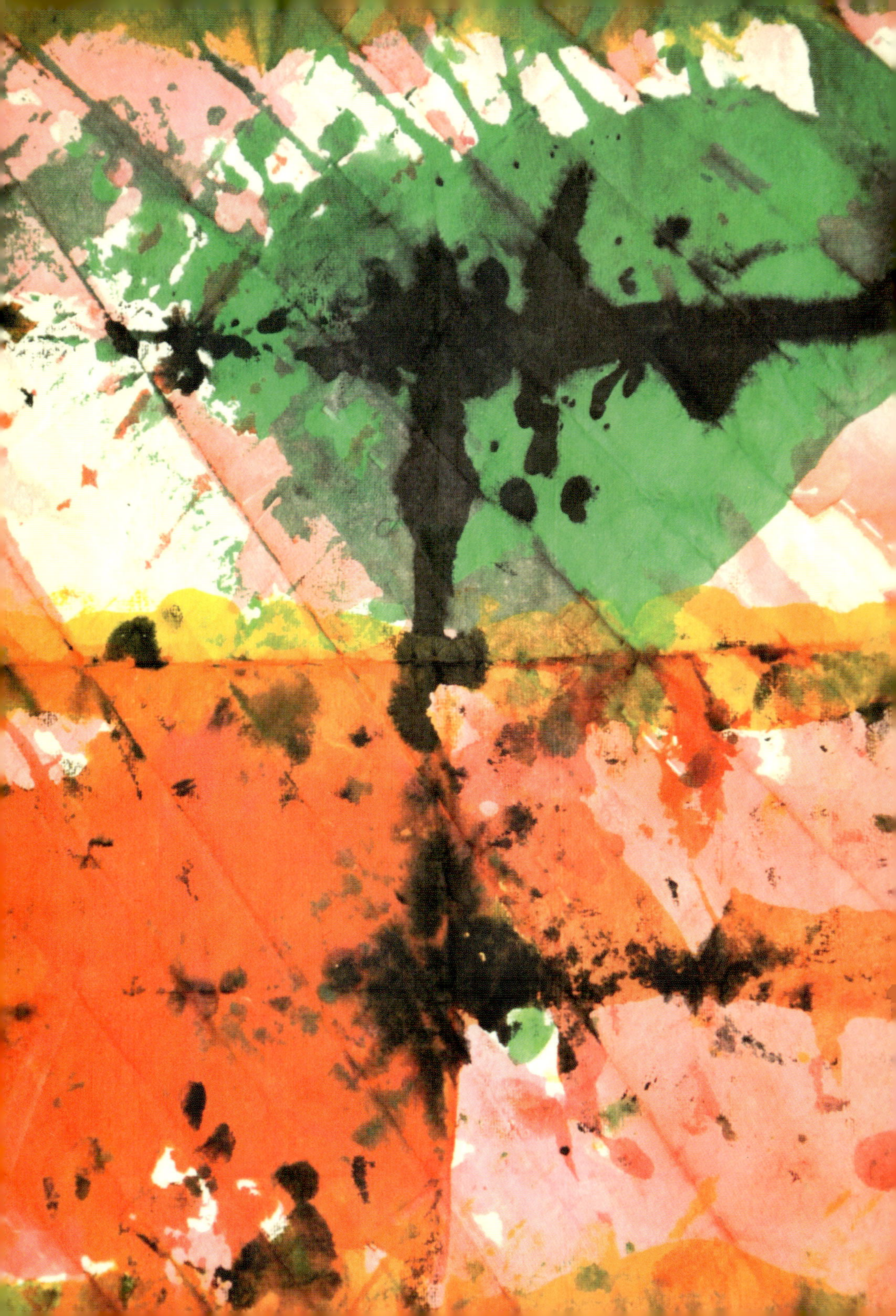

Things begin to take shape – an exhibition is scheduled to open in Bangalore early next week. So we decide to work towards it. The bookmarks – initially with vegetable prints – potatoes and okra – and then pasting bits of fabric on them. Some paintings, which I hope to use on posters.

Have been taking some photographs without quite knowing how to set the camera.

One of the issues under discussion is whether we could continue to work on the terrace, and if the landlord would agree to put a roof on it. The other option would be to rent a place – 5,000 as advance and 1,500 as rent.

Accommodation – a room at the Institute of Behavioural Sciences? Monthly rent 1,500.

How am I feeling? Better, not so pent up, now that I have begun. Hopefully it will clear the way for my painting as well, and I will be able to go beyond feeling so empty.

Azra came down on the 30th – a day of confusion. The girls had promised to come at 11, we were there at 10.30. No sign of anyone, the centre was shut. Went to Faizal Park and met the lot on their way to Shah Alam for a wedding. Dressed to the 'T', lipstick and the works. They promised to be there in an hour, I decide to wait and let Azra attend to some other work in the city.

The girls came at 2; I called Azra, who arrived at 3.30. We managed to work till 6 – she taught them how to make envelopes, and some elementary book-binding. I was tired at the end of it, having waited without lunch – except for a cheese sandwich. Decided to put some swatches of fabric on the paintings and have them printed as posters – so worked on that for a bit.

Had met the landlord the previous day, he had agreed to have a roof put over the terrace – initial expense mine, to be deducted from the rent.

Good.

Zaid will work for me, for 2,500 – that's ok.

All this quite factual –

29th

Back in Baroda, arrived last evening. Met Sharmila Sagara again at the Kanoria Centre to enquire about the workshops that she had mentioned – they sound good. Batik, papier mache (handled by Karl Antao) painting, calligraphy – 11th, 12th, 13th – have decided to send two girls to each workshop – I will attend the workshop conducted by Madhvi Desai – architecture – on the 12th and 13th, so I can be there and have something to do at the same time. Looking forward to it.

On the morning of the last day in Ahmedabad, met our neighbour at Mayur Park – an elderly man and a relative of the landlord, who does *bandhini*. A surprise – asked him if he would teach the girls and he agreed. The family is from Jodhpur, Rajasthan.

A discussion with Zaid before I left – he suggested that we have a counsellor come in once a week, as a couple of the girls were very disturbed. Tasleem, who had to stay with her widowed sister, Shaheen, in order to look after her two children – Shaheen's mother continued to live in Naroda Patiya. Tasleem quarrelled with the neighbours and with her sister as she had to stay at home while Shaheen 'played around' – the connotation including the kind of gossip that a small, conservative community would indulge in.

Rehana, who was married and had lived with her husband for a month, had returned when tension built up due to monetary demands from the boy's family. Her family feared for her mental and physical well-being in the circumstances. Her attention span was severely limited, she had very little idea of what the sessions were all about, and could sometimes withdraw and remain sullen for extended periods of time.

As we discussed things, we decided to approach an art therapist whom Monica knew – a very good idea. I could learn a lot from him – will meet him the next time.

Now, in Baroda, will go to Lalita to have the posters formatted and printed. Met some nice people on the trips to Ahmedabad – Arvind from Madras, Prita Jha from Manchester – a lawyer. She was taking interviews – working on criminal law and justice.

Feelings, my favourite subject? Relief at having begun, though it is impossible to predict how it will go.

Painting by ----------------------------------: 2005, Himmat, Vatva, Ahmedabad
--------by ---------- Artist/Activist Collaborative: The Himmat Workshops,
2005. Vatva, Ahmedabad.

Just spoke to Karl – the paper pulp workshop involves colour as well, so
that's good. Tasleem!

Papier mache Madhubani Batik Calligraphy
Tasleem   Farzana   Rehana   Tahera   Rabia   Shahjehan

Fees have been waived.

All this still part of the orientation – towards art as expression.

Rehana broods a bit, and is very unskilled. Tasleem is a little slow. Pent
up – picks fights and takes it out on her sister. During the first session,
she did not attend class for a couple of days. According to Shaheen, she
had threatened to stab herself. Shaheen stopped her, offering to immolate
herself instead. All very dramatic.

The visit to NID was exhaustive, the staff very helpful. We had the paper
for the bookmarks cut there – by a huge and complex machine – a
demonstration as well as giving the activity a value – the value of straight
edges and skill. Back at the centre, we made some cards and bookmarks
with the paper that we had cut.

1st Feb

Now in Ahmedabad again at the Kanoria Centre – 3.15 in the afternoon.
Have put the girls in their respective workshops – Karl's workshop cancelled
– a problem with the paper pulp, a disappointment.

I was hoping that there would be at least one artist handling the girls. So
it's Tahera, Rabia and Farzana in the Madhubani workshop with Shatrughan;
Shahjehan, Tasleem and Rehana in batik with vegetable dyes, conducted by
Praveena Mahicha – supposedly very good.

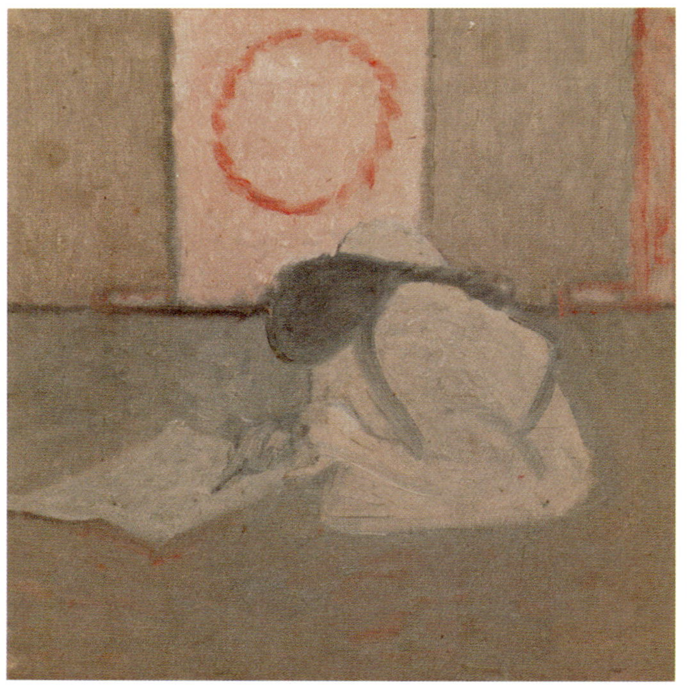

Met Ashok Shah this morning at the BM Institute of Mental Health – investigating some kind of a tie-up with the institute. I suggested a session every two months, he says two every week for one month and then maybe someone could come to the centre for two more months. Will have to find out more about the institute and its workings before getting involved.

Hope to meet Riyaz etc. this evening.

On the 10th, was unable to get through to Majidbhai (the contact in Faizal Park) so went straight to Vatva from the bus station – met Kulsum Apa (Rehana's mother) first – buying vegetables – or it could have been her husband's *lari* – who directed me to Tasleem's – they seemed happy to see me, a good sign! Farzana's cheque – which paid her school fees – had to be collected, so she could not attend the first day of the workshop.

Tahera (detail), 2006

Went to Tahera's and met her mother, who was working on her sewing machine – making underskirts for saris. Tahera was keen to show me the photo album with her father's photos in it – she had told me the last time round that he used to work in Saudia as a carpenter, and had come down to Patiya on leave when the riots broke out. There was a photograph of him in his apartment – tall, light-skinned and well-built – celebrating New Year's Eve with his friends – and several shots of him in his room. I felt sad, as I hadn't felt in a long time. I rarely feel anything these days – apart from superficial ups and downs – all somewhere between the surface layers. Feel at peace too – especially since the project got under way. As if I am finally doing what I should be doing.

I met Tahera's younger sister – bright and light-eyed, very pretty – I remembered her as the little girl that I had met, years ago, the one with the ice-candy.

Asked Tahera – on the rickshaw to Kanoria the next day – about the little boy who had also been there – she said he was her *mama*'s son, and lived elsewhere. His father was trained as an electrician – but had been shot in the leg during the *dhamal* and was now paralysed.

Saw Tahera's and Farzana's schools on the way – looked good, clean and cheerful.

Hung around at the sessions a little and then decided to meet Ashok Shah.

The Madhubani workshop – it occurred to me that it would be a good way to help the girls render/draw very simply. The tradition seemed to correspond with their level of skill and their perception of the world.

And yes, it has given them a fluency at the end of it all.

How awkwardly I write – as if after a long time, as if another being/person.

The batik workshop – for Tasleem, Rehana and Shahjehan so they could do simpler drawings with wax – will help loosen them up. To handle colour and cloth – to develop their tactile sensibilies. I think it worked well, they were still at it when I left at 4.30 yesterday. Some curiosity from other participants. I did give them some details just to let them in on the reality of Naroda Patiya.

One plump, aggressive young woman said – you must give them a pep talk,
tell them not to worry about what they should be doing. Uncalled for advice
– I felt they had integrated quite well with the rest of the group and were
very actively engaged – including Rehana. And – are you from an NGO?
What is it that you are trying to do? Empower them?

Is it so easy to explain?

I thought of the several proposals that I had written.

February

Came back for a three-day visit on 25th evening. Mainly to fix up things for
the next session – with Shatrughan, and to have a chat with Ashok Shah,
the art therapist – to see if the association could be taken further, especially
after my project is through. He suggested/offered use of the premises to
conduct sessions, but that does not serve the purpose.

Met with Roumanie, a designer friend, and had her visit the apartment
– showed her the screen and the output from the Madhubani workshop/
discussed how it could be translated onto fabric. She thought the posters
were fabulous – people suggest that I approach CRY etc. to have the drawings/
paintings printed as calendars/cards/stationery – perhaps they can be.

Monica is leaving on the 6th so I have to fix up accommodation – checked
with the BSc – they agreed to block the guest room for a year – spacious,
with a balcony looking out into the green environs of the St Xavier's
campus. In the meantime, other developments.

We had decided to put a roof over the terrace where we had worked during
the first session. That was in January and the weather had permitted it,
though the sun was still a little sharp in the afternoons and we had to
retreat towards the shadow cast by the west wall. By March, this would be
impossible. I wanted Sarosh and Riyaz to design something.

It was almost time for Monica to leave and five women were no longer
interested in working at the centre. Most now received compensations from
NGOs and from the govt. – enough to cover school fees etc. Monica held a
meeting to take a decision on handing over the centre to Jana Vikas – who

would employ a supervisor to oversee production – but with only a few women left, this was no longer feasible. The five that were left could pay Rs 500 towards rent – and I would have to pay the rest. And if the roof was done, I would have to pay 700 more.

That decides it – I will stay at the centre, it will save me a major chunk of expense.
The girls are free on the 7th, so will have a session 7th–11th and then 15th–21st – all tentative.
The first session (colour and drawing) – helped with the Madhubani workshop –
Farzana's drawings – her forms/sense of design seem based on *mehndi* patterns.
The girls' favourite colours – *kesar* and *gulabi*.
Shahjehan initially chose black.

27th

Lokesh and Viplav, former students of painting, came over to talk about the project – I showed them the work that had been done. Shatrughan had spoken to them about it. Good.

28th

Painting since the last couple of days. Visited Lokesh/Viplav/Ashutosh in their studios/gave them a critique.

The posters – text has to be augmented

Artist/Activist Collaborative: The Himmat Workshops. Funded by the IFA Bangalore. Coordinated by Vasudha Thozhur. Painting by Rehana. Ahmedabad 2005.

4th March

Day trip to Ahmedabad – to shop with Roumanie for cloth in Manek Chowk. Waiting for her at NID.

1. One metre in each colour/print
2. Base fabrics – cottons/synthetic/transparent opaque
3. Yarn – threads, needles

Directory of stitches in different kinds of yarn

5th March

This journal finally comes to an end on 6th March 2005.
The first entry – 13th Nov 2002. Started with the red book – but that's hardly
portable –

- - - - - - - - - - - - - - -

The Second Notebook/begun 28.4.2005

Staying in the BSc for the first time – session 25th April – 1st May.

One and a half hours in a queue on the 25th, waiting to get on to the bus
to Ahmedabad – very hot now. Left Baroda at 10 – finally arrived at 12 – no
time for anything, so straight to Vatva, there by 1 – started immediately,
upstairs again under our new roof. No fans, sweated it out. In Baroda, had
prepared material for the session: formatted some cards to show to Oxfam,
enlarged some of their drawings for the work on fabric – was very happy
with the results. Started with the running stitch exercise – 16 by 16 pieces
of casement – pink, orange, green – for cushion covers. Wool, threads/gold/
silver etc.
Resource person: Sharifa, who was good with embroidery, showed us how to
fit the fabric onto the rings, and to sew. Stopped at 5.

Accounts
35+60+45+75 – transport
Water: 24
Coffee and sandwich: 60

On the night before I left Baroda, Zaid called – back from the peace march,
a huge relief. To have someone here.

On Saturday, had called the BSc to confirm the booking for the guest room that I had made earlier in the week.

Unprepared for rudeness – one Father Amalraj – found out from Zaid that his was a higher position than the director's.

Anyway, he said – I was told you wanted the room for the whole year – this is not a guest house. We only let it out to NGOs. This upset me for a couple of days. He finally agreed – told him I wanted it for a week + had made no other arrangements – but the encounter left me with a bad taste. Saw him again late evening, but he was leaving for Kutch for a couple of days – and agreed to meet me on his return.

Was that the 26th? Yes I think so –

25th – was exhausted and dazed with the heat – on coming back around 6, slept for a while and then went out.

No – it was the 25th that I met him.

On the 26th, continued with the work upstairs, but aware of tensions in the group –

Met Zaid in the morning, which was nice –

Accounts – 26th
75+75
Food – 100

Tensions worsened – scrap/shouting/abuses between Afsara and Tasleem.
O yes
On the first day: talking to the girls about the literacy classes.

Oxfam had bought five posters for Rs 6,000 – we decided to start the classes in the morning for the girls – all except Tahera/Farzana. Started on the 15th of April – Shahana teaches them – as a resource person – she had been associated with Himmat earlier. Zaid fixed it up.

Of course we can only run it for two months with the money we have. Girls will be paid Rs 10 a day – as incentive to attend.

On the 25th, asked Tasleem about the classes – got to know that Shahana
was teaching them to shape eyebrows/wax arms/legs + *mehndi* – I didn't
mind the *mehndi* but did not want the rest.

27th morning I told her so.

Accounts
75+85+15 – auto
Food and water – 100
Electrician – 200

27th

A peaceful day. Tasleem hasn't come for a couple of days. The girls say that
she is not well. Maybe. Substantial amount of work done: looking back,
in such a short time, the girls have had a variety of artistic experiences:
Madhubani painting, batik, vegetable dyes, drawing and painting, work with
fabric – running stitch, embroidery/appliqué. No display boards, so unable
to draw inspiration from work done – prioritize. Also, a small exhibition to
celebrate the opening of the centre upstairs – next month? Who to invite?
Would they come? Maybe this should be the focus of next month's session –
but it is the height of summer??? Tahera out till the 20th of May, so session
will take place after that. Good. That will give me the time to catch up with
painting. 9th–11th – exams at the Dept. of Painting + I am the external
examiner again, this year.

The girls also have to learn how to paint in oils – next session.

As I told Chaya, I feel lonely, doing this work. Not very many who would join
me – very little glamour or romance or promise of rewards.

Arrived in Ahmedabad almost too late – and the nature of my contribution is
different from what it was intended to be, namely a documentation of bizarre
times/resistance to fascist forces, expressed in different ways. Times now, three
years later, are not so bizarre; the administration is being held responsible for
what happened – Modi refused a visa to the US, a public rebuff thanks to the
barrage of e-mails from activists/NGOs to the White House?? The Congress at
the centre – so many cases coming up for hearing: no results as yet, but still.

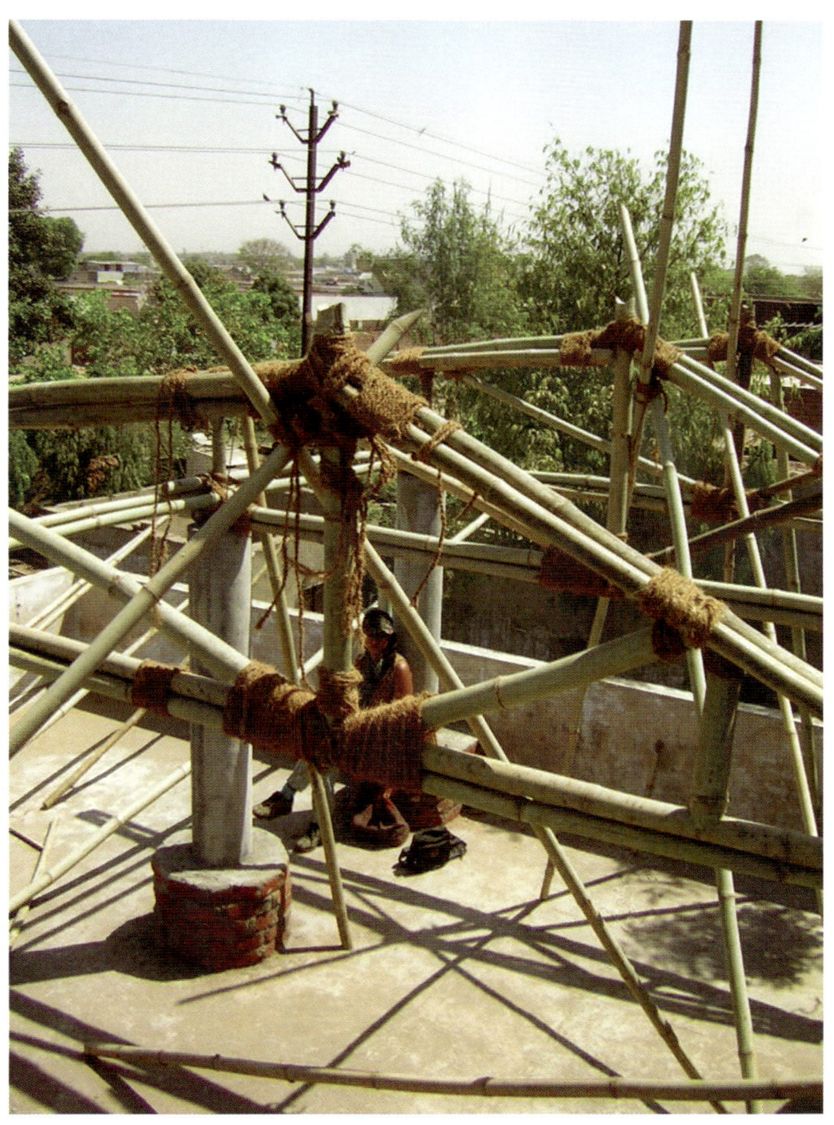

Constructing the Centre at Mayur Park, Vatva, 2005

So what am I doing? Something, yes, for certain. Giving my time – that most valuable resource – building a relationship – educational inputs into the girls' lives – seeing the grant through, delays and all – making the best of things. The rebuilding of trust, yes. The therapy angle perhaps would have been more acutely felt post-riots; still felt however –

Occupational therapy for sure –

Does this community still need us? They receive adequate compensation and subsidies –

Walter Benjamin and the state of emergency –

Chaya said – it is almost impossible to change people, but we can set up institutions which support progress, and things will gradually change – what will I have left behind at the end of it all?
At the moment thinking of continuing the workshops for a year on the whole – till January 2006. Need about six months, or more, to compile the work.

Something else that I think about is the framing/presentation of the work that we have done: would cost a fortune. How to raise funds? Far in the future, though.

Reading *Surviving Hitler: Corruption and Compromise in the Third Reich* Adam Lebor and Roger Boyes.

Very illuminating.

Accounts:

Breakfast: 10+5+24+20+20
Food + drink – round it off to 100 Rs a day?
Transport – 75 + 66

Must do accounts tomorrow.

30 x 5 = 150 x 6 = Rs 900

For the last session of 5 days
+literacy classes:

24th = Sunday

18–23 = 6 days + 2
17th = Sunday
8 days + 4 girls + 10 Rs a day = 80 Rs x 4 = 320 Rs

27th / evening

Cheque for Zaid – 9,500 Rs – towards building costs. 10 – meeting scheduled with Shipra and Avinash at Oxfam to collect remaining posters, cheque, and to discuss cards – they had no time – barely ten minutes – we rushed through my agenda – gave them card/bookmark samples – no cheque, promised that they would drop it off tomorrow.

Dissatisfied. Also spoke to Zaid about the tensions within the group – decided to meet with the girls – so we did that – also decided to draw up a set of rules, impositions, etc. to ensure peace – was a good meeting. Tasleem did not turn up, as a result of yesterday's flare-up. Girls instructed to go to her house and ask her to attend from tomorrow – let's see.

The meeting relieved me.

Also asked Z to do some team building sessions with the girls on a regular basis.

Class went reasonably well after that – let's see.

Tried to meet Fr Amalraj this evening – scheduled for tomorrow at 10 a.m.

28th

7.30 a.m. actually did a 15 min run/walk.

Glad I finally started writing again.

So much action that it is difficult to record – I realize when I sit down to write out all the details.

Many dreams come to nothing

This year – I do not know.

I work – no tangible results as yet – too involved with the fieldwork still.

Need some more time to compile and edit. Did a photo shoot with Z – from Sabarmati to Vatva, the Ashram to Faizal Park – a good day, sometime last month – the 14th/or so. Have to put it together.

In a book? Or a long panel – horizontal? Both.

Each photograph framed separately?

Keep your desires small and within reach.

29th

All journal entries now few and far between but better than nothing I suppose –

This is a post-session reminiscence.

Actually, about the project: so much happens, so much density that it is impossible to record/do it justice, unless I do nothing else but the project. Occurred to me as I read through *The Story of Five Posters* – such trivia recorded, as it was easy to isolate from mainstream living/working. Now it is the fieldwork that is the reality, the mainstream.

This time round, at Xavier's, nightmarish.

Beginning June always the hottest days – I had a small, stuffy room with doors and windows which opened into the corridors instead of the grounds – no breeze, lights on all night, no privacy – uncomfortable and slept badly for the four nights that I was there. Did not eat very well either – result – fell ill the last night and day, throat on fire, temperature, disturbed dreams. Lucky that I had a good seat on the bus, at the window, alone – got a rickshaw to drop me at home. What a blessing to have a home! And things exactly as I want them – water at room temperature instead of icy cold – had some coffee and went to sleep.

And some dinner later. I leave the door open and look through the grill – heaven! The breeze at night – Baroda so much more comfortable.

At Ahmedabad –

The first couple of days spent in completing work on fabric. Started with oil painting – with the small-format canvas sketch pad that I had picked up in Baroda earlier. Also, six small canvases, 1" by 1" – which they started to work on the last day. Left them all to dry, due for a second coat by the end of the month.

N came in one day – someone P had put me in touch with.

She was a former student of MSU printmaking. I had considered having her do a session with the girls – painting the cement pillars at the centre. Found her passive, with no real focus or vision of how she would proceed.

Important:

Before this trip, one more trip on personal work – went to the centre with Sarosh, Zaid, and the others came later. It was good – felt people were beginning to come forward to participate in the project.

Rewind again, yet another omission – was one of the external examiners this year at the Department of Painting – as I was last year, too. Prayas called me while all that was going on – from Ahmedabad. He had conducted an elective at CEPT where he had met Riyaz, and had spoken about some artists' residencies that he wished to organize in the poorer quarters of Ahmedabad. Wished to tie up with our centre, I thought that was a fabulous idea. He had published a journal called *Crimson Feet* – a collection of short stories, essays, poems – folded up due to lack of funds but continued online – I was impressed – so we met in A'bad, I was also keen that he should do a poetry workshop with my girls – we came up with some good ideas about how we would go about it – some of them don't write – so – spoken poetry, playing with sounds, syllables –

In A'bad, he came up with a further idea – do an exercise around their names – toss them around, combine them in different ways –

Well – he was supposed to continue where I left off, after four days – but when I called to confirm, he had taken on a full-time assignment and was free only on Sunday. By which time Zaid would no longer be there. And I, back in Baroda. No point. Disappointed.

Rewind again. Session last, end April. Dates a bit scrambled, but the gist –

End of session coincided with Mayday and the group was participating in a rally – the women – Monica/Zaid wanted the girls to make posters for the rally. We did it very quickly, during the last couple of hours –

Still, they turned out well. Mayday was Himmat's 'birthday' as well – so a celebration that evening, and many friends of Himmat were invited. I was to leave that afternoon, but at their persuasion, decided to stay. A very enjoyable evening, especially since I met some nice people –

Shahrukh and Som, both lawyers working for Action Aid, both from Bihar. Neha of Awaz – Prasad had also come. They picked up some of the bookmarks that we had made. We all promised to keep in touch. I left the next morning, early.

12th June 2005

To continue where I left off – back in Baroda for an entire month – scheduled to go back 21st or so, but Tahera and Tasleem called and asked me to go after the 1st – Rabia called on the 20th – are you coming tomorrow? I was confused, but Zaid wasn't there either, so I decided not to go: I needed a break to catch up with my painting, which I did. Worked on *Do Not Swim Without Knowing* and on the Pachmarhi series which is turning out well. But growing beyond its original intention – a pity I have to part with it. No more camps/workshops for me.

Back to session 5

Managed to do four days, ill the last day, oil paintings – 1st coat done. Will try and do three more days end of the month for the second coat.

It is time we thought of doing an exhibition, at the centre itself – motivation – I feel it waning; after five sessions, why do they still need to be told how to proceed?
We bought about three display boards, for inspiration, which will be fixed to the wall upstairs. Will buy the rest later –

The show itself will take some organizing – one session devoted to setting things up? When – before/after monsoons?

Scheduled to go back on 18th for three days but not too well – bad cough –
so will put it off till the end of the month.

So many precious things broken.

The heat – many ways of describing it.

Liquid heat

like hot syrup

like hot sweet syrup, suffocating,

syrupy heat lapping around me.

Liquid heat like scorching sweet syrup ebbing and flowing around me

hotter still, it is now dry, charring to the bone.

Did not feel it so intensely till I fell ill. And now I wait for the rains.

Temperature/fever just for a day, but it has taken me a long time to surface.
I still feel tired and unable to face A'bad in a hurry.

I fixed up with Shahrukh Alam to do a session with the girls.

One module that I plan to do is about posters – which could express their
current needs or talk about relevant issues. I asked Shahrukh if she would
discuss these with the girls, get them to think politically. She came up
with the idea of a film-based module where films could be screened and
related issues discussed later. I thought it was a great idea. We fixed up
with Shahana – whose brother had a video/TV shop or something – and it
happened – apparently went off very well. They watched *Bombay Hamara
Sheher* – borrowed the cassette from Stalin of Drishti.

Is it all going the way I wanted it to go? Yes, and quite logically I think –
even in terms of how their skills and thinking are developing.

I am uneasy about how it eats into my painting time though – commitments
there as well, needing a lot of peace and quiet. Now that the house is
more or less set up the way I want it. Most of the work done, except for

the water proofing – ideally done before the monsoons but I cannot face
it – the workmen, the mess and the tension of getting them to do things
right. The IFA wants me to speak about my practice/work at MICA Mudra,
31st July. Should do it, but more painting time lost. Have to put a couple of
presentations together – shouldn't be too much of a problem – as many of
the images have been scanned – are on the hard disk at Lalita.

14th June

For the presentation at MICA Mudra, I finally sit down to write. There are
entries in the diary, yes, handwritten. The flow is different, I can do this
faster, put down things soon as they occur to me.

Floods in Gujarat. Today, the situation is a little better, the sun shines
and there is hope. We have been all right here, though the highway was
submerged, and on 30th night, when water was released from the dam, it
came up to Ranjit's gate. Fifteen feet of water in Sayajigunj, they say, both
the under/over bridges submerged. Today, eight feet of water in Raopura.
Schools of course closed for the past week, almost.

The IFA would like me to do the talk in two parts – one about painting, the
other about the project. Looking through the PowerPoint presentation that
I had done last year at the NCPA. Will also look up the Art/Activism seminar
presentation.

Where shall I begin? Will be speaking to students of Business/Management/
Mass Communication and so –

Part I

Since it is communication that we are concerned with here, it might be
relevant to focus on that aspect of art practice that has to do with language.
Art as a language, and the specific faculties that we bring to bear on it.
Those faculties that are best exercised in art, and the recognition of their
particularity is one way in which we can draw certain limits around what
could otherwise lose shape/coherence. Especially today, when it functions
as an experimental area where boundaries begin to blur and merge – the

visual arts are democratic in that they allow varied contributions from various disciplines. This is a situation which works both ways, towards its detriment and development – but that is not what we are looking at now.

In our own times, we have witnessed a relentless repetition of destructive events which have taken different forms – war, oppression, communal outbursts – and which have one common denominator in that they are engineered by greed for wealth and power. This also leads one to be able to define one's own ideology vis-à-vis other motivations. I realize that this has impacted the way I work, the kind of aesthetic that I choose to prioritize over others, an aesthetic which by the nature of its grammatical structure and its pace, resists appropriation. Again, this is premised on belief – wanting to believe in the possibility of formulating a vision which reaches beyond immediate gratification.

Earlier, one thought of a viewership more in terms of an absorbed fan following than as a relationship based on mutual respect. This was in tune with the nature of what one understood as the dynamics of art practice, and did not question its tenets. Nor realize that these tenets emanate from situations that include, by whatever means, a certain basic quality of life. To expect its members to have attained a level of attention for detail and nuance would not be unreasonable – they are for the most part not beset by doubts regarding physical survival from one day to another.

But is it unreasonable to do so here – apart from the fact that it is sometimes difficult to continue to practise in the face of social problems of such enormity? One realizes this more and more as one leaves one's student years behind, and faces reality as it impacts life in India. But does that mean that we exempt sections of society from participation in a practice we believe is vital to society? If not, how does one form relationships that enable a common tongue? How urgent is this need?

For me, the urgency was brought home by the fact that human life, especially of the underprivileged – was cheap. What happened in 2002 bore this out it quite clearly. The poor in times of crisis are the shock-absorbers – and feel the impact of every kind of misfortune most intensely.

There is no end to this – I should stop somewhere?

To return to the idea of democracy, and of art being democratic. What is true democracy? The space and the right for each one of us to be heard, for a political structure or resources to be available accordingly. In art therefore, concern/respect for the other, optimum use of resources, towards a form which allows participation, fosters understanding and knowledge.

Groups and sequences/montage – each spoken in a tongue which suits it best – can include other panels, other tongues, others who wish to lend their voices. The flow also allows entries and exits – that which we leave behind, other things that we seek, yet to be fully explored, all visible at once, we confront time as a continuum; we allow these relationships to change or to create new forms, to focus on one thing or another, priorities are redefined endlessly, according to the need of the moment as one experiences it. Further, it is a completely transparent procedure – it can still accommodate that which is about to fade, that which might yet appear, that which is in doubt, that which is less or more important – in a kind of a confessional mode, almost – it de-mystifies itself, communicates its making to the viewer, it does not intimidate. It is this effort, not the 'perfect' artwork, which creates a viewership.

Part II

For the second part of the session, I would like to start again from the same point – of art as a language, something that requires a common basis in terms of a culture and shared experiences; the lack of it, when seen as something undesirable, can be redressed.

With the years, the realities of this country began to replace the idea of an 'art world', which was earlier seen as defining one's worksphere.

It might be interesting to actually examine the idea of the art world – what is it? A historically constructed idea of art is certainly a prominent part of it, and its roots are from all over the world. Its functioning in contemporary times is a network of related activities which include the publishing of catalogues, mounting of major exhibits, curators, critics, galleries and institutions that are responsible for making it accessible to a public beyond the studios and workspaces where art is made. They could occur anywhere in the world, and still be relevant to us here. For a practising artist who works outside institutional spaces, this begins to seem like a surreal construct in terms of its remoteness and sometimes, invisibility.

I am very distracted, unable to focus. You know the answer to this, now that you have identified the problem.

Take care, time, over it. Work around your weakness.

In 2002, the lacuna in communication was brought home to me with great force.

It was of course a disturbed and a disturbing situation for all of us, and the rationale for the proposal that I drew up for the IFA was quite simple. How does one continue to function as an artist in a politically disturbed state? Does one shut oneself off? Or engage actively with what's going on? Given one's lack of experience with such things, how does one go about it? Therefore the thrust of the project was precisely this – to discover ways in which one could engage with the sociopolitical environment and yet remain outside institutionalized spaces. One recognizes that this environment, however hostile, is a vital part of one's own make-up; the connectivity manifests itself in overt or covert ways, and without this underpinning, the relevance that in the final analysis marks a work of art, or qualifies whatever we do, becomes questionable. It creates an unhealthy situation, a lack of a discernible future – and somewhere, between the immediate response to the prevalent violence, and the desire for freedom from the institution, the quest for relevance continues.

Monday 4th July, 2005

- - - - - - - - - - - - - - -

Working on Shahrukh's posters – six b+w posters

Bina in Baroda, a nice evening at home, drinking jamun wine that Raj Kumar's wife had made – visited her at her home.

a.   Have to put all the posters on a CD for Urvashi Butalia and send it to Delhi

b.   Call Zaid and ask him if he can come up

Will schedule the next session end of the month – will give me hopefully enough time to catch up with myself.

1st–10th July – flood-related chaos

10th–18th – digital work – cleared some amount of backlog.

18th–25th – A'bad

25th–1st – my sister's visit

July *18th–25th*

Is this possible that a month should go by so quickly? June and July chaotic in terms of work, except that the project goes on regardless. Some writing, finally, thanks to having to do the presentation at Mudra. Happened on the 31st – Sheikhbhai's on the previous day, part of an elective course conceived by the IFA.

Peaceful, at Seminar Hall 2. The campus at Shelagaon – 18 km from Ahmedabad – arrived on 30th night, left 31st after lunch. Beautiful, but very quiet – green – removed.

Visitors at home, 25th–1st August – very busy – no work, apart from the talk. Confusion over flight connections – all via Bombay – flooded beyond belief, worse than Baroda –

Anyway, finally resolved, they took a car to A'bad, flight to Delhi; and then on to Bangalore.

Oh yes – was very ill in A'bad – every day.

Took the girls to the Calico Museum, Zaid and Shatrughan came along – with two other young artists.
Have to format those posters as well + have them printed on OHP film for screen printing.

Recall

> Lapping around me –
> liquid heat, like hot sweet syrup
> Not
> Now of course –
> wet, wet, wet.

Then,
Waves of liquid heat, liquid despite the dryness –
masses of heat.

Bina asked me – what insights have you gained over these past months?

Actually, none? I just get down to work – to teach – the insights came as I was writing up the project proposals – all those months of it.

Do I feel a great sense of achievement? No, at least not yet. No regrets either. I am doing what I set out to do. Seven months have passed, five more left – at least, five sessions – I want to spend more time painting – is that an insight? Cut down on the length of my sessions – delegate work – to Zaid to Shahana – to Sharifa.

Today the 3rd

Started painting – *Do Not Swim Without Knowing.*

Swimming since three days – It's 8 in the evening and POURING in a way that reminds one of the floods – God Forbid.

Do not, not Look?

I need to write up a preface for my books –

4th

Painting since the past four days. Started a new painting yesterday – earlier one still unfinished, but I need a bone-dry surface, so am waiting. The session this month conducted by Shanta, this is the third day and she tells me that it goes well.

Have written up the interim report, the financial report still to go. Should be done in a day or two.

20th Oct

Financial report done! The lot couriered – on the 24th I think. A huge relief.

The new painting progresses quickly. It's a view of myself from the back – seated – the photo taken by a photographer, Gottfried Junker, who had visited sometime early this year – and sent me some contact prints.

Three panels, one of them *Sanctum*, my old, old, painting – that I had made in England in '79, now destroyed.

Planning a quick trip to A'bad on Friday, to discuss the work that the girls have done – to discuss with them how to format the other sketches – from the session with Monica.

26th Oct

A two-day trip to A'bad to fix up things: the next session, how it will go, the next stage of the project. Farzana has got engaged and will not continue. Rehana is moving back to Naroda Patiya as her father was unable to make a living selling vegetables in Faizal Park.

Also to review work done during Shanta's session – very good – scrolls, the theme – Mother. Met Shatrughan + Piyush.

Met Kaumudi of Drishti Media collective.

1st November – Diwali

Painting: the idea has been put down, now the best/most truthful way of expressing it –

The carpet is driving me crazy.

Always the most simple things.

Veracity x expression without sacrificing either –

A concept note for Drishti. Applying for a two-month scholarship on behalf of the girls.

16th

- - - - - - - - - - - - - - -

Drishti Media Collective/Public Art Grant

Against the background of the above text (the interim report for the IFA) this is a short concept note about one of the ideas that we had vis-à-vis a proposal.

The girls have built up a bank of sketches and paintings, some of them on issues relevant/of interest to most of us. The Ahmedabad Hamara posters, for one: they have extended the idea beyond the images on the posters; one session was devoted to paintings, about the difficulties that they experienced during the floods.

I have also involved young artists who are currently working at Kanoria Centre; most recently, Shanta – who did a session with the girls around the theme of 'Mother' – we decided to format the paintings into *patachitra* scrolls consisting of four to five frames each.

Yet another session was about life in the Shah Alam camp, post riots. We will be working on enlarging the drawings from this session.

The girls had also attended a workshop in Mt Abu where they learnt a game which they performed/played at the Sahiyar workshop. It was about unity – a recitation which is enacted with the participation of the audience – something between poetry, play, theatre.

We now propose to paint/write a set of narrative scrolls, as a backdrop against which games regarding the themes outlined above could be invented and played – through which they would learn to vocalize and think constructively about solutions to what they face on a day-to-day basis. The scrolls would be screen printed in black and white on khadi, so they can be rolled up and carried from place to place without fear of damage.

We have a few resource people in mind: Shatrughan, who will help us with the aspect of performance and with the screen printing, Piyush, who is a young artist/writer in Gujarati and Shanta, who will help with the image formulation.

The grant award will go to the group of four girls – Tahera, Shahjehan, Tasleem and Rabia. The cost of materials and payment of resource persons etc. are being budgeted separately.

As far as I am concerned, applying for the scholarship works in several ways – but primarily moves us away from the protection afforded by the IFA grant, and into Ahmedabad in a very real way. It would put the girls in touch with creative people who are also actively concerned with social issues, and thereby open up other possibilities for active engagement with these issues. I have worked in the field for almost a year now, and will soon begin to withdraw, to compile and format the material gathered – I would by then like the girls to be able to function artistically independent of my presence.

17th November 2005

Back from A'bad yesterday –

No entries for such a long time, it's hard to negotiate that gap.

Today – Sharmaji working upstairs on my stretchers. 3.30 appointment with Azra, so three hours to re-organize things. The girls have won the scholarship – not undiluted joy, though – many adjustments (in thinking/ attitude) to be made with Drishti.

The first day of the Drishti interview – met the girls at the CEPT canteen, dropped them off at the CEE (designed by Chaya, incidentally), left them in Gaurang's charge. Kabirbhai entrusted with ferrying the girls back and forth – only four of them now, anyway.

Three days of shortlisting – apparently, there were screenings, discussions – etc. – they made it to the finals.

Met Jayaram Poduval at the Faculty of Fine Arts a few days later, he had been on the committee for the final selection of the candidates – and was very impressed with the confidence with which they had presented themselves. As I said – feedback from Kaumudi similarly worded – good. Maybe, then, it is the truth?

Did a three day session with the girls – working on the sketches that they had made with Monica. It was based on a game – folding a piece of paper into four, choosing and changing partners, exchanging confidences with a different one each time – the content of which was sketched on paper. Some sad stories, so the last space to be filled with happiness.

Before that, the sessions had been troubled for a while. Waiting for the second instalment of the grant, wondering how to proceed – Farzana had left, so had Rehana, only four girls left. Felt that it was time for a re-inforcement of motivation – a show, yes, but that isn't going to happen so soon; it's important to continue with the work, a show could be a major interruption. Was unhappy with how the oil painting exercise had turned out. Difficult to handle the medium in such circumstances – the paintings had gathered a lot of dust, the girls were not handling them well, they looked dull and muddy.

In the meantime, there had been a week-long workshop with a group of school children from Poona – through Monica's initiative – and they had painted on the walls with enamel paints. So, decided to use enamel paints for Monica's exercise – worked very well – fresh bright surfaces, the girls also enjoyed them, I think, so much more. Mixed them in with turpentine, and so dealt with the problem of drying time.

Was also wondering about this – now that they were painting larger and more complex work, how to manage it in terms of time, my time? Resource people cost money.

So – we worked for three days, and then the girls were to continue after I left. We wondered if that would work, and it did.

12th Dec

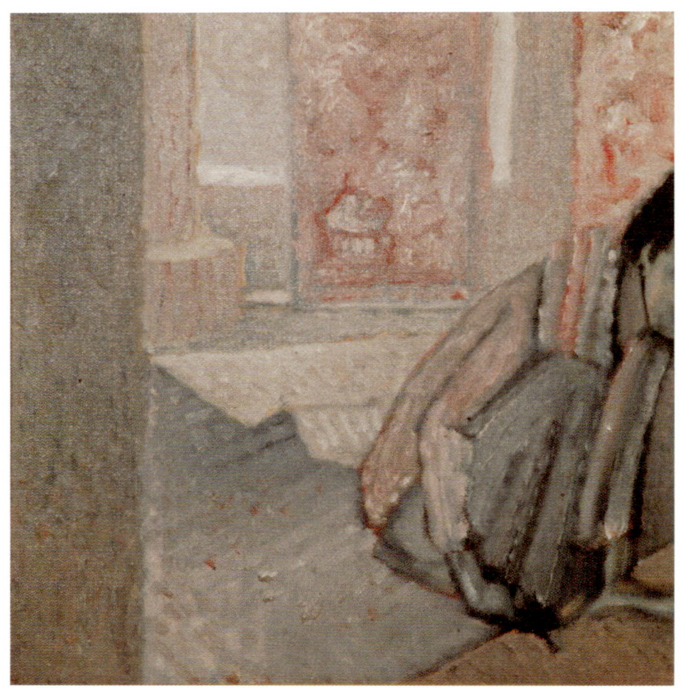

Mixing colours is like tuning an instrument – or warming up. Especially if
that particular palette has been unused for a while – it takes a long time.

14th or 15th

Night – put the three panels together, and looking at them – the swimmer.
Learnt to swim at last.

18th

Completed the Swimmer.

22nd

Shahjehan (detail), 2006

Went to the Faculty for the Fine Art Fair in the morning, felt disconnected and disturbed the whole day. A vacuum, maybe. Tomorrow, a trip to Ahmedabad. I don't enjoy crowds, actually.

23rd

In Vatva

Kaumudi and Gaurang visited a couple of weeks ago. Gaurang is an actor.

The girls came up with a few ideas for plays – based on their own lives.

For example, on a conversation between Tahera and her mother regarding education. Hopefully, Piyush will put it together in the form of a script.

Zaid has been talking with them and they have been making sketches for the paintings that will be used as backdrops for the plays.

Tomorrow, a Sunday, I will go to A'bad. Prem will meet us between 2–4, and we can firm up ideas about how exactly the paintings should be done, how they will be put up, etc. Will be able to proceed after that.

This vacuum is weird. I feel spaced out.

A good visit. Set off at 11.30 with Vishnu, bass guitar, printer etc. Had lunch in A'bad first thing. Zaid joined us a little later, dropped off stuff at Vishnu's, picked up Uma at CEPT and headed for Vatva. There are fifteen women working there now, and they use the small room downstairs as well – so from next month, I will pay less rent. Maybe, I should pay Zaid more, as he is taking on the additional responsibility of the Drishti project.

Looked at the paintings from the previous session again, they really are beautiful. The girls performed one of the skits, the one on literacy – I was impressed – we all were. Saw the sketches – will develop them into scrolls that could be mounted on bamboo frames.

It is cold. There is a cold wave in effect in the North, including Delhi. That could account for this dullness that I feel – the hormones freezing as well or at least feeling the cold.

Need to go back to A'bad mid-week to get them started.

25th

Drishti has proposed the following:

Prabhat Pheri 8 a.m./Play 10–11 a.m. every day at:
Mayur Park

Navapura

Chunaravas

Ektanagar

Faizal Park

Unrealistic
1.   Buy paints – Fevicryl
2.   How are the screens designed? How will they be fixed?
14th – Zaid leaves/5th Feb – returns

Ambavadi Circle – Nehru Nagar Circle

Naman's near Ambavadi circle for art materials.

13.1.2006

(recorded in another notebook)

Was in Bombay the last week for an international conference at the Mohile
Parikh Centre. Wanted to catch up with the theorizing/thinking.
Before that. A month of teaching at the Faculty, three days a week, in the
form of discussions with students from MA and third year BA. Have spoken
to all except two. Went down with a viral infection towards the end of it,
carried it to Bombay with me, thinking it was on its way out. But it went
on – headache every day, sniffles, congestion – was great meeting so many
friends from all over the country after such a long time – though I began
to wilt after two days of lectures and discussions. The headache went away
but the muscles of the lower back went into spasm – three days of limited
mobility – moving against pain.

Last day, met George and had a long chat – about the project too – and
confessed the fact that the journal had suffered. He said that it had been
one of the most precious parts of the earlier phase of the project – and I
suffered more pangs of guilt, so here I am, trying to catch up with what I
should have done. Back in Baroda now, and recovering, I think.

So, where to begin?

Yes the Drishti Fellowship. Ran into all kinds of trouble from the very
beginning, because of the expectations.

Several meetings with the coordinator – did the idea of the games come from
the girls? I said no, it was mine, but it had emerged from an understanding
of what they were capable of – not in those very words, maybe it should
have been. She insisted that they rethink the whole thing, so I left them to
do it with Shahana and Zaid – and they came up with the idea of putting up
three plays, based on water and education – in the form of conversations –
between Ayesha Bibi and Tahera, etc. – which was a wonderful idea, that their
stories would be about themselves – and we had discussed already that we
would have resource people from local theatre groups to work with the girls.

We had, in fact, fixed an appointment with Soumya Joshi, to discuss this,
much earlier – had a good meeting with him and he had suggested a few
names. Had also discussed with him my reservations regarding the way
the programme was being implemented, but he felt we should apply, and

then adapt it to our circumstances. It also turned out that he was informally associated with Drishti.

The girls went through a rigorous interview process – something like five days of progressive shortlisting, and they did well by all accounts. They were awarded the grant in December – I was very happy, the community was, too. Subsequently, more problems – demands that they report at Drishti once a week, attend screenings, exposure trips – all at their expense. We had to intervene, brought it down to once a week. Zaid was unhappy too, a minimum of fifteen performances was expected – one a day for fifteen days.

They had recommended a budget of 10–12 thousand, but released a bare 2000 – we were put to expense, to be reimbursed later. Hasn't happened so far. They insisted on paying by cheque. We recommended otherwise – but the cheques were released, and the girls were to start a joint account. That ran into trouble as well – some did not have birth certificates – by then, the rehearsals with Prem had begun, but were sporadic. Our initial meeting with him was good – Soumya and his troupe had put up a superb play in 2002 and had actually worked in the camps – Prem spoke about this with a lot of feeling, which impressed me. But – he seemed to have lost interest, was distracted with other commitments, the girls did not do too well with him.

The painting of the screens went very well, however. There's just one more that needs to be done. We decided on using enamel paints on canvas – they had just made a very beautiful series of paintings around the session with Monica. Earlier, Himmat had commissioned them to paint on the walls of the centre – on subjects that were to do with the growth of the organization. As I had mentioned earlier, did not have much success with painting in oils – The drying time, lack of appropriate storage – dust, neglect – the paintings looked dull. The enamel paints worked extremely well.

In discussion with Shahana, a script had been produced for the play on education – there were two plays, one emerging organically from the other. Prem had further done a few sessions with them –

Zaid was to be in Hyderabad mid-Jan to early Feb for a workshop on how to combine art/craft with social work. We advised K to wait till he came back – she was adamant about the deadline.

19th Feb 2006

Have been teaching at the Faculty over the past couple of months – ill most of the time with the viral that I had picked up. Amma here till yesterday the 28th. Veda's 10th board exams are over. They have both left for Bangalore. Went swimming early this month, and had a relapse.

Grounded again.

Project on hold, Zaid in Pakistan. Will resume first week of April. The next preoccupation: hope to complete most of my fieldwork over April, leaving mid-May for Bangalore with Vishnu.

Am alone after a long time, will be for the next month and a half. Am writing so this silence will begin to take shape/form/find form.

The journal hasn't been such a success, has it?

29. 3. 2006

Will complete the large triptych in a few days – *Sanctum*. Relieved. Teaching done. Three presentations, which involved a little updating – one about my work, one on the project, one on the colour courses in Ahmedabad and Jaipur.

Have been painting since the last entry, intensive. Scroll/*tanka* prints – *Four Ways of Reconstructing Pain* – framed and looking rather stunning.

Recovering from the relapse. This silence is very restful and very healing – I can get back in touch with myself, my inner world.

Today – priorities – painting – the shadow painting needs a few finishing touches –

But also a trip to Ahmedabad, this time extended so I can finish off all that needs to be done this month.

2nd April

Got back yesterday, Wednesday the 10th. Had taken Hanna Hoyne along with me – a student from ANU Canberra – who was in Baroda to interview artists. She had a video camera, and seemed interested in the work I was doing in Vatva – a good opportunity to implement the filming session that I've had in mind since a long time. We did it over two days – the camera was shared between four girls.

They filmed the two plays that they had rehearsed, interviews/conversations between themselves about the work that they had been doing over the past one and a half years, a walk to Faizal Park and visits to each of their homes – all this, on day one.

Day two – a walk to the market. And then bicycle rides.

The market and Qutb-e-Alam Dargah – very beautiful.

Hot in Ahmedabad, also the nights – felt a kind of lassitude settle on me, Zaid felt it as well, Hanna too, especially on the first day. Very full, and dense, the first couple of days – much shared laughter, exchanges and bonding within the group. A lot of excitement in Faizal Park about the filming – the girls and their families enjoyed it thoroughly.

Day three – started drawing on the canvases – Tahera and Shahjehan showed up, the others didn't. A performance had been scheduled for the evening at Ektanagar – had to be cancelled. Tahera sulky – so we had a chat in the evening to clear up things – tears, as usual. Upsets me as always, but Zaid remains unruffled – that teaches me a lot.

Apart from the lassitude, there is very little that I can do anyway, after starting them off. This time, I took my sketchbook along, for the first time, and made a few sketches, but the heat soon robbed me of all initiative. The fan outside has been removed –

Day four, the girls began painting, Tahera progressed very quickly as usual. The small canvases that we had worked on with oil paints several months earlier – I've given them those to re-work with enamel paints. The script for the play on education has to be written out too, on two pieces of khadi. All this can be done without my continued presence.

Saturday evening moved to Chaya's, Sunday with Sarosh – discussing the chair – the listening chair – for my voice CDs, which I also have to work on. And now, back here in Baroda – some repairs/re-painting going on, and I need to gather my thoughts again.

11th April, Tuesday

Today I am at a loss – so – in the beginning there was the Word.

Zaid is somewhere in Maharashtra, his grandfather passed away. Waiting for him to come back so we can get on with Shanta's session – we need to buy material from Manek Chowk. Shanta will be busy with the workshops at the Kanoria in May, so we must finish before that.

Had a call from Pooja Sood of Khoj – and we spoke of a month-long residency in Delhi – to compile the documentation of the IFA project, maybe meet people who might be interested in what has been done – sounds good, exactly what I need – a team that I can sound things out with. That should be sometime in July –

22nd April

26th – day trip to Ahmedabad – mainly for the Drishti meeting. Met Sarosh about listening chair – went to Vatva to pick up girls/Zaid/some work to bring back to Baroda. Shah-e-Alam work completed but not quite – disappointed with results – seem to have lost spirit, they admitted as much. Shahjehan is getting married 18th May, only two girls left – Rabia and Tahera. That's one reason – but hopefully they will work on the paintings a little more.

In the meantime – panic – can't find the *kichadwali* paintings – black + w, ink, fabulous – they are in a roll somewhere, unable to locate them – have been carrying them back and forth – to Azra's, A'bad, Baroda – will turn up, hopefully. Met Shanta to fix up embroidery session based on sketches. Will happen 11th May – for ten days, five days a week. Shanta's good. They have worked on the small format series with enamel paint – looks brighter though there is loss of detail – again, hastily done.

Meeting at Drishti went well, the girls were grilled. Showed whatever documentation we had – photos, dialogues on khadi – which were never really used – the girls have been paid – 2,750 for Rabia and Tahera, 500 for Shahjehan who did not perform. The experience discussed – most important. Some of the other projects have suffered because the grantees cannot express themselves visually. Stalin asked the girls if they could help out, which I think is a FABULOUS idea. He also wanted them to work on the walls of a few schools. I must push this a bit, also discuss it with the IFA in relationship to the extending arts programme. Also spoke to Nimmi of Drishti about setting up a screen printing unit – they have trained a community to do it, some of them could come round, instruct the girls and set things up. Meeting the IFA in Bangalore between the 18th and 20th of May.

27th April

Surges of strength are as difficult to deal with as depletion/ and to be used accordingly –

The heat robs one of energy though.

28th

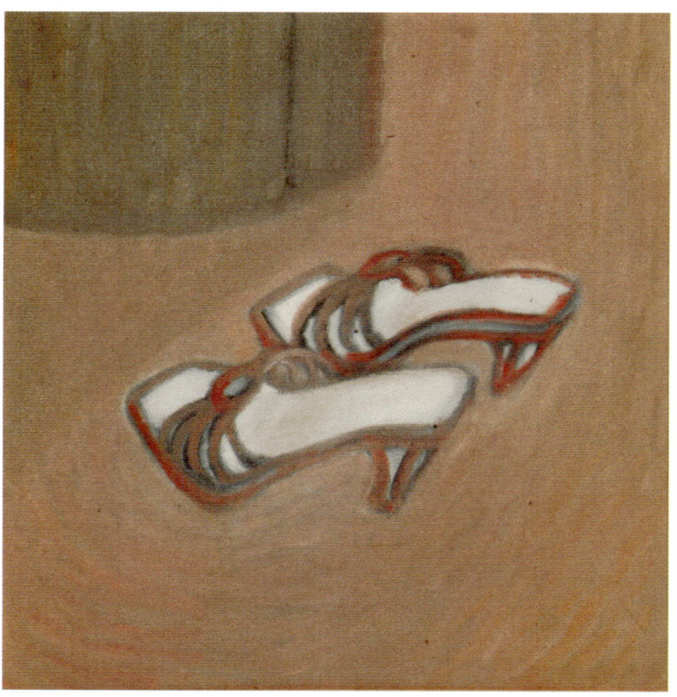

Detail (one of 13 panels), 2006

Prajna Kuteera

An ayurvedic clinic for two weeks

Brought books/music/writing, so time well spent.

Typing out my journals for the Voice project

Working with Sarosh, my architect friend on seating/listening arrangements for my audio CDs. The visual part of the project is a set of four prints entitled *Four Ways of Reconstructing Pain*.

Left Baroda on the 16th, arrived in Bangalore on the 18th – crazy city, increasingly.

Before leaving Baroda, spent a day with my girls in A'bad, they are doing a session with Shanta. Zaid on the point of applying for another job with Pratham – just spoke to him – he's got it.

Typing out my journals, 1996–2006 – am struck by the singularity of it all – the nature of my work at that time/most of it done alone.

After the project – now involved with the world outside the studio-self, what with teaching, etc.

Actually, feel a disinclination to start writing about myself – have to find a way.

Reading Benjamin's *Illuminations*

Ruminations on the world

26th May, Mysore

Getting a grip on the diverse matter of the past several years, things that I had been meaning to compile – at least I know where they are located – and feel a greater sense of control, gain an overview of myself in temporal progression – as against a fixed notion of oneself as rooted in the present – too many empty spaces in that notion/which perplex me.

This spell, this retreat is a much needed one, physically. A bonus that it has also turned out to be productive workwise. I had carried my:

1. laptop
2. music for *riyaz*
3. books to read and write on from Baroda. A lot of baggage, and wondered if I had been stupid –

But I'm really well set up here. Thinking of acquiring an antique French organ.

In a way the work of compilation – of both the voice project and the A'bad project – has begun.

I am not an irreplaceable/component of any/an identifiable or stable component/of any social circle. I am never there/I am always not there.

Edited the scar images – surprisingly fast. Just a few left.

30th

Baroda

Back here – two days settling down.

Today most things in place, including repairs + maintenance, so turn attention to work or the beginnings of it.

Start painting? Not much time left for the solo in March.

14th June 2006

Trip to Madras again 25th–30th July – rains – mess to face on return. A week to recover, rains again Sunday night – flood warning, Surat under water. Work schedule upset, due to leave for Delhi end of next month, so it is time to start preparing for the residency. One disaster after another, very disruptive – just dealing with basics of life/dysfunctional phone/water filter/ domestic help. One learns to remain calm in spite of everything.

9th August

Now barely ten days for the Khoj residency –

Have to stop painting again + this causes severe disorientation, loss of strength, imbalance – again having to pursue people to have work done, in preparation for the residency: a trip to A'bad to collect material and review embroidery workshop.

Have started working on the books again – a reprint of the *Story of Five Posters/ The Project*

Compiling photos – why does it all take so long?

1.   Must send off the paintings for scanning
2.   Put all the stuff on a CD for talks –
Planning a trip to A again next Saturday, to show the film footage to Drishti
3.   Must pack and send off all material to Delhi and plan for four weeks there.

I am involved with the books, for now + would like to pursue that direction

Work on paintings – *Of Journeys and Emptiness* Part II

Edit film

There, you have it – more than you can manage

Have started calling up old friends that I had lost touch with –

Why?

Looking for a new life?

After the fieldwork – not quite over though.

A sense of peace that I don't have to make those frequent visits to Ahmedabad –

17th Sept

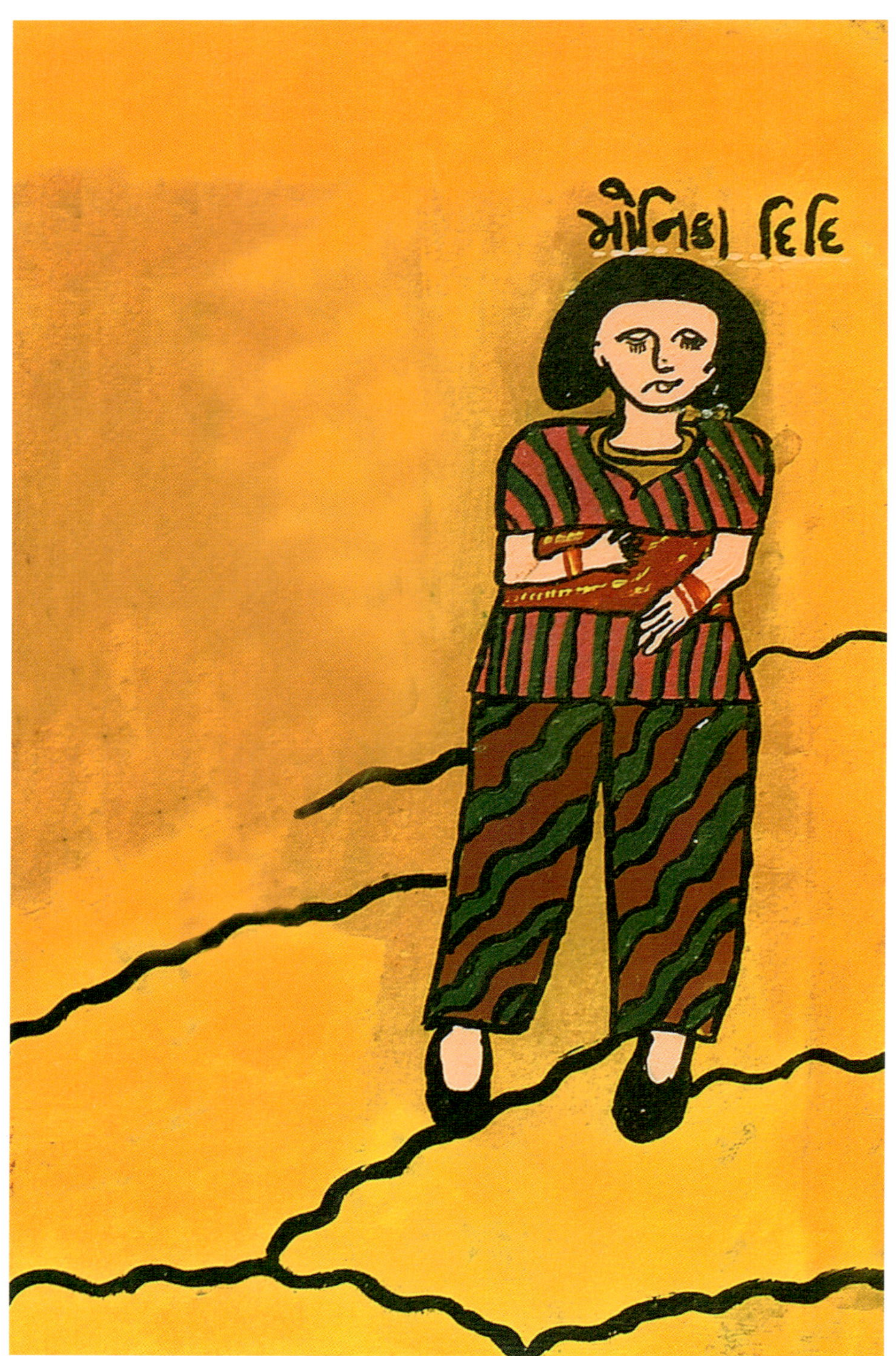

મોનિકા દિદિ

MONICA WAHI: AN INTERVIEW

You have been working with the community in Faizal Park ever since I met you – in 2003 was it? I'm curious about what happened before that, your experiences when you first arrived, from Delhi. When did you come, why did you come and why did you stay on?

You know, every time someone asks me why I came, I think of all the stories that would answer that question. I think it was not just one particular reason, but the stuff that we were reading, the e-mails that were being sent around and what we were watching on television. It pained you but it also angered you. As citizens of this country, this was not what we stood for, but we could do nothing to stop it. So, the fact of going to Gujarat to help in relief camps really became a way of doing away with one's own sense of impotence. Then when one came here, we met a whole lot of other young people from all over the country, who'd come as volunteers, either attached to some organization or on their own, so slowly, one got into the rhythm of doing, working.

Had you been doing this kind of work before?

No, not like this at all. It was, of course, while working with Anand (Patwardhan) that one interacted with a lot of activists, and got a glimpse of what they were doing on the ground. One realized that one could do things instead of just making films or stories around things. Earlier, I would take part in *morchas* and meetings, but not on this scale. I didn't think that I would ever be doing something like this.

How long did you work with Anand?

About three and a half years, and then another year of freelancing on my own. When I came here, there was no set work which organizations wanted volunteers to do. There is an assumption that volunteers come in the way, and therefore you don't give them work, but that in a way worked out really nicely for people like me. There were a lot of gaps which were left by the NGOs, though they were well-intentioned – like for instance a lack of certain kinds of infrastructure. So we started filling in those gaps. Those three, four, five months of doing work on health and education, entirely on one's own, gave us the confidence that we could do without the base of an organization. But that was very small in scale compared to what has happened with Himmat.

Monica Didi, by Rabia Sheikh (detail from poster), 2005

Who were the others that you worked with initially?

Some volunteers had come and gone, some stayed for two to three months. One of them was Shri. He was an Action Aid volunteer, I think he came before me in May and stayed on till September. And there was Shambhavi who came for two months at a stretch and again for another month. There were a lot of students, and other volunteers – really lovely people who wanted to do work but didn't get work from organizations, so we finally had a situation devised. For example around August 2002, in Jehangir Nagar camp – this was in Vatva, camp no. 9 – there was one woman who lost her newborn twins. She didn't have money to go to the hospital, just that 100 rupees that she needed to reach medical care. One of the twins died and the other would have survived had she reached the hospital. The fieldworkers were not sure if they were supposed to give her the money or not, silly things like that …

… because of the bureaucracy involved?

NGOs are not bureaucratic, but the fieldworkers were newly recruited and not necessarily people who had a background in social work. The NGOs themselves were fighting too many things on too many fronts. There were a lot of people in that camp and most of them were not employed anywhere, so we recruited four or five volunteers and devised a system whereby they'd collect people who had health issues and take them to the hospital. If it was something that couldn't be sorted out by LG Hospital which was nearby, they'd take them to VS Hospital with the funds we collected from family, friends and NGOs, and from Xavier's Social Service. We would pay for the travelling costs and initial expenses and if it was something serious, they would call us to meet them at the hospital. Then it was not only people from here but also from Chunaravas, which is a Dalit community, who started coming to us. This went on for as long as we had the money, but it gave people a sense that they could do things – devise systems on their own and execute them without assistance or guidance from anyone else.

This influx of volunteers to Gujarat at this time, it seems unprecedented – or am I imagining it?

No, I think that the way Gujarat was portrayed in the media, especially the visual media, made a big difference. The visual media, really, was soaring on emotion and it touched a lot of people; I think it's got a lot to do with that.

That's become another point of controversy, that so much horror should not be indiscriminately publicized by the media, what do you think about that?
No, definitely one should not be seeing dead and mutilated bodies every day – but one has to address it, especially in a carnage like this which is not a riot. One has to address the question of who is being killed, and who is killing. Before this, because of a certain kind of media portrayal, of say even the Bombay riots, everybody in the rest of the country assumed that it was a riot, and that it was, you know, two-sided, which leaves you with the sense of an eye for an eye. This was not like that. This was more planned.

Comparisons are being made with the anti-Sikh riots – and there is sometimes a kind of anger that it didn't get the kind of media and public attention that is now being paid to Gujarat.
Definitely, terrible things happened even then, but it was mostly over within three or four days. What happened here went on for months. And there is a point of difference here because at that time there was just Doordarshan, and the print media. I think a lot has to do with how much people are exposed to things, and in the '80s people didn't have access to that kind of media.

What was your first impression of the Shah-e-Alam relief camp?
We went there twice, sometime in July. Somehow it seemed, at that point, like a sort of safe haven – there were volunteers, some of whom were teaching the children. It seemed like some kind of a family – if one didn't see it in the context of all that had happened. Some of the women were actually going to work. I didn't get to meet people who were injured or in trouble because of the time that had passed. The president, Abdul Kalam, also came to visit the camp, and it received a lot of attention. Vatva and the other camps were really badly off and Jehangir Nagar especially was a horrible situation, and continued to function that way for more than two years. Shah-e-Alam was really luxurious compared to the others. It was overloaded – whether with food or clothes or whatever.

Was that because it was larger? Or the first ?
It was a really large camp. Shah-e-Alam is a dargah, so it was a place that people came to. With the other camps, you had to put up tents and things which were very makeshift – while there you could always find somewhere to lie down or sleep. This is not to deny the kind of things that

had happened to the people who came there, you know, but I'm just saying that because of all this attention you tended to neglect the other camps, especially when it came to poverty and resource distribution. Jehangir Nagar and the other camps were much worse off.

So you worked there mostly?
Yes, that was my main area of work. There and at Vatva, for a long time, until Himmat started.

How many camps were there in Vatva?
There are two – Qutb-e-Alam and Jehangir Nagar. There was another one called Zia but that wound up in the beginning of July – these two camps were my long term engagement, and all my activities were focused in that area till these women came to Sehgal Park. Till Himmat started, a lot of work still had to be done at Jehangir Nagar. And Himmat – the idea started forming in Jan./Feb. 2004. None of us had thought of it as a specific group, but the fact is that some of the women were very despondent, especially two or three of them – Ayesha Bibi, Nur Jehan – they would talk constantly of committing suicide. They didn't know what to do with their lives. They would constantly say – you know we don't have any skill …

You know, one year had passed, and when the carnage was commemorated, of course they remembered what had happened and realized that there was no point from where they could move on. They had nothing to do, even in terms of earning; for many of them, their widow pensions had not come in and they had picked up a lot of debt. And also there was no hope – they would go looking for work here and there but find none, because of their lack of skill, and also because Vatva is not a place where one could get work easily. And I'm sure Sehgal Park must have been depressing after Patiya. Even though Patiya was small, there were a lot of basic amenities for which people had worked years to acquire. They had managed to rent, from the municipality, things like electricity and water. Sehgal Park could not even guarantee that kind of thing. It was all very, very depressing. And they would talk either of killing themselves or poisoning the children.

How did you get acquainted with that particular group?
I used to play with the children, and obviously through the kids I got to know the mothers.

Was that mostly in Shah-e-Alam?

No, in Sehgal Park. It was in September 2002 that I started doing this Sunday thing with the children. The moment the houses were ready, they had shifted out of the camp. I'd met a whole lot of other people in Shah-e-Alam, not just these women – I don't even particularly remember meeting them.

I used to feel terrible that the children in Jehangir Nagar had to stay in a camp without education. Their parents couldn't afford to send them to school, and some had tried sending their kids to other schools which at that time were coming up, set up by the Islamic Relief Committee and GSRC – but the children came back. Then in August, Zia came along – she's a corporate person – she said she could do something. We had heard about this school in Raigarh, and she spoke to Dr Ungre, who had started it, about the problem.

At that time Tahera Park and all those other settlements had not yet come up, it was all open ground where we could play. You know that little street that you see, that little maidan – that was much bigger, huge. When we played, kids from all over – there would be at least 100–120, they would all come like little bees from here and there. It was a big circle and usually it would be just me and one other volunteer, at the most two volunteers, and we would handle all of them at the same time. And when the kids were tired they'd invite us to their homes. When the possibility of a school like Raigarh happened, the parents at Jehangir Nagar were keen that the children should study, but it's actually the children who forced their parents to let them go, forced their mothers to get their names written down. I think they assumed that we would be playing there the way we were playing here, forever. So they insisted on going, and literally dragged their cousins along.

The first batch of kids was from Sehgal Park, originally from Patiya. During October, this was the first batch that went to Raigarh. And from then on I must've gone to the school at least four or five times in those four to five months. Every time I went, I'd take letters or *chahana* as they call it. Things to eat, from the parents to the school, and we'd bring back letters for them. I got to know their mothers intimately because when you go as a postman, as I suppose it happens in villages, they sit and talk to you about their lives, and they disclose a lot – and you know what their children are saying, because you have to read the letters out, as the parents are not literate. So that's how I got close to them. But a point came when I felt very embarrassed about going there again and again. That was – you remember, Vasudha, you had also come – the first time we'd gone to Sehgal Park? That was when they were really in a state of despondency, and each time I'd visit them, I'd cringe.

... because there was nothing you could offer?
... nothing that one could offer, and because all the things that one would hear, all that depression. ... One felt that it was too embarrassing to just go there to talk. There were not so many women then, but there were about six or seven that I would interact with – especially that one *chaali* where all the widows were. Till then, one had got things done, like collect funds or put pressure on NGOs to have things done. For instance in Jehangir Nagar, if something was happening, one would go to Action Aid or Sahyog to bring it to their attention. One tried the same thing here, consulted several NGOs about the livelihood problem. But it was always – you know that this is not our area and this is not something we can do, we are not based in Vatva, or even if we are it doesn't fall under our purview, and livelihood is something that involves too many things and that is hard – and really now, in retrospect, I would also think a thousand times before getting into something like this.

It needs dedication, I suppose.
No, not merely that. As an NGO, if I had to generate funds and guarantee results, I would think a thousand times before coming to a decision. If I were alone I'd still do it, but NGOs have a different way of working, one can't be spontaneous and answerable at the same time.

Do you think that most of the things that you have been able to do are because you have worked as an individual?
Yes, but one can't blame the NGOs for not getting into it. At that point of time I used to be livid about it, you know, why can't they do it – that sort of thing, but now I can understand from their standpoint that so much goes into it, that with all that funding and everything, it's a roadblock. As an organization the risk factors were too much.

These women had sewing machines that were donated by SEWA, except for Shahjehan's which was given by Saharwaru, but most didn't know how to use them. Some of them were trying – Zubeida was trying to teach Shaheen, and we were trying to make some *godhdis* so we used to get really paltry kind of money. We were doing this two-rupee kind of work, which Ayesha Bibi does – 1.50 rupees for a salwar. So how much can you make in a day? And the work is not constant – 1,000 jute bags for 50 rupees, you just have to do the running stitch, but even then – how much can you make? And they would want me to get them that kind of work – but one didn't feel nice about it. So we thought we'd work for traders, you know, *vyaapaaris* or *saits*. We tried locating those, one didn't think big at that point in time, and without references no one would give us that kind of work. Initially, I would talk to the women individually, and then I started getting meetings together, of all the women who had livelihood issues. Everybody would give their suggestions, but we still couldn't find work. So two months passed, and to me it seemed like time was running out.

They were so depressed, tomorrow I didn't want to go there and see someone kill herself, to me it was urgent, and each day was too much. But we sat together and said – okay, this is the kind of group that is forming repeatedly, these twelve or thirteen women were coming together, and we felt that we should come up with a name. So we sat together and thought for a while – and Shaheen came up with 'Himmat', which instantly everybody agreed with – *'Haan, haan, yeh theek hai'* – so we had a group before anything started, before we had anything to look forward to. We had a group and we had a name. Himmat was something we felt that all of them needed, something which would help them and open doors for them. So you know, it was just like a small *mahila mandal ka* meeting. After that we got duped – this charlatan sort of fellow who must have sniffed out this group of women looking for work. In fact, we invited him here. We'd gone to Patiya, and in this one room, there were some women making clothes. One or two of them were Aman Pathiks, and they said – There is this guy called Tabrez, and we are doing some work for him. So we approached him, we told him we were looking for work, and he agreed to come to Sehgal Park. He was from Bombay. He came down and said we'd have to give him a deposit for the clothes as a guarantee against damage – this was the usual practice. When we completed the work, we would get our wages and the deposit, unless we wanted to quote it again for more work.

The women of course were inexperienced, they used to work from home and their husbands would procure the work. So he gave us some cloth, and asked us to make some samples. We thought we were being very smart about all this – we got his signature and all our signatures on stamped paper, and paid the deposit. After that, I went to Delhi for a while. The women were trying to get in touch with him – he had a mobile, and kept promising to visit the next day, and then of course he disappeared altogether. We tracked him from place to place, but he had always left just a day earlier, after having duped someone or the other. That's when we decided that this was not our area; even if we'd found him, if he had two or three goondas working for him, what would we have done? I felt that this was not the kind of work that one could push the women into. Even if they were safe, what if they didn't pay them on time?

The market is very ruthless – plus, why did we have to depend on someone like Tabrez? Because the women didn't have any skills. They could just do this running stitch … and with that level of skill, they could only go to these kind of people, who would take advantage of them.

That's when we decided that they had to be trained to do work which was not dispensable, which could pay them proper wages – and find outlets and boutiques which wouldn't make fools out of them. At that point, I was trying to get some organization like Sahyog to manage it, again, one didn't think one could do it on one's own.

I was constantly writing to people. Because of Raigarh, I would go to Bombay a lot, and would try to put it across at seminars. I also tried to put it in context – of the thousands of people, who had lost their livelihood during the riots, some of whom who had been pushed into doing manual labour. Everybody was talking about Gujarat, about law, about relief camps, about women – could livelihood also be addressed ? And the question of economic boycott?

Was it not addressed?
No. People had differing opinions, they felt that anyway the industries that had employed them had shut down a long time ago. But I believed that the way people, especially the Muslim community, had been deliberately pushed towards poverty, over years, had a substantial part to play in the riots. At the first meeting of Teesta Setalvad's Citizens for Peace and Justice in Bombay around March 2003, I spoke about it again, and people came up to me and

said, you're being too simplistic, this thing cannot be done, or – yes, this is a problem, good that you are so intense or whatever, but things don't happen so easily, you're just somebody who's come from Delhi, who has no idea how activists and NGOs work and you're being very romantic about things.

One has sort of realized that now, to an extent, but that was also a time for testing things out, and one felt – why can't things be made to happen? So, I just told myself – forget it now, I'm not going to waste my energies here and there, I'll just do it on my own.

I was in constant touch with Anand of course. He supported me through and through when I came to Gujarat. For the first six months, I lived on my own savings – staying here also takes money and nobody's paying you. Then I spent all my savings but I really wanted to stay on, so Anand offered to give me living expenses. He's also this person who's is in the loop of things and has a lot of friends abroad. He knew an organization called the Singh Foundation, which had some money left over from the time of the earthquake in 2001 and they wanted to give it to some riot-related work. They asked him to suggest a credible organization that they could donate it to. So he asked me to write up a proposal and a budget. I had no idea who to call in for training the women, but I wrote down the basic premise, and sent it off.

I also went to meet Uma Didi at Verchi, because I had volunteered with them earlier on these fact-finding issues …

… related to Gujarat?
No, nuclear basically – tests and radiation – in January. They were doing this survey on radiation effects in Pokhran. I had corresponded with Uma Didi and Suren Bhai, who is a physicist, earlier, but this time I decided – I am not calling them, I'm just landing up there. It was crazy because they'd just had a meeting – I reached at 12 in the night and we must have spoken till about 3 or 4 in the morning. I returned to Ahmedabad at 5. I think the urgency of it got across to them, and Uma Didi said – Look, of course you need to train them and I'll come and help you with that once you've got the funding to keep it going. Even if you don't get money from somewhere, we and Sampark Kranti Vidyalaya have some, so go ahead and start. She was basically sort of touched by the whole thing. And then, one just had to wait through this period before the money came in, in March.

We looked for a place in Tahera Park, but that place could only take in about four to five machines. It was too small. So, the ones who didn't know the work at all, we decided that their machines should be kept there, and devised this system, whereby those who knew a little bit could teach the rest. It was a sort of three-tier teaching system. We also tried locating a tailor. When we finally started, we thought of this thirty-rupee stipend – because if they don't get something while they're learning, they are bound to start doing other things to just get the money in. A lot of people donated for the centre, including the women themselves – someone gave a *pankha*, someone else a *matka*. All of us together started building it up. Zaid, in the meantime was working for Action Aid, and I used to help him, so when we had to get tables for the centre, I roped him in. For two days, Uma Didi taught us how to do measurements and things. Finally, on the third day, we located a lady tailor, and that's how the training started.

When I approached you, you were very supportive of the proposal, even when I was doubtful of the time that we had lost while waiting for the grant. What is the role of art, according to you, in a situation like this?
Initially, the idea was that they would be able to give vent to their trauma, and what better way than art? At that point they were so despondent that one felt that this kind of intervention would help them to get their feelings out – what they were frustrated with, what was pulling them down. So somewhere I was looking at art, and I still do, as therapy. It doesn't have to be therapy in a methodical sense, but any kind of letting out, any kind of creation, gives you a sense of self-respect and joy, and a sense of power. That again is something which has not been addressed, even though so much has been said about the pain and the trauma – it's barely been touched.

... the therapy part of it or the art part?
The art part. In some ways, the psychological counselling that some of the organizations did touched upon it – the children were told to make pictures of what happened during the riots – but I think it worked more as documentation than real involvement. First of all, there was no long-term engagement. They would do it with a set of children and move on to another set of children – so it really became, in a sense, their documentation. These pictures of people killing people or people shooting at people – they'd go on about how horrible it was or how beautifully these

children had drawn it. But what have the children got out of it? Whereas you have been coming here since two years, and you were saying that you could teach – to me that seemed to make sense. I felt that it could help the women. Of course, later one realized that maybe it wasn't so much about the women because they had a lot of livelihood issues, and that it would be best to involve the girls – one, because the girls had never been spoken to and also, the women have had more exposure than the girls have had.

... in terms of having the opportunity to tell their stories?
Yes. They're at that particular age when so much anyway doesn't make sense, and then something like this happens, how do you fit it into your thinking? And the displacement from one area to another, whether it's the women or the girls, they'd always talk about Patiya. Vatva is very barren, while I think Patiya was full of activity, with all those many little lanes – it was full of life.

They had a culture there, families ...
They were born there, and they'd grown up there, got married there and the whole fabric is torn apart – also because there are 45 of them who were displaced at once.

Don't they want to return, or have their houses been destroyed?
No, their houses have been rebuilt, but they don't want to go back because it was in those same houses that terrible things happened to their family members. And I think with the widows, they feel more free here.

Could you tell us something about Bibi Banoo? That is one major tragedy which has happened within the group after the riots.
I think Bibi Banoo has a special place. Wherever she went she touched people – or rubbed them up the wrong way. She was somebody you could not, you know, debunk or look away from. One, she was definitely the only person who was extremely political. The other people in the community – they lack the sense of empowerment that I think Bibi was probably born with. She had it in her to do her own thing and use her own mind always. Of course, the fact that she lost so many people of her family also put her in a position, financially as well, where she could get away with it – she didn't have to rely on anyone, her in-laws or her parents. She was entirely on her own financially, and she was a very headstrong person – very

articulate, extremely articulate. She would also endear herself to a lot of activists and NGOs. Here was this person who would actually speak your language without having been trained into it. Whatever you were saying, she would understand – she would grasp it without having it explained to her, you know. It is another language – trying to explain to the people in the community is not easy because they really have to cross a certain mindset in terms of being able to understand the politics of it all, but Bibi somehow knew everything.

How did she get involved with the man who finally killed her?
I think she dared to step out. Now, how many women, especially widows, would dare to step beyond a certain boundary into having a relationship in the first place? You know, everyone is human – everyone is an emotional, sensual being. I'm sure the other women also have a desire to form a relationship. But that whole idea is blocked not only by society, but when they tell themselves – no, you know, if we step out there, what is going to happen? What are our children going to say? Apart from what society's going to say – you know, all that.

What exactly happened with her?
The fact that she and some other women like her dared to step out of those constraints – and then – it's such a tragedy that the only people who are ...

... available?
Not only available ... they literally locate them. I mean, I'd say that – I don't think Bibi located somebody, I'd say that she was located by somebody. She was located by Tanvir, and similarly people like her are located by other people – here is one woman who has money, and at the same time, she has no qualms, and Tanvir thought that he had found somebody who he could exploit later. Get her into a relationship, then marry her, and control her.

Do you think it was thought out from the beginning?
Definitely it was, because you see, even the marriages ... the widows, none of them need to remain widows. They can all marry, because there are so many men who want to marry them. So many single men who have never married before want to marry them, and in normal circumstances, why would a young man want to marry an older widow and not another young, unmarried person? Because of the money.

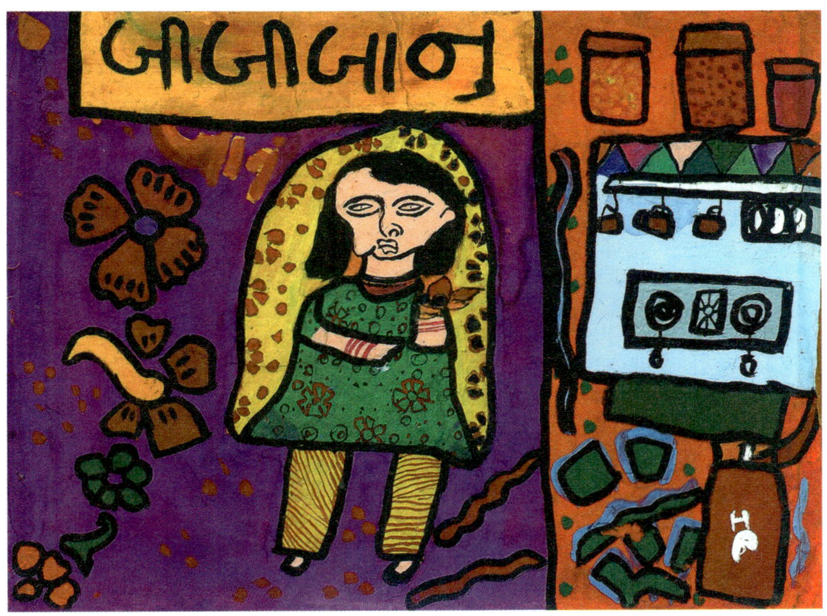

Madina, one of the women in our group. She got married to some person who has put her in a burqa (she had never worn a burqa in her life) – who does not let her go out of Jamalpur. The women have seen this with that one marriage, suddenly all your freedom is curtailed ... money is in his control, everything is in his control. So I think this is something that they talk about, and decide – we don't want to marry. And Bibi was also very smart. Tanvir assumed that – now I have a relationship with her, she's going to marry me – but she was smarter than that. She said look, first of all I'm not interested in marriage, and even if I marry you, you have to write it on paper, before we marry, that you will have nothing to do with even one paisa of the compensation that I have received. That has to go to my children. And even if something happens to me and my children, you will have nothing to do with it.

Very, very radical, and of course it angers the man, he thinks he's got you under his control by seducing you, she was saying that look, she's got a mind, she can think, she knows what is what, tomorrow what if he does

Bibi Banoo, by Tasleem Qureshi (detail from poster), 2005

something? This really angered him and he started becoming aggressive.
He came and beat her up, started throwing things around in her house.
That's when she lodged an official complaint saying that he had threatened
to kill her – *main acid phenk doonga, yeh wo ho jayega* – then he got arrested,
but got out on bail. A week later, he came and did this.

It was also revenge for having him imprisoned?
Not because he was sent to prison, I think, but – how can she do this, one,
she's a single woman, and first of all to him she must've been a *besharam*
woman … you know, which is in the first place why he wooed her. How dare
she do this … so, I think it's frightening that the money that she received –
you know, finally it was used against her. Even when she was in the hospital,
everybody in the community, they were so unsympathetic, they were
saying look, she has stepped beyond certain limits and this is why this has
happened and it is what she deserves.

So I think it brought out a lot of debates within, especially with the women.
At least we tried to bring in debate; even in the group the women had this
kind of attitude that she deserved it – we tried to tell them – what about the
man, nobody's saying anything about him, and why should you not step out
of what is 'written' for you. It's a horrible thing that she had to meet a man
who wanted to exploit her – there is nothing wrong in having a relationship
per se, but the situation she was put in, the guy of course poured kerosene
on her and burnt her, he's now in jail, but it's horrible how it ended.

I think this kind of thing would never have happened in Patiya – the way
that she was burnt in broad daylight, because there is a community which
has been there for decades together, nobody would have dared to come
in and do this kind of a thing. But here in Faizal Park, people have been
uprooted and placed in a different situation which is not really their home.
It's to do with emotional displacement and social displacement - something
like this, on this scale would not have happened in Patiya.

**Yes, it is strange that in broad daylight, somebody just walks in, there's a
struggle and nobody hears it? How did it get that far without someone
noticing that something was wrong?**
You see, there was an ongoing thing with Bibi and Tanvir. When you're in
a relationship it's very difficult to get out. And I think for a long time, even

before her (formal) complaint, this had been going on. He would come and threaten her, and then she'd go back to him after a while.

Finally, when he beat her up that day, and broke things in her house, that's when she lodged a complaint. The people around assumed that this must be the usual thing, of course our women were not there, they were all at the centre at that point of time because it was a working day. That *chaali* was more or less empty. There were a few people, Tasleem was there, the kids were all there, the kids and the younger people – but the elders were not there. But again, as I said, they'd already given up on Bibi as somebody who'd crossed her boundaries – so why meddle with something like that – it's a very gendered kind of society you know. They feel that *voh jo ho raha hai vo hone do …* we won't bother with that.

Even when she passed away, there were not many people who came to see her. There wasn't even anybody to pick her up immediately and take her away; for half an hour, she was apparently lying like that.

The children were in school?
One child was in Raigarh, the other was in school. Apparently when the auto came, she walked herself up to the auto, she had that kind of courage. Of course it speaks (negatively) of the attitude of the people around her too, but she herself had that kind of courage.

Who was it that had her taken to the hospital?
Majeedbhai and the people around, but that was after some time. They wrapped her up in blankets and let her lie there because they didn't want to make a decision. They're already involved in their own cases, so they probably didn't want to be involved in something further.

But, even in the hospital, she gave her statement the very first day. She was conscious from the very beginning, and the first two or three days, she showed some improvement. She had so much in her, so much fighting spirit – but for the last week when she started going down, she had also become our baby, you know. She had always been the outspoken one, who would tell you off and be rude to you, and not be ingratiating – and somehow she became such a baby. One started getting attached to her in other ways – while before that one really admired her – it was like nursing a little child.

And it was horrible when she went, because we thought, there's no way
that she could go. She was a survivor of those times, and even now, it's sort
of unbelievable that somebody like her who had so much courage and so
much strength – how could life go out of her, somehow death has to stop
at her door. This was somehow our conviction – I just feel that if things had
worked out differently, then people would not be left saying – this is what
happens to women who cross the line. I wish she had survived and come
back to work.

You know, her machine – she was very possessive and she wouldn't let
anybody sit at it or touch it. When she was in the hospital, I thought she was
worried about it, so I told her that I would get it shifted to her house. And at
that point of time she wasn't speaking any longer, she just shook her head
as if to say 'no' – in her eyes, the way she shook her head and the way she
tried to use her hands, it was like she was saying 'no', you know – I'm going
to come back to work, leave it there. When I remember that I feel terrible.

Her children, I think they have lost a lovely parent in the sense of somebody
who would've thought far ahead for them. She really resented the fact that
she hadn't been properly educated. She had studied till the tenth standard and
was married off after that. Her mother had come to look after her in hospital
– she was telling her – this is all because of you. I'm here on this bed because
of you, because you didn't educate me. If you had educated me, I would be
somewhere else today, not lying on this bed, not married, not widowed.

For her children, she was very sure that she wanted them to really study …

The amazing part about her was that she would depend on her own
mind. Even when Raigarh happened, she came with us, when we were
taking the kids – she came to Raigarh, saw the school for herself and was
really impressed. She was not somebody who would go as part of a herd
anywhere. She would have been a very different parent, compared to the
others in the community who would get their daughters married and say,
okay this is enough, you've studied enough …

**What do you think displacement has actually done? I'm looking at the
community which has been relocated here, do you think they're getting used
to it – how has it harmed them – or even helped them?**

I think that it's worked both ways. One, of course there is definitely emotional
and social displacement, because the kind of relationships that you had in
Patiya – whether it's the children, the women, the elders – obviously, that
has been lost. The people that you were close to, even that whole system of
things. And even the people that are now living together, they're not the best
of friends. They have taken a lot of time to adjust to each other, because of
having to live in such close quarters with somebody you either did not know
or somebody you previously didn't like, or didn't get along well with.

Also, somewhere the displacement and the compensation money which has
come in has skewed the social hierarchy that must've been there before.
Within our group too, you know, somebody who was previously socially or
economically higher up has now come to the same level as somebody who
was badly off, and those that were badly off have climbed the social ladder
– so that also creates a dynamics within itself.

But I think for the women, the single women especially, one could say that it
has helped them too. When you look at Bibi's case you feel – you know – the
fact that you can gather that kind of freedom now to stretch your limits. Of
course that's the process of being single anywhere, but also you're in an area
where there's nobody to hide you or guide you, you've taken things upon
yourself. If you talk to the women, they will tell you that initially they used
to be very timid – even to approach the guy who supplies them electricity –
or to call for help when there was a theft. They would go in groups… .

Over a period of time, they became this gang of women who would go and
thrash someone – *ki tune paani nahi diya, electricity nahi diya* – and that guy
would just … he would normally not be scared of men walking towards him,
but he would be scared of this gang of women coming towards him. They
are able to chart out new roles for themselves in an area where roles had
previously not been defined. So, I think in that sense it has been very liberating.
The fact is that they go out on their own, they dress up as they like and go and
do their fun things. In Patiya, that kind of thing would've been frowned upon.
Here, there's no one to say anything because they're on their own.

How do they get on with the older residents of Faizal Park ?
Initially, the older residents were very resentful – because they would see
so many visitors coming to talk to these women – that they belonged to

the same station economically, but were being paid so much attention. The women were also at the forefront in getting this drainage system done through one of the organizations, their drains were getting clogged up, so they had new wells made. They got the others to contribute, and that made them resentful – they felt that they had all the money to spare, so why were they asking us? But I think now it has more or less settled down.

You will soon be returning to Delhi – how do you feel about it?
I'll definitely miss all the fun. I think that from the kind of despondency that was there even a year after the riots, to now when they're exercising their freedom and actually looking for fun – I think that's the spirit that I love most, which drives me to continue working here. When I watch films about Gujarat or any kind of tragedy – what I feel people miss out on, you know – they always tend to look at people who have been victimized as victims forever, because they tend to relate to them through that incident or event or whatever. I feel that the fact that they can seek happiness or have the spirit to enjoy themselves and have so much fun – that spirit should be celebrated. Definitely at Himmat, whatever's happened or whatever happens, when it comes to fun, they know that this is the space for them to find it. That's what I'm going to miss most – I haven't had as much fun with my friends as I've had with them, and they are also so *bindaas*. You forget everything, where you are or what you're up to and you just get into this celebratory mode.

At the WSF, for the first time – that night when we checked all the three stalls, we'd sold everything except for a few odd pieces – they spontaneously broke into song and dance, I've never seen anything like that – they were just so overjoyed. There was this spirit of we've done it, you know, this is the first time we displayed our work, and we've sold everything – my god, it was beautiful. It was at night, everyone had gone, we were all packing – of course there were no clothes to be packed. The women were all divided amongst the three stalls at different places on the grounds, and finally everyone came together to count the money – *kitna bacha, kiske stall se kitna bacha* – and they were trying to compete with each other. It was amazing, it was something about their energy, nobody said anything, and then they just broke into song and dance. They just danced and danced and danced, it really touched me ... and it's also because of their being single that they're able to participate so freely, in a way that their married friends might not be able to.

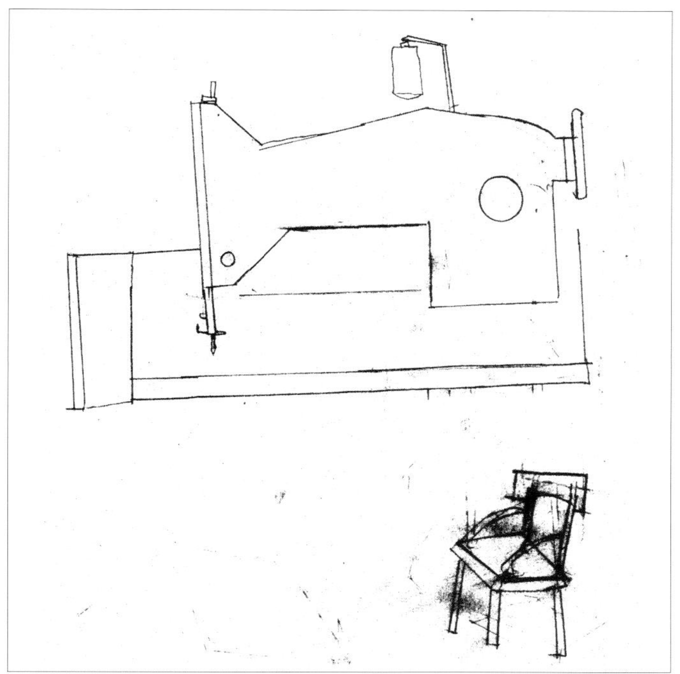

You remember Vasudha, you came there – to the Window to Gujarat at the WSF – that space that spoke about what had been done in Gujarat during the riots. There was that sort of commemoration of pain all around. These women did their little dance right there, in that very space. They got the watchman who was there to click their photographs. They also acted out, for fun, instances of how they had duped customers into buying defective pieces. It was such a joyous, joyous moment – to infuse that space which was commemorating their tragedy, with this sense of celebration. Things go on, and I think people who work with issues or with communities somewhere have to be able to create such spaces and acknowledge that in spite of pain, in spite of whatever happens, there can and will be such moments.

Ahmedabad / 2005

Drawing by Shahjehan Sheikh, 2005

SECTION THREE

SECRET LIFE

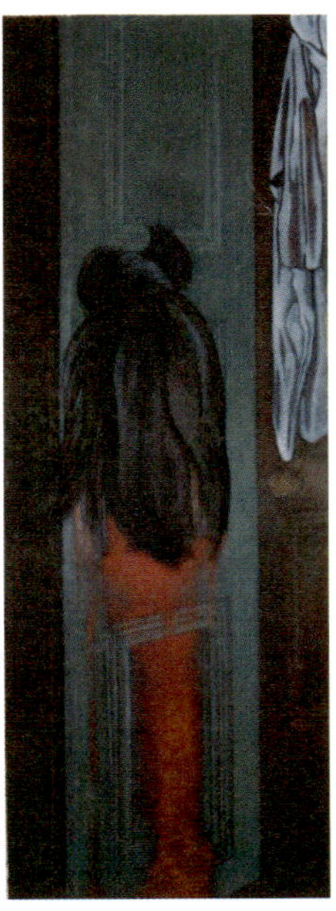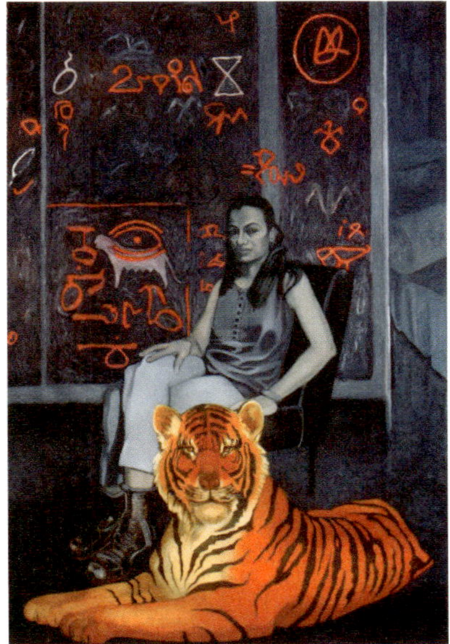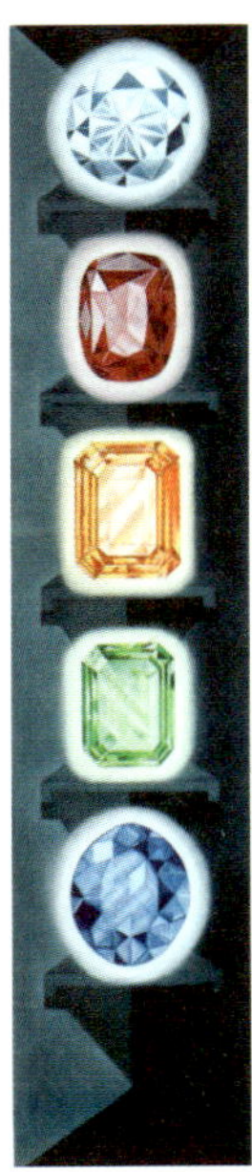

Secret Life is a body of paintings made between 1997 and 2001. It was conceived as groups of narrative sequences, involving temporal progression from one frame to another. The matrix within which individual frames were composed was based on the idea of a 'House' with its many rooms, its different kinds of spaces, metaphoric and functional. The script for the enactment of the narrative was based on life – aspects of it which are an unspoken taboo during the course of 'normal' social interaction – and therefore lived in private, subterranean realms. How does one edit life? What are the parameters of retention or erasure?

Obsession, as an editing tool: the most stringent, the acknowledgment of which compels its cultivation and the inherent dangers therein; but when one works with something as large as life, there is no other choice. The origins of obsession are traced back to the self; without its inclinations and impulses there would be no concept and no form, no ideology or attitude; one does not adopt these things as intellectual choices, they have their origins in desire. And therefore I place myself at the heart of my narrative, and my story stems from desire.

The choice of visual language for the fleshing-out of this desire is perhaps a logical one, and it is at this juncture that the notion of structure becomes central: the limits of a single frame are insufficient to contain the complexities of what I wish to engage with. It is necessary to evolve a working process and a method of display elastic enough to accommodate the negotiations which are inevitable in a narrative which is continuously in the making.

I now use a similar textual structure, flowing towards affinities as places of clarity, choosing to trace continuities which underlie the seeming disruptions of logic. I include excerpts from my writings on my work, which is an ongoing process, and therefore expressive of an immediacy which could be lost in a retrospective text. The one below pertains specifically to the title of this text.

From a paper written for a symposium, 2002

Late in 1994, I began working towards a structure which could accommodate changing patterns of living and working. It was a phase marked by frequent travel, which meant increased mobility offset by an unwillingness to give up the discipline of an everyday practice. It was difficult to work on the scale that I was used to, at least on a single surface. Further, change was an essential component, which needed to be physically incorporated into the work – like grit in an oyster shell, visually and visibly transforming it without negating the logic of the processes at work. The idea of progression of any kind naturally brought in the question of time, again as something that needed to be made visible. Earlier paintings were large works expressive of movement within an overall stability, thereby representing an entirety. I now began working on segments/sections of larger schemes, as solutions to transitory working situations in studios in different countries, allowing them to 'find' each other in time to make a coherent whole.

What emerged was a visual vocabulary that straddled different kinds
of languages, and a format capable of expressing interrupted, parallel
and sometimes divergent streams of experience. There were spaces in
between for many things, for reminiscence and recall, for projections
into relationships as yet unexplored, not merely in terms of ideas but
as possibilities for the embodiment of these ideas. These groups and
sequences contained passages which belonged to different points in
time; the viewing moment was used as a focusing device rather than as
something which dictated, spatially or in a temporal sense, the limits of
what could be expressed.

Distances, absences and speed were things which had to be confronted at
all times; it seemed to me that they need not always create more distances
and more speed, but could be subverted towards closeness and greater
intimacy. I made studies of the interiors that I lived and worked in, fitting
them within the notion of a house, claiming them as personal territory. The
structure therefore is very much more than a formal device or solution.
The events which animate it encompass the internal and extend beyond
it into the realm of common concerns – the reclamation of identity in the
personal and collective sense, the recognition of the vitality of the 'popular'
as a bridge for communication at various levels, the conception of a new
aesthetic which begins to deviate from previously accepted norms. Still, they
remain components of a larger body whose essence cannot be summarized
or fully comprehended. It is a continuing dialogue, with its attendant doubts,
convictions and emphases that shift with the passage of time.

I see my presence in the painting not merely as a self-portrait, but in the
light of one who introduces the piece and the actors, becomes an actor
herself, distances herself when necessary, and detaches herself completely
in the end; taking several forms and incarnations in successive roles and
lifetimes, thereby creating illusions through the mixing of virtuality with
reality – like the *sutradhar* in traditional theatre. The distinction between
the real and the reflected begins to blur.

For a lecture at the Department of Art History in the Faculty of Fine Arts in
Baroda, I wrote down some thoughts on the physical aspects of structure.

March 2001, Baroda

I think of my scale as life-size, or as a space that one can comfortably enter; architecturally it has to do with the actual scale of a middle-class home in India. The height of the paintings is about 8–9 ft, dictated by the height of the ceiling, and the fact that I can reach the top of it standing on a chair. It is as much as I can handle, physically. While on display, the paintings are hung a few inches above the level of the floor. In spite of their size, they then become part of the wall; they are not intrusive and do not need a great distance to be viewed. The entire body of work can be hung close together and considered as one painting, one piece of narrative. People tend to refer to them as diptychs or triptychs; the term seems to limit the connotations exclusively to the realm of the visual, and is further inappropriate in the context of my work. Montage might be a better word, the links are conceptual and intellectual as much as visual and temporal.

Earlier groups were more loosely constructed, one could replace a segment with another. I also duplicate segments when I feel a certain image to be integral to another group, or when I want to refer to it as a quote or a memory. How is the temporal made visible? In the fact of composing a sequence, yes, you step from one space into another, one room of a house into another – and there is a lapse of time in this passage, things have changed in the next frame: it is a different space animated by different events. Like a comic strip or a cinematic narrative, with shifts in scale and perspective; a long shot juxtaposed with a close-up, a narrow frame with a large one. The fact that the frames are separated by a few inches enables them to retain their differences and not attempt to fuse, artificially. There are also formal differences in the handling of the paint which render time visible, or a shift in the way the grey is constituted which makes a different kind of sound altogether. Panels executed a year or two apart, or more, contain such disparities. I re-introduce earlier paintings into current groups on the basis of their affinity – of concept, but also in enjoyment of this dissonance. Looking back is as important as forward mobility or 'progress', recovery as much as discovery.

The unity we seek is a larger one and we have to go beyond appearances in order to find it. This structure makes possible inclusions and exclusions dependent on current pre-occupations; nothing is destroyed or effaced, one area merely illuminates another.

February 2002, Baroda

With a painting entitled *Veda*, the conceptual and formal elements that I
have been talking about attain greater definition. It comprises three panels.
The first describes my studio at the Cite Des Arts in Paris, with my paintings
on the wall; my overalls, which I think of as a second skin, are draped over
the sofa. In the centre is my daughter, wearing my skin, a magical garment.
Around her, what appears like cabalistic symbols are in fact quotations of
drawings which repeat themselves in her sketchbook. The face is classicized
and typified, the colours used are reminiscent of early film posters, indigo
and white with a touch of rose. The last panel has a row of shelves from
studies of the toilet in the pump house at Oserian in Kenya where I did
a residency in 1998. On these shelves are Sacred Hearts extracted from
popular religious posters of Christ and The Virgin. These melodramatic
reproductions are specially significant for me in their recurring depiction
of fire and blood, violence and pain eroticized to the pitch of fantasy, the
aesthetics of pleasure privileged and retained beyond the persistence of
suffering.

At the level of the sensual, I use these and similar elements as vehicles for
colour, which came back into my life after a long grey spell.

At the level of symbolism, they find spontaneous meaning within an
internal context but are still recognized by most people and would hold the
attention while less obvious areas revealed themselves in relationship.

At the level of play, I think of all those things which fascinated me as a
child, which I loved to paint but later came to believe were artistically
embarrassing. Released from that prison of good taste, the universality
imposed on us by the art school culture, they began to acquire the power
of larger-than-life dreams.

A different aesthetic seems possible, neither revivalist nor postmodern,
deriving its energy from the contradictions of a turbulent country; capable
of expressing the complex and explosive realities of a specific geographical
and cultural location here in India and of a life lived within that location.

These groups and sequences enable me to do several things at the same
time: for one, to convey the experience of time as something pervasive and
cyclic. Also, to juxtapose disparate elements in a manner which does not

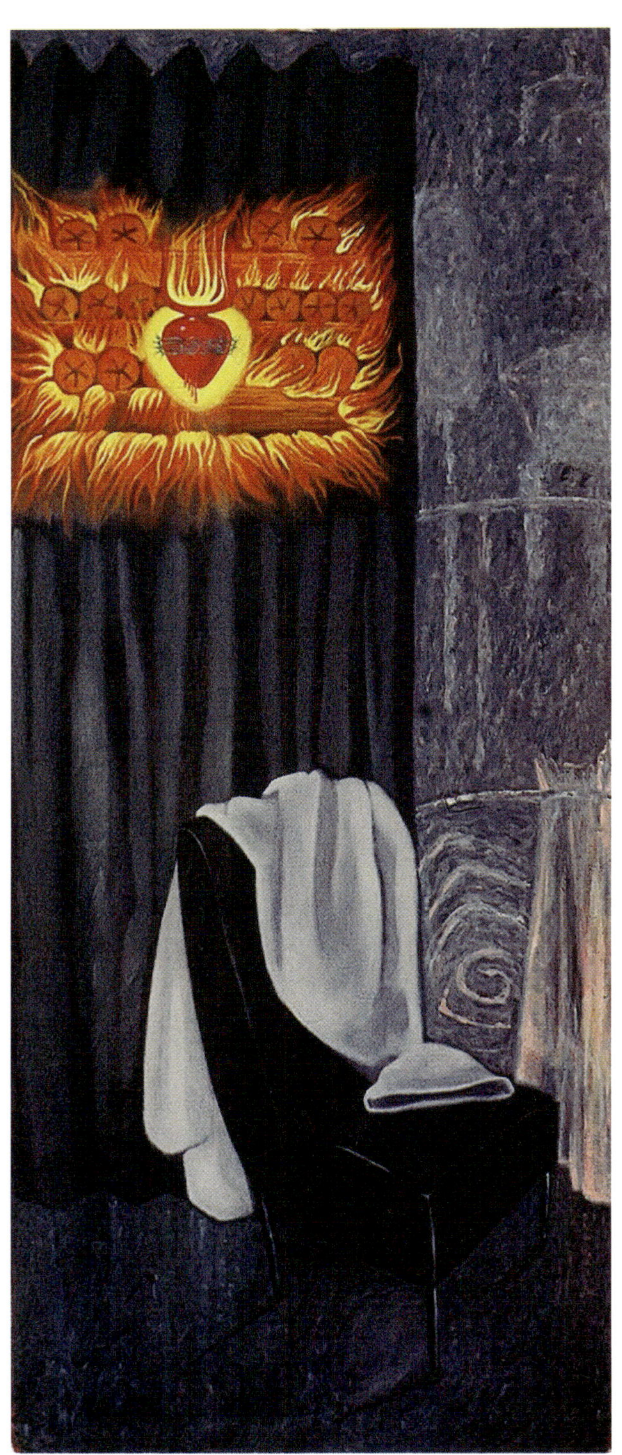

Veda, 1999

demand a compromise or a dissolution of boundaries and differences – co-existence or indeed the inter-connectedness of polarities. My most recent painting is one of myself seated in my studio at the Cite Des Arts, with a tiger at my feet. The idea of a tiger in Paris is of course incongruous, and at a superficial level touches upon the notion of the 'exotic'; so too the jewels on the right.

It is also a story of loss and enrichment.

The title of an earlier body of work is significant in this context: *The Secret Life of Objects*. It derives from a comment made by a friend when he saw my paintings for the first time in 1996. When he saw them three years later, his feelings were that what had seemed earlier like a display of sorts had now become more like an environment dictated by the objects in question, or a virtual space.

I had begun working with interiors by then, rooms which were large in scale, logical in disposition but still far from real. The experience of watching people enter my studio and become part of my painting was a strong one, so too the sight of my dog curled up at the foot of a painted bed. It was at this point in time that the human figure, which I had not painted in a long time, re-entered my work in *Veda*.

September 2000, Mysore

Secret Life was shown in March 2001 in Delhi. The accompanying text in normal circumstances would have been in the form of a catalogue. Instead, I made an audio CD of readings from my journals over four years, 1997–2001. They are reflections on work, life, anecdotes, bits of poetry, other excerpts from my own writings; meant to be heard through headphones, in the gallery, so as not to intrude into viewing space. Not quite secret but as something between two people; an oral catalogue. It enabled me to use voice in an area not usually associated with voice.

Current-day art practices evolve in conjunction with text as critique, interpretation or as a complementary trajectory. Ways of weaving text into the fabric of the visual narrative are several, and below is a response to a letter from a student whose dissertation required the information.

In the early nineties, I began to set aside in my paintings a vertical strip which I treated differently – I used symbols and hieroglyphs in a more literal manner than I did the painted image. Some of them were recognizably from a collective rather than an individual vocabulary; the reference to early manuscripts and miniatures with their narrative inscriptions was an intended one. A significant change occurred with the birth of my children and with the experience of watching them learn how to write, my daughter in particular. She learnt three languages in school, and in the process, evolved her own sets of symbols which crossed the boundaries between these languages. It was no language, it was an attempt at formulating a language. I found what I had been looking for. I used these symbols, tracing them from her notebooks and drawing books. They were repeated and taken a little further with each painting, the very repetition imbuing them with a contextual meaning within the body of my own work. I print them in vermilion, the language of shop signs or political slogans in India. When the paint drips, it is also blood.

The script is unreadable in the same sense that we experience the forty-odd languages in our country as we travel. It is a sub-text to the creative/working processes, which are obscure places of origin rather than known sites. Like painting and life – incomplete, the meaning half-visible, being created with every step.

From text for catalogue

UNTOUCHABLE
Paintings from 2001 to 2007

The following text collages fragments written over the years, since 2002.
It was compiled in February 2007, and is by no means complete.

A Letter

In relationship to the conversation we had, some thoughts on what I am doing now – as a starting point? The best way to begin, as far as I am concerned – sorry about the length, but necessary for precision.

A run through –

My show in March 2001 was entitled *Secret Life*. The accompanying text in normal circumstances would have been in the form of a catalogue. Instead, I made an audio recording, of readings from my journals over four years, 1997–2001. They are reflections on work, life, anecdotes, bits of poetry, and other excerpts from my own writings; meant to be heard through headphones (in the gallery) so as not to intrude into viewing space. Not quite secret, but as something between two people.

They were also meant to make the vital connection between life and art, easy to forget during times like these when the kind of visibility demanded of the arts exerts a pressure to remain on stage till performance deteriorates into posturing. I was amazed that it was so much cheaper (!!!) than printing a catalogue – the visuals were the paintings themselves – a perfect solution to lack of funds.

My next body of work will be entitled *Untouchable*. The idea was spontaneous, but in India the term carries with it a heavy semantic load, focusing for the main part on caste taboos. I implicate these connotations but widen the context to include other forms of marginalization/exclusion/ subordination. It includes the notion of the 'untouchable' as someone who falls outside the hierarchy/convenience/status of classification but is used as an intermediary who provides access to the darker, mysterious forces of life (there are various social practices and interactions which bear out this relationship).

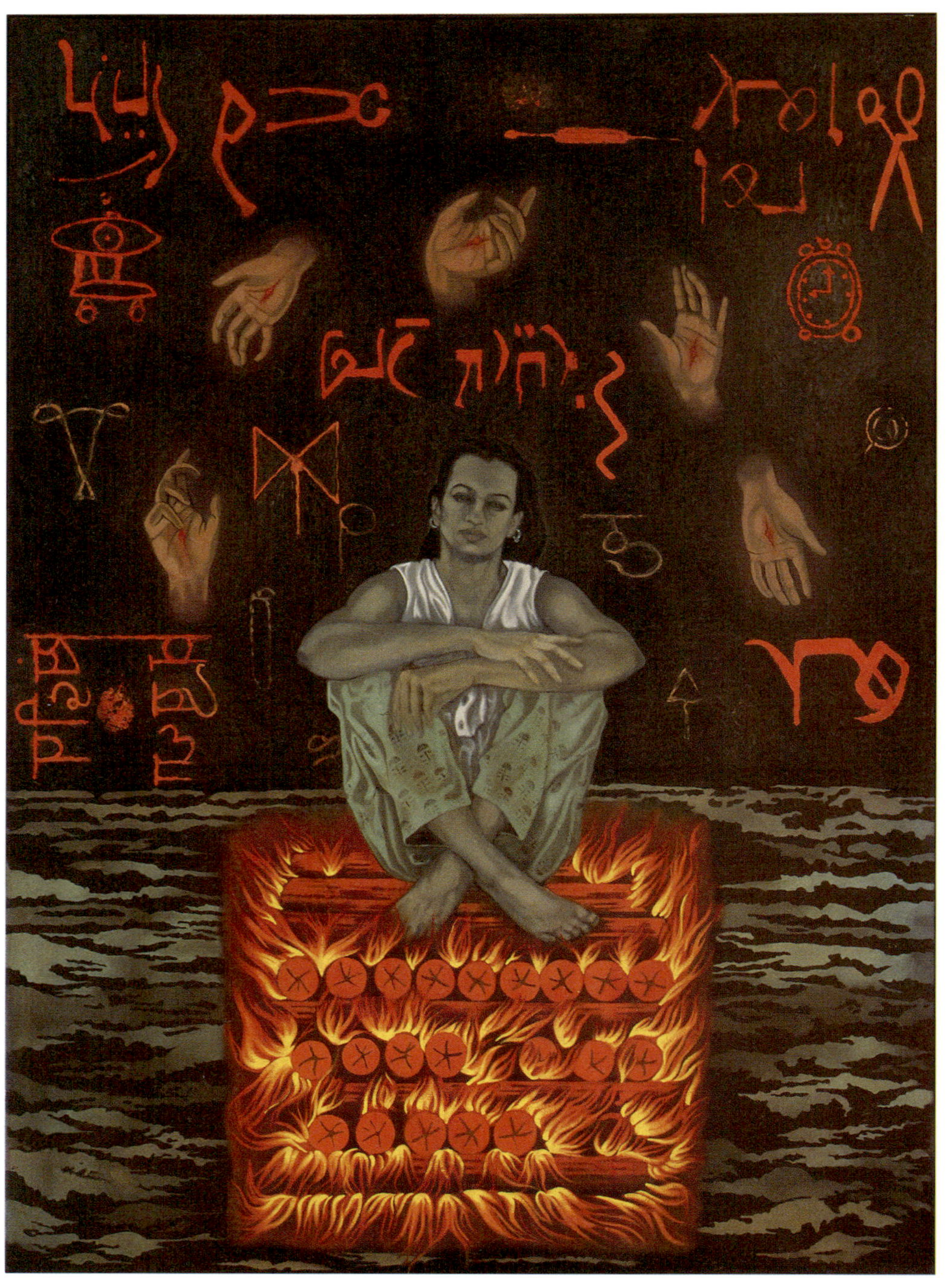

Untouchable, 2001

I have just completed the first painting in this series – framed within the act of self-immolation. The context emanates from the self – a personal history which is partially narrated in symbols within the painting, possibly the most inscrutable area. The impulse is not initially an intellectual one, but one of those things which occurs in a flash, a visual flash in the context of painting, a vision to use a more dramatic word? The analysis comes later, but I notice increasingly that if the matrix/structure is strong, there is a convergence of perspectives, and I see it unfold through my practice. A collective reading is also possible through the use of images which in India would be identified across all economic and social hierarchies. Revulsion and awe/worship render the object of either beyond access; extremes create dualities that actually collapse divisions and exclusions. Symbols of sati and other rituals of purification, rites of passage into states of deprivation, renunciation – the entry points are therefore multiple – social, personal, topical, fantastic and historical, both in the artistic and temporal sense.

An arc of hands bearing stigmata spreads above the figure in benediction – hands/touch/heal/untouchable/redeem the unredeemable/ – touch – love or defile the sacred? Stigmata carry specific religious associations; there is an overlap with *mudras* as in classical dance.

Contentious ground, and I wouldn't take such liberties with an image other than my own.

The next painting – the self-image framed within the context of widowhood/sacrifice/loss of sexuality through the shaving of one's hair – part of a group of four, with the peacock as the central motif. The first panel is a piece of text; a letter, to be precise, in vermilion and gold.

The second panel is based on a press photograph, which appeared in the newspapers during the months after the earthquake in Gujarat, of a man whose hair is being shaved off by a barber in preparation for rituals of death and mourning. I have substituted my own image for his in the painting.

The third panel is a painting of a peacock.

As for the fourth – one of the most moving stories that I read early in 2001, during the aftermath of the earthquake, was of a young girl who was crushed under the debris of her own home. As rescuers toiled to pull her out, she scratched a plea on her bare leg, with a piece of the rubble – do not stop one who wishes to go.

The peacock as a national/notional bird is an intended cliché, I recalled later the fact of his being male. There are two broad aspects to this panel – one is personal loss, the other is the nation, or rather the play of forces that seeks to define it in exclusive terms – embodied by the aggressive display of opulent plumage, and the intended seduction.

The third painting will be constructed around the fountains of the Brindavan Gardens in Mysore, the city of my birth. And so on.

The clichés are as much ideas as repositories of brilliant colour. The 'catalogue' for this body of work will be a book/books of poems in Braille, (which tends to be a lengthy affair, longer than the written word) also with the same title. They would be chronologically ordered, dating from 1995. Braille is written by puncturing the paper to produce an embossed script and can be read with the fingers, by touch, which also brings with it possibilities of healing. I do not seek to set a precedent, merely to materialize something which is intrinsically connected with the concepts that I work with.

I would, through the course of my work, make things which could possibly initiate a quest, as extensions of a larger, deliberate event such as a show. For me, it would be a quest for a different conceptual space than the one created by mainstream practice, which is an assertive act – I exhibit my work and in a way demand its viewing, demand a critique. The objects/books/ CDs which I make will be limited in number and free from compulsion or self-consciousness of any kind. They would exist as authentic, subliminal records of processes related to work, but would in fact be easy to overlook; those wishing to access them might be put to some effort and the giving of time. The impulse which prompts their discovery could be curiosity, or the conviction that it might be worth one's while to attempt to break the code – an open question, to which I have no answer. Of course, it becomes possible to present these due to an existent viewership.

The objects however are largely autonomous and from the moment of their completion increasingly independent of control – I set them free to go where they will, to remain undiscovered or to be found. Discovery would

involve communication, not through confrontation but through compassion
and understanding – and journeys into unfamiliar spaces. Like a treasure
hunt. The personal property of whomsoever it may concern. They could be
duplicated on demand.

I would like to work with recorded text transcribed into morse code. I have
not yet decided on the text, the idea is still in formation. Have to see what
it sounds like and in what way it would hold the attention, if it needs to be
modified, additional inputs, voice? Would like to actually see the machine
which produces the sounds, see where that would take me. The idea of
working with outmoded technology interests me.

I make work from a routine which clarifies my senses and gives me peace,
it is demanding of my life but will not kill it. Regenerative as opposed to
degenerative. I would want it to remain that way.

February 2002

Lost Years: A Reconstruction is a portrait of Vishnu, my son – the missing
component in *Secret Life*. It has developed from a complex set of
associations – a photograph which Valsan, his father, took of him, and from
Vishnu's stay in Mysore, my own birthplace. The fountain is one of the star
attractions of the Brindavan Gardens just outside the city: the subject of
many postcards, available in digitally enhanced colours, designed to attract
tourists. It is also the site of magical memories from childhood: of nights,
lights, chill sprays of water carried by the breeze, the sheer scale of the
fountains and their landscaped surroundings.

In time, though physically related, it stands outside the earlier body of work,
Secret Life. I had hoped to make it the predecessor to a project involving five
children, survivors of the massacre at Naroda Patiya, now rehabilitated in
Vatva.

The project has run into trouble; the current series of paintings, entitled
Untouchable begun in 2001, continues. I had envisioned *Vishnu* as a powerful
strand which would strengthen other continuities between two succeeding
bodies of work; the precise nature of this relationship will only be revealed
in time.

There also arises the question of interpreting a loaded theme – one belonging to a cabaret of national proportions, spectacles of enticement, repeatedly, desperately paraded to gloss over extreme deprivation. How does one therefore paint, or choose to paint a fountain, a peacock? And why? With the many languages now at our disposal, given a particular kind of training, a set of skills which are irrevocably hybrid from a purist point of view, can one dare to look for an original impulse? How can one reclaim that fascination in the face of so much violence, and weave it into a narrative of wonders, intimately related to one's own life?

September 2003

Of Journeys and Emptiness: A Painting in Thirteen Parts

2005 – I began the year on a note of emptiness, wondering, for no immediate reason, where I, in particular, and artists in general, fitted into the scheme of things.

My friends, Robin and Ranjit were organizing an artists' workshop in Pachmarhi. I did not respond to the invitation initially, due to the demands of a recently initiated project. The time frame offered by most workshop situations does not correspond with my work process, nor with the concept of continuity and interconnectedness that supports this process.

I agreed to go however. I began with thinking in terms of long walks and treks, and of recording, in photographs, the paths that these would take. It seemed closest to the reality that I would experience in Pachmarhi.

I took along two boxes of small canvases measuring 1 foot by 1, in case I felt the need to paint. My sketchbook began to fill with random images – landscapes, flora, fauna – a groping towards coherence in a situation that was empty of prior meaning. I decided to present them as they were, but rendered in paint, almost like studies.

On one of the walls in the courtyard beside my room was a chalk drawing of a strolling donkey followed by a trail of misaligned strokes, resembling question marks, each assigned a name – representing several unsuccessful attempts at pinning a tail to the donkey's backside, blindfolded. The

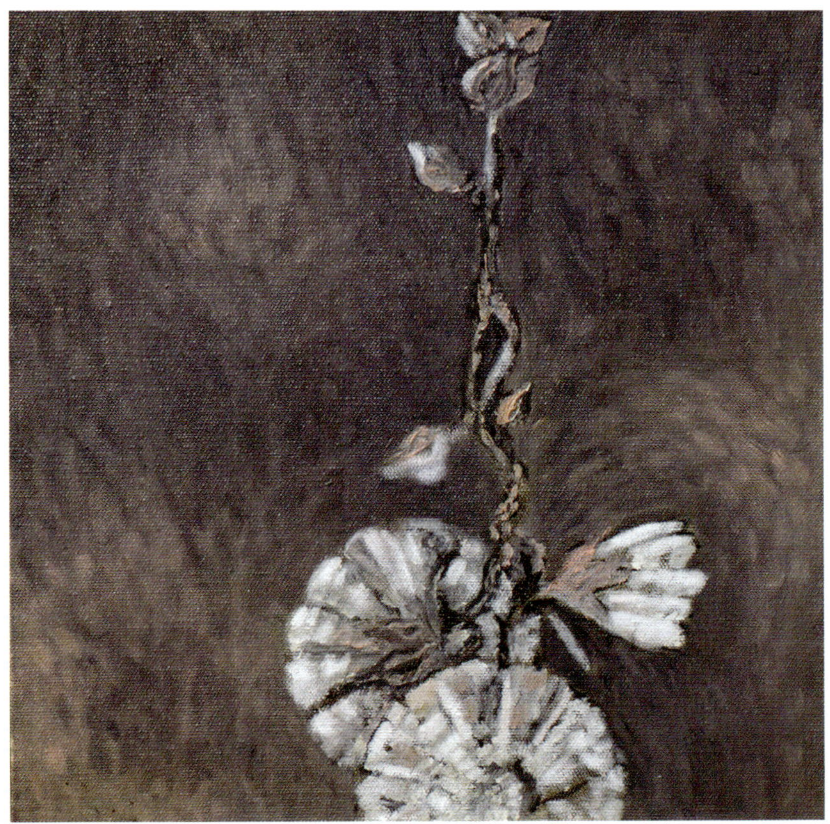

remnants of a bygone birthday party – it seemed an apt metaphor. I spent an afternoon sketching it exactly the way that it was.

Put together like a set of 'hieroglyphs' as Pushpa put it, a story did indeed emerge.

I was reading a book about pigments at the time, entitled *The Story of Colour*. It was interesting to collate the text with the rock paintings of the region, and to work this relationship into the narrative.

Of Journeys and Emptiness (detail), 2005

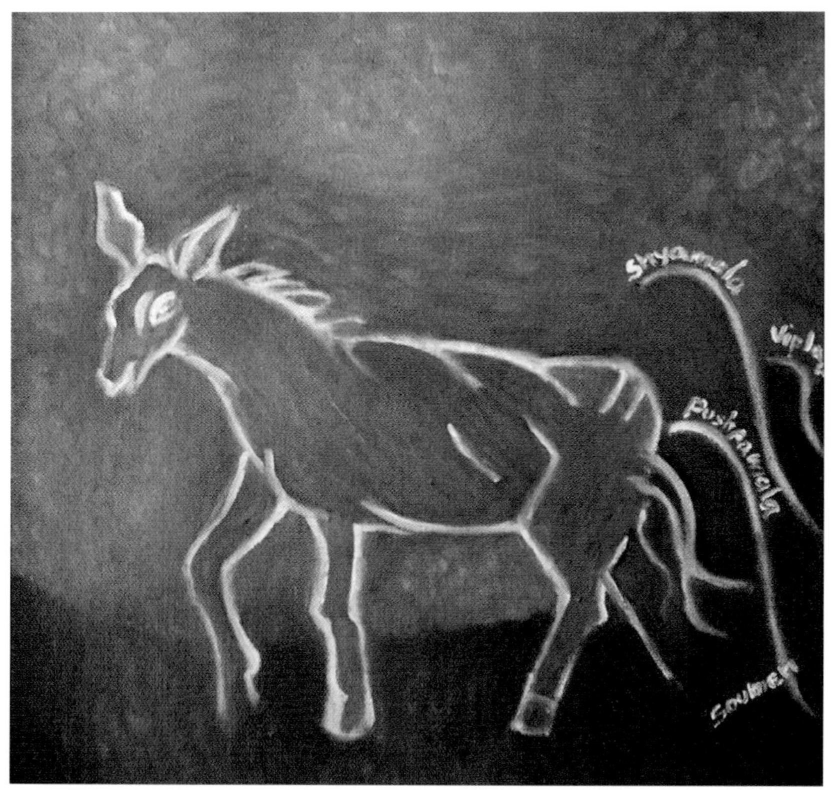

The main keys are of course the primaries, in three frames, and moving through the others in a series of tonal variations. There are moments of discord with the introduction of a sharper and more strident pitch – two old posters, digitally reconstructed, that I unearthed in the shops outside the Mahadev caves. The content is correspondingly potent.

On my return to Baroda I examined the photographs that I had taken. I was surprised. A parallel set of equations seemed to emerge, inclusive of the colour relationships – but one read love and the other, death.

January 2006

Of Journeys and Emptiness (detail), 2005

As far as the title is concerned – the idea of variations and multiple ways is in keeping with the possibility of accommodating differences, the inclusiveness that is also spelt out in the sequences that I work with.

At the Khoj International Artists' Workshop in 2000, I constructed four pieces collaged from layers of newspaper and nylon sarees from the local market at Modi Nagar on the outskirts of Delhi. They seemed to me like subaltern tankas, as opposed to the silk/brocade/material and sacred content of those traditional scrolls. I had intended to embed, in the centre, miniature portraits of the staff who maintained the Modi mansion where we were housed.

The two weeks that we had were insufficient, however, and the work remained incomplete for several years.

By 2005, I had completed four 'self-portraits' (not in the strict sense of the term, rather they were enhanced in order to extend beyond the personal into areas of common relevance) of epic proportions – in terms of physical dimensions as well as the range of experiences that were embedded in the imagery.

I had found the core – the iconography could be transferred from the painting and set in the heart of the scroll, amidst the maze of text and fabric. I wondered if it could be painted directly, or separately and then superimposed onto the surface. Neither would work, considering the state of deterioration the scrolls were in. The sheets were brittle and had begun to crumble, further, they were bulky and gathered dust. I had often thought of throwing them away.

Years ago, while travelling in Germany, I had visited an exhibit of a project documentation by students of one of the universities – I don't quite remember which one. It involved digital reconstructions and light projections of the synagogues that had been destroyed during the Nazi pogroms. To see them rise again in all their beauty, if only in reproduction – it is a memory that has stayed with me; I remember thinking even then that technology could retrace – as opposed to a ceaseless forward motion that never looks back – the path to 'progress' in order to discover value.

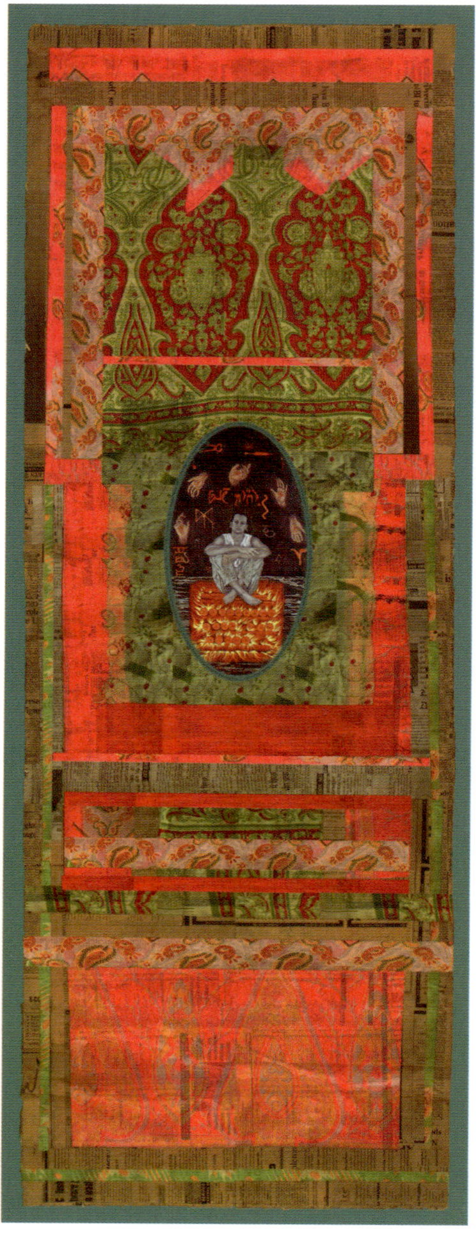 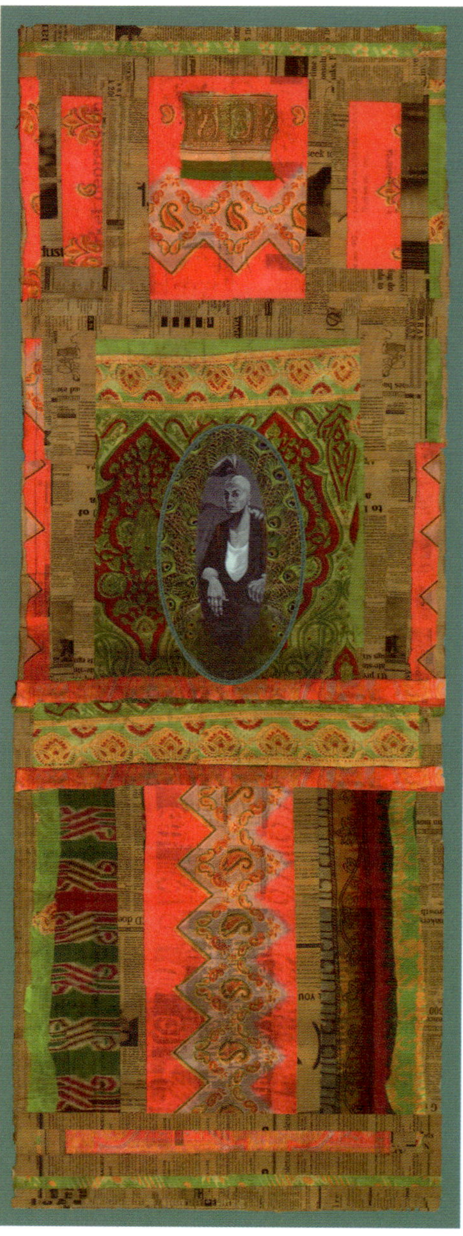

Four Ways of Re-constructing Pain, 2005–06

I decided to scan the scrolls directly, and restore the damaged areas digitally. The available scanner could not accommodate the size of the scroll; Azra (the technician) and I cut each piece into several sections, scanned them separately, and reassembled them on the computer. Strips of newspaper and fabric were extracted (on Photoshop) from the original, in keeping with the manner in which the scrolls were originally made, and used to replace lost bits. The portraits were extracted from photographs of the paintings and superimposed.

A revelation – it was the layering, physical, temporal and in terms of memory as implied by the temporal – that was integral to the work, more than the medium itself, which was merely a means of rediscovering or affirming the concept and the process of its actualization, at a different point in time. Medium as an outward manifestation of inner process, which makes use of whatever is available in historical time; therefore divested of pre-eminence or hierarchy in terms of artistic value, or of the 'new'. The work itself something of a document that bears out the processes of its making – the term 'document', in this case, all the more significant considering the time involved – five years.

And the work, though materialized digitally, is beyond medium. Through the process of layering strips of newspaper and fabric, pieces of text emerged or survived in a manner that created new meaning; one of them read – 're-casting cybermaps for the old economy'.

Sanctum: An Explanation

Sanctum is the title of a painting that I made as a student in 1979. One panel in the present group is a re-construction of that painting, it had been one of my favourites. Among the memories that it evokes is of hours spent at the Tate in London where I was studying at the time, and of wandering into the room with the Rothkos – and somehow linking it with the theoretical study that I had so recently left behind in India – of temple architecture in the south of the country. The plans had fascinated me, even visually, as plans: they revealed a structure which was somehow obscured in viewing the actual monument, by virtue of the sheer scale, weight and the ornamentation encrusting the surface. They also embodied a philosophy, a spatial and sculptural organization that transformed movement through those spaces into enactments of passage.

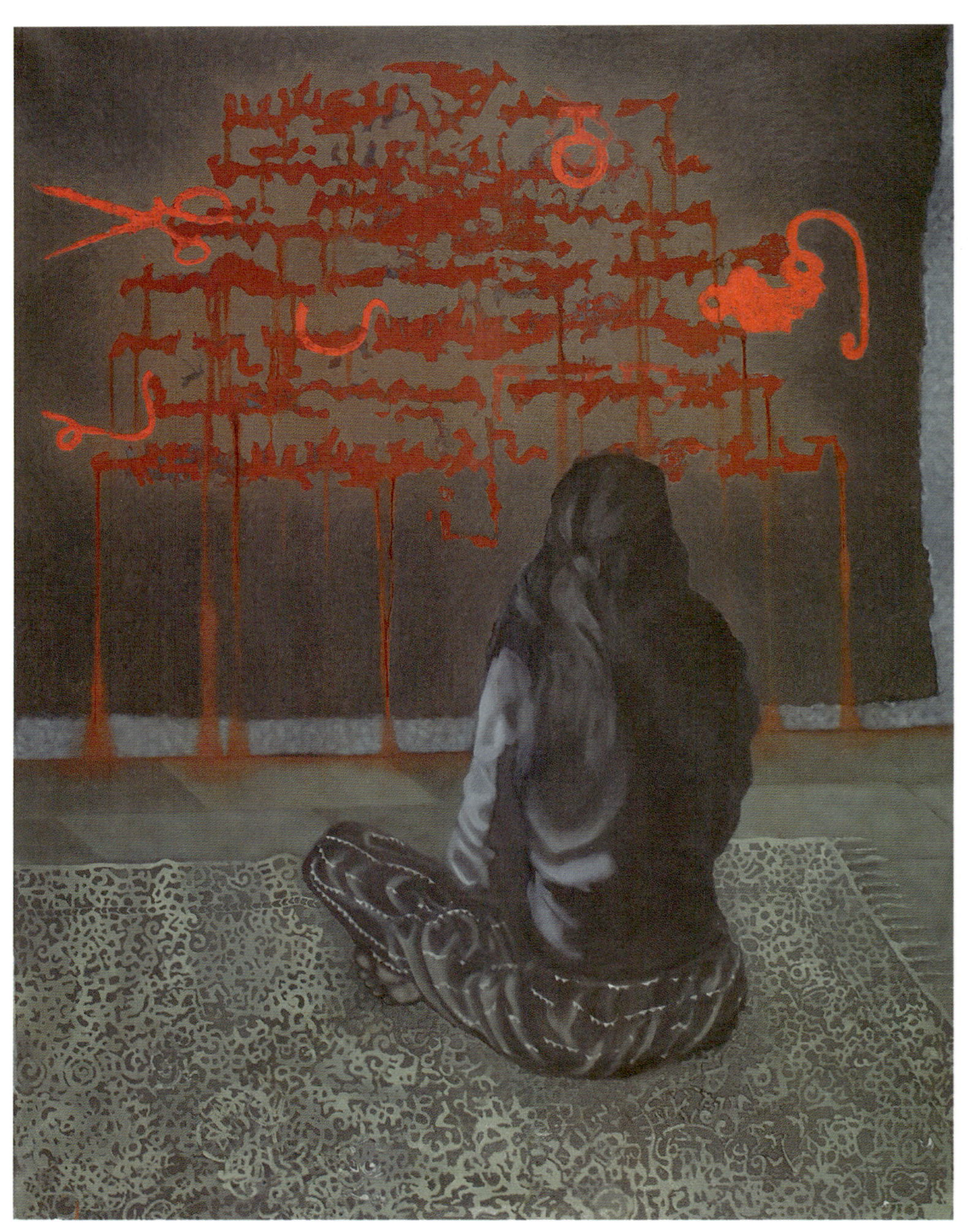

Sanctum (detail), 2006

I found a resonance, in the Rothko room, in the colours, the reds and maroons, and in the mysteriousness of the interior spaces from which they seemed to emanate.

The original painting has subsequently been destroyed by time, damp, and termites – and I wanted to bring it back to life.

In 1998, I had conducted a workshop at the School of Architecture in Ahmedabad, where we had worked around the idea of shadows; my contribution was an installation where I traced out the silhouettes of my hands, spelling out my name in sign language, one among those that are used by the hearing/speech impaired. I drove nails into the hands. Red beads in the shape of drops, which I had found coincidentally in one of the local shops, were suspended from the nails by pieces of string.

I had, at the time, recently moved to Baroda from Madras, and had been struck by the profusion of rust-red splashes on the walls of buildings – on staircase landings, convenient corners – caused by the habit of chewing paan and spitting (or rather squirting) out the juice.

I had, for long, wanted to make an artwork around that rather strong visual impression. I splashed red paint on the wall beneath the hands, and then nuanced it with another splash of gold – to create the duality of desecration/worship, among other things. At that moment, a piece of saffron-coloured paper floated into the room and settled on the floor beneath. I pasted it on the ground, exactly where it lay, and splashed it with red/vermilion. I had taken a photograph of this installation and again, had been wanting to re-create it, as it would eventually be painted over.

The central panel is adapted from a photograph taken by Gottfried Junker, photographer and film-maker, who spent a morning in my studio. I was seated on a dhurrie with an intricate pattern. Looking at it later, I wasn't quite sure how I would paint it, much of it was not really visible. When it finally worked itself through, it was a combination of attempted rendering, and tracings from the actual carpet which were printed on the canvas and then re-worked. Layers emerged, decorative as well as script-like – cobwebs, bits of tattered lace – like preserved but crumbling body tissues. I was facing a blank canvas in the photograph, which I covered with inscriptions that grew into a tree – a banyan tree with roots of blood.

Looking back, other correspondences emerge. At the time that I started working on the first panel (with the hands) early in 2005, I had completed a series of paintings which saw me through very painful times. I had also begun working on a public project which I saw as a vital responsibility. Unfulfilled, it would render my practice as a painter meaningless, and there still seemed such a long way to go. I needed to see some sort of manifestation of faith within my own studio as well, that forsaken space – a writing on the wall, even if it was nothing more profound than my name, nothing more than a pledge: Vasudha.

The photographer had appeared unexpectedly, leaving me with the beginnings of the second panel.

The sense of ease that I then began to feel enabled me to look back and reclaim other things of significance gathered but not quite resolved in earlier years. It was something of a triumph – that with so much destroyed, one could still regenerate the best from the worst, and watch it grow.

September 2006

HIMMAT: THE REPORT

January 2005/Posters

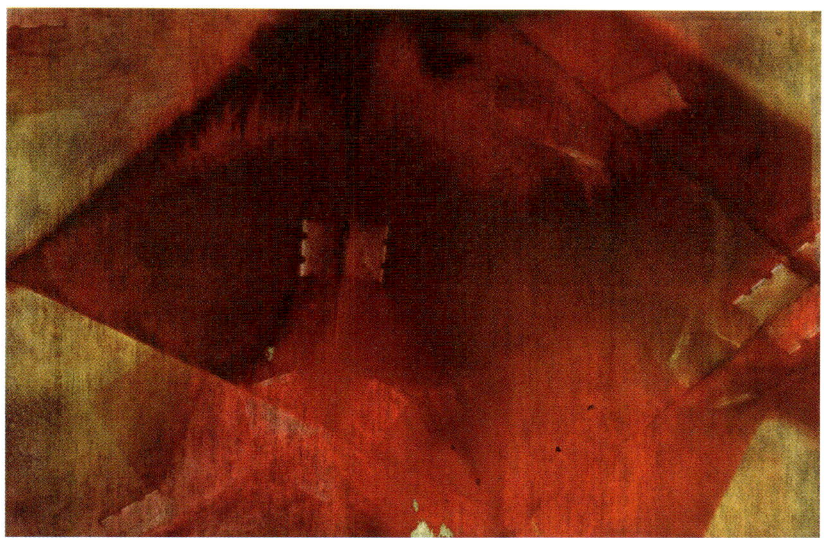

The first couple of sessions dealt with colour – marbling on paper, some tie and dye, some drawing, printing with vegetables, collage with fabric. Bookmarks were made combining the vegetable prints with fabric collage. There were sacks full of waste fabric at the centre which were used.

The girls were given notebooks that they could draw or write in, so they could keep records of the process.

We went on a visit to the Kanoria Art Centre, where we met Sharmila Sagara, who invited us to participate in the arts festival that was scheduled for February. We also visited NID, where the staff took us around. We had the benefit of short demos in every department, and interactive meetings with the students.

Azra Khan came over from Baroda on the last day as a resource person and showed the girls how to make stationery, and some simple book binding techniques.

With the output from the first session, six posters were formatted for the sale of garments which Himmat had organized in Bangalore and in Goa.

Later, six of these were sold to Oxfam and with the proceeds, we started literacy classes for the girls. A local resource person, Shahana, was willing to conduct them, for an hour and a half every day.

The girls began their lessons and by May were able to sign their own names.

February/Participation in the Annual Festival of the Arts, Kanoria Art Centre, Ahmedabad
Madhubani painting/Resource person: Shatrughan Thakur
Batik with vegetable dyes/Resource person: Pravina Mahicha

The second session took place at the Kanoria Art Centre. Tahera, Rabia and Farzana took part in the Madhubani workshop. The selection was made on

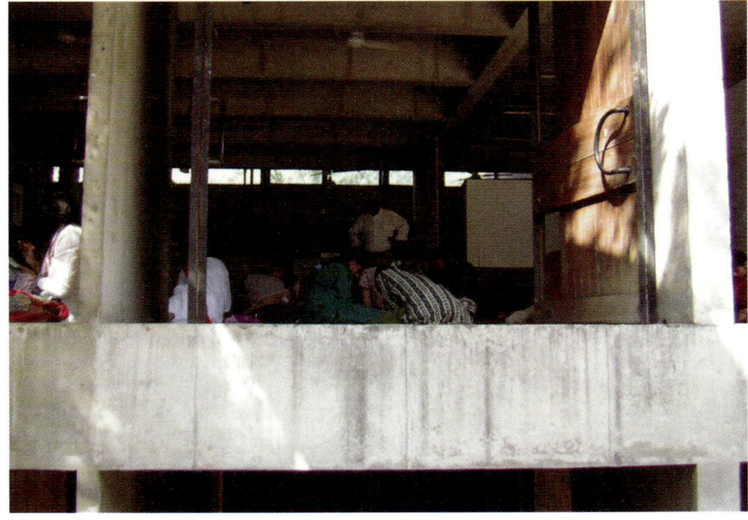

At the Kanoria Centre for Arts, Ahmedabad, 2005

the basis that the three had a reasonably good hand, and were more fluent with drawing than the others. It was conducted by Shatrughan Thakur. The idea was to use the Madhubani tradition as a teaching aid, to help them to arrange elements spatially, on a flat surface – the girls' level of perception and expression of the physical world corresponded with the strong decorative sensibility of folk and indigenous forms. They were also familiar with *mehndi* patterns, which appeared frequently in their drawings.

The other three, Tasleem, Shahjehan and Rehana, participated in the vegetable dyeing/batik workshop conducted by Pravina Mahicha. They were inhibited about drawing, and the tactility of the medium and the dyeing process would hopefully give them a sense of freedom as well as control. They later did a three-day workshop with Shatrughan at the centre.

April/Fabric Collage

Resource person: Sharifa

We were finally able to begin working in our own space upstairs – convenient, obviously – for several reasons.

We began working with fabric, and Sharifa, one of the older women, was our resource person. She could work on the haat, was an expert at embroidery and basic appliqué.

She showed us how to transfer our cartoons onto the fabric, and guided the girls whenever they needed help.

We a made a set of experimental pieces, with appliqué and overlapping areas of transparent fabric. It was also an exercise in colour-mixing.

The work extended over two sessions, into May.

April/Fabric/Embroidery

Resource person: Roumanie Jaitley

We worked with the running stitch on a set of six pieces of fabric which were originally meant to be cushion covers, but as it turned out, too beautiful to be used as such. They were also significant in that the motifs

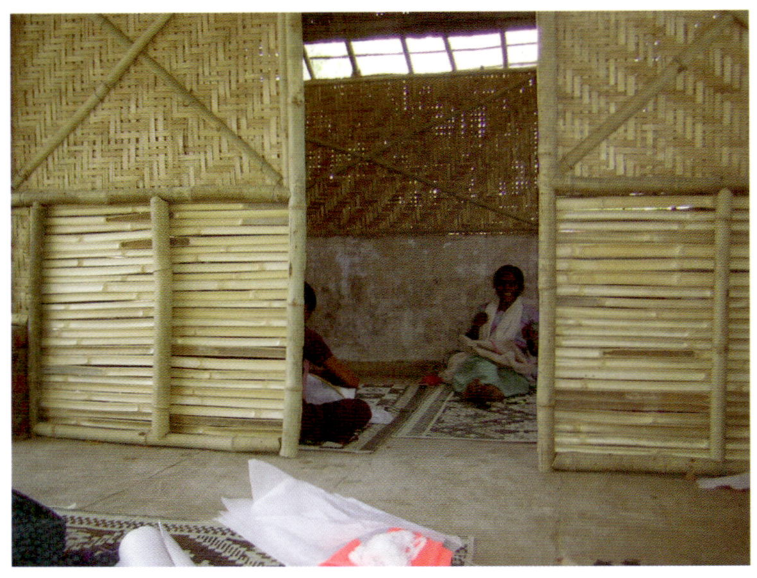

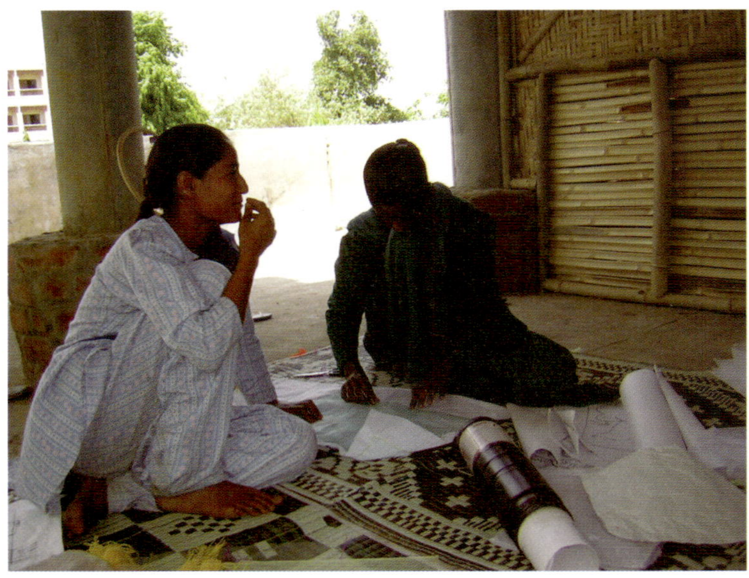

Tasleem (above), Rehana and Shahjehan (below),
at the Himmat Centre, Mayur Park, Vatva

used were recurrent in most of their work – including their paintings, drawings, collages, etc. They are framed and presented in a manner that is in keeping with a more complex narrative.

Mayday Rally Placards

The 1st of May coincided with Himmat's founding day – the organization also participates in the Mayday rally every year. On the last day of April, the girls made a set of placards, very quickly, which were taken out on procession during the rally. The slogans were composed by Monica Wahi.

June/Collaborative Painting

The girls painted six small canvases, each one square foot in size. Later, in October 2006, at a residency in Khoj, New Delhi, I added seven more of my own. This was to be a partial fundraiser for the framing that needed to be done for a trial exhibit in Delhi.

June–July/Ahmedabad Hamara

Resource person: Shahrukh Alam

Shahrukh Alam, a lawyer associated with Action Aid, was involved with a stay order vis-à-vis the demolition of *bastis* in an area called Mahakali, after the mandir that stands there. We asked her if she could conduct a few sessions that would work towards rights-based empowerment. To begin with, she decided to do a film-based module that would enable the girls to critique advertising/media and the visual language in general.

Between June and July, Shahrukh did six sessions with the girls.

A VCD was hired, and set up in the centre. Shahrukh screened different kinds of films – documentary, Bollywood, activist – there were critiques and discussions afterwards which were very animated. They culminated in a set of montages, using old newspapers and magazines, around some specific themes under the wider rubric of 'Ahmedabad Hamara', the topic of their choice. They were representations of the city from different gender and economic perspectives.

Resource person: Shatrughan Thakur

Tracings were made from the photo montages, a process which simplified the forms. They were recomposed into a clearer articulation of the given topics and guided as to how to convert the completed drawings into a graphic form suitable for silk-screen reproduction. We were thinking in terms of an affordable print medium, entailing hand skills that the girls could acquire.

The drawings were scanned and printed on transparent film. The image could then be transferred on to the screen through a simple photographic process.

Shatrughan Thakur offered to help us, as a resource person. Sharmila Sagara gave us permission to print at the studios in the Kanoria Centre. In September, we made six editions of twelve prints each. The posters are about building a critical relationship with the city, and affirming a presence within it.

September/Pen and Ink Drawings

Resource person: Shahana

We had developed a methodology – Shahana discussed current issues (in Faizal Park) with them during the literacy sessions, and helped them make small sketches in their notebooks. They also wrote about what they had drawn. They had developed a good understanding with her, based on shared experiences during and post the carnage. One of the themes that they had worked on was the floods during the monsoons in 2005. They had drawn and written about the absence of a drainage system and the resulting difficulties.

September/Paintings by Tahera and Farzana

Resource person: Shanta Rakshit

During the screen printing session, we made larger pen-and-ink drawings using the sketches as the basis. Tahera and Farzana completed their printing sessions before the others, and one of the young artists working at the centre, Shanta Rakshit, took them out for some sketching and painting.

Tahera made a painting of the façade of the School of Architecture, and Farzana of the sculpture on the grounds of the campus.

October/Four 'Pats'

Resource person: Shanta Rakshit

Shanta Rakshit conducted a module with the girls, the theme chosen was 'Mother'. They made scrolls in the tradition of the Bengal *pats*, and the narrative describes daily domestic routines, difficulties, struggle – also related to the aftermath of the riots of 2002 – looking for work, lining up outside the government office where death certificates were issued, visiting injured relatives at the hospital.

October/ 15 Paintings

Resource person: Monica Wahi

Monica Wahi conducted a session with the girls – based on three questions that they were to ask each other in private. They made rough sketches based on what they told each other, about their families – which included depictions of their daily lives and portraits of those who died during the carnage. Apart from other things, this was an exercise in bonding; the session would help to build closer relationships amongst the group. Fifteen paintings were made on the basis of these drawings, in (industrial) enamel paints on canvas.

November 2005–March 2006/The Drishti Fellowship

Resource person: Prem from Soumya Joshi's Troupe

The girls won the Mirror Amdavad Fellowship (for two months, to be followed by an exhibit/performance) after intensive interview sessions with Drishti. The concept discussed combined painting with performance in the form of four long scrolls on canvas and the script for two plays, in a similar format, written on khadi. The plays were developed from discussions within the group. Two broad themes emerged, one around the non-availability of

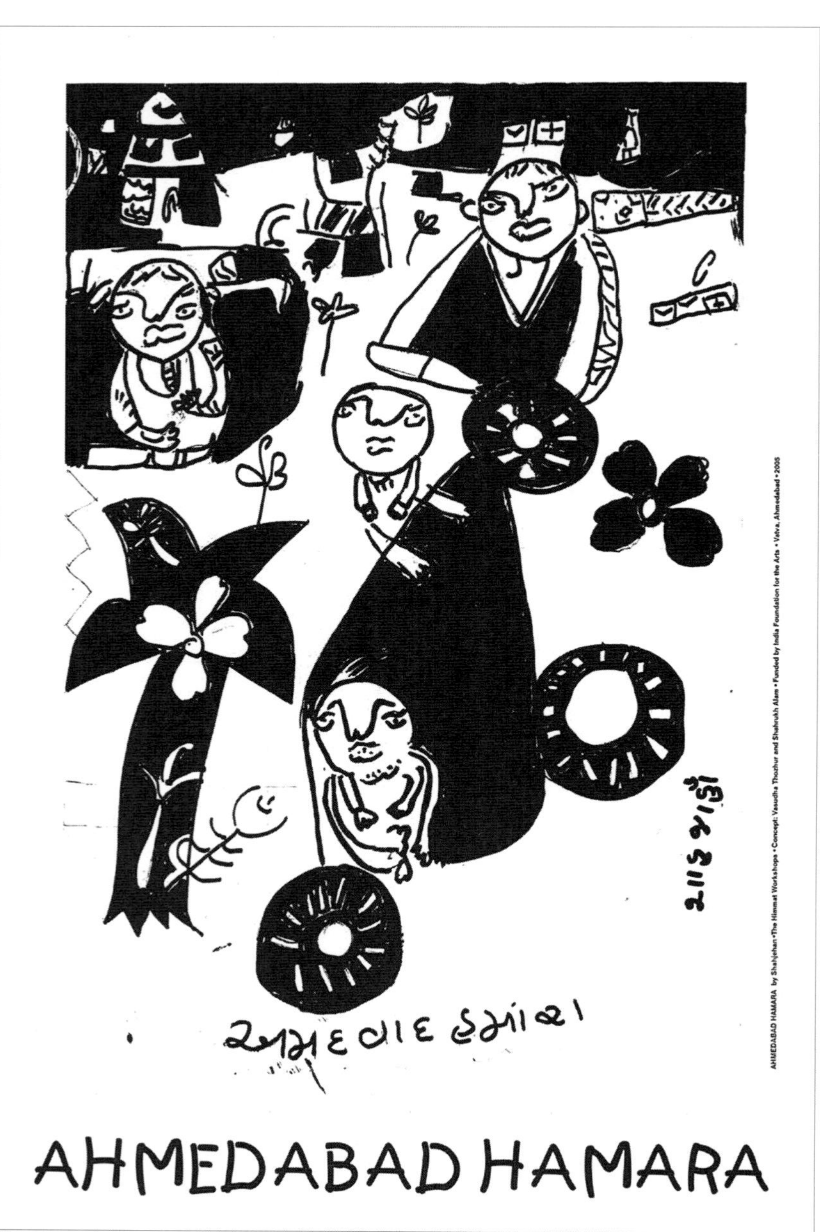

Ahmedabad Hamara, by Shahjehan Sheikh, 2006

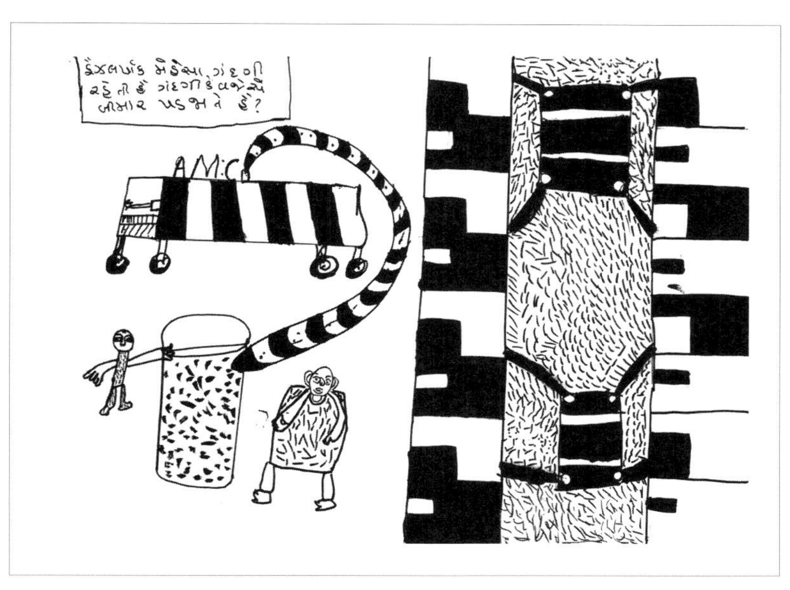
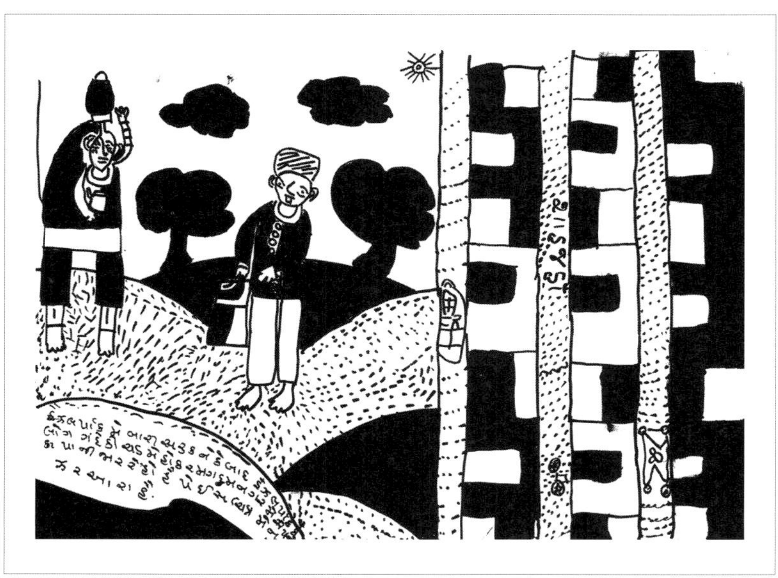

Faizal Park during the floods, 2005: (above) by Rehana Sheikh,
(below) by Shahjehan Sheikh

water, the other around education. Prem, from Soumya Joshi's troupe, trained the girls for a few days and the plays were performed at the centre. The scrolls were toured locally, in the neighbouring *bastis*, as a background for a narrative performance, and also taken out on a rally. When mounted in an exhibition space, they take the form of an installation.

Resource person: Johanna Hoyne

This module was conducted with the help of Johanna Hoyne, an art student from the Australian National University. The girls learnt how to handle a video camera, and created footage related to whatever was current in their lives – the plays that they had produced, learning to ride a bicycle, visiting the Qutb-e-Alam dargah, interviewing each other about the project that they had been a part of. Six films have so far been edited from this footage, most of them of a documentary nature. The editing was done during a residency at Khoj Artists' Workshops in Delhi. The longest film, *Cutting Chai*, is about visiting their homes in Faizal Park. It has been screened, independent of the other exhibits, by Vikalp in Bombay, and selected for an experimental film festival, Experimenta 2007, to take place in March at Max Mueller Bhavan, Bangalore and Bombay.

May–June/Embroidery on Fabric

Resource person: Shanta Rakshit

This being the last formal session in terms of the sequential development of the project, the task was to translate the drawings, paintings, and other forms of visual output into motifs and narratives on fabric. They could then be sewn onto cushion covers, curtains, wall hangings: functional household and other accessories that could be sold to generate an income. The girls learnt to work with the traditional kantha form of embroidery. An important aspect of this module is the originality of the motifs and other elements used, evolving as they did entirely from the girls' work – thinking about the market does not necessarily preclude creative expression arising from the experiences of a community. They can in fact enter the commercial stream

as personal expressions which have the added component of sustainability
in the financial sense of the word, while still remaining an authentic record
of an evolving cultural consciousness. We framed the cushion covers
because they were rich in imagery and narrative.

September

Completed four books using written documentation compiled via the
project: *The Story of Five Posters, Mahakali versus Megacity, The Project,* and
Bibi Tere Naam Himmat.

October/The Quilts

Resource persons: Neha and Deepa Sharma

The samplers that the girls had made while learning embroidery were
combined with pieces of hand block-printed, vegetable-dyed fabric to
make two quilts that are installed along with the other exhibits. Deepa
Sharma runs a boutique, 'Arankri', in Delhi, which promotes the use of
vegetable dyed/hand-printed/handwoven fabric and garments.

September 2007/Paintings

**(for 'After-Images', at the Faculty of Fine Arts, Baroda, curated by Ranjit
Contractor)**
A four-day workshop was conducted at the centre, and a set of paintings
were made by Tahera, Tasleem and Rabia to be exhibited later at the show.
All the original pieces in this archive will be preserved as a resource from
which things can emerge.

– – – – – – – – – – – – – – –

Chronology of Shows, Displays, Scholarships/Residencies

2003

'The Story of Five Posters', an installation at The Canberra Contemporary Art Space, as a guest exhibit in 'Witnessing to Silence: Art and Human Rights', an Australian National University Humanities Research Centre Project, curated by Christine Clark.

2005

Posters and bookmarks were made for the sale of garments that Himmat periodically organizes, and are displayed in the stalls.
Placards were made for a Mayday rally, and are used every year.
Placards were made for a rally in memory of Bibi Banoo, and were taken out in procession during the event.

December 2005 to February 2006

The girls won the Drishti Media Collective Fellowship for a public project which involved painting and performance – entitled *Paani ki Museebat*. It was performed at Faizal Park, Navapura (two performances), Ekta Nagar, Mayur Park (at Himmat), the Gujarat Social Forum (at Ahmedabad), and informally for visiting groups on several occasions. The performance was also filmed by Johanna Hoyne and the girls, for a documentary by the same title.

October 2006

A month-long residency at Khoj to compile work from the project and to think through ways of displaying such material. Six films were edited from footage shot by the girls: *Cutting Chai, Paani Ki Museebat, Paani Ki Museebat: A Narration, Himmat, A Film for Bibi Banoo* and *Interviews*. One of the earlier exercises in painting involved six small canvases, one each by the participants of the project. I made seven more, from sketches made on site during the workshops. Put together, it is a sequence of thirteen, entitled *The Himmat Workshops*. A trial exhibit was mounted, very successfully, at the Khoj premises. The painting was bought by Vadehra Art Gallery; some of the proceeds went towards exhibition expenses, including a later display in Ahmedabad, and a commission for Khoj. The remaining was divided equally between the girls and myself. The narrative scrolls, the excerpts from the script, and the curtains that were sewn during Shanta Rakshit's module were mounted as an installation in one room, with 'Interviews' showing on a monitor. One of the quilts was spread on the floor, for people to sit on.

Paani Ki Museebat was projected on the wall of the landing as one mounted the steps to the first floor. Rabia and Tahera attended the opening, Monica and Zaid were also present. The paintings, posters and collages were displayed in the other rooms of the building.

Before the event, we were also required to do a PowerPoint presentation of the documentation of the entire project.
Yet another presentation at the School of Art and Aesthetics at the JNU.

Chandita Mukherjee, a reputed film-maker, contacted us for a film that she was making on three artists' responses to the riots. She spent about two days at Khoj, filming the mounting of the display, and later, the opening evening. The presentation at JNU was also filmed.

For expenses related to the framing and display, we managed to raise about 50,000, generously donated by the Bodhi Art Gallery.

Some of the paintings were also shown at the WSF in Delhi, at the Himmat stall, and later at a peace festival in Bombay.

February 2007

A large exhibit was mounted in Hutheesing Gallery at the CEPT campus, as part of Sach ki Yaadein, Yadon ka Sach, organized by several NGOs in Ahmedabad, on the fifth anniversary of the carnage. There were other events like film screenings, and a display of Madhubani paintings – comments on the carnage, by Santosh Kumar Das. Students who had been involved as resource people during the project helped with the display.

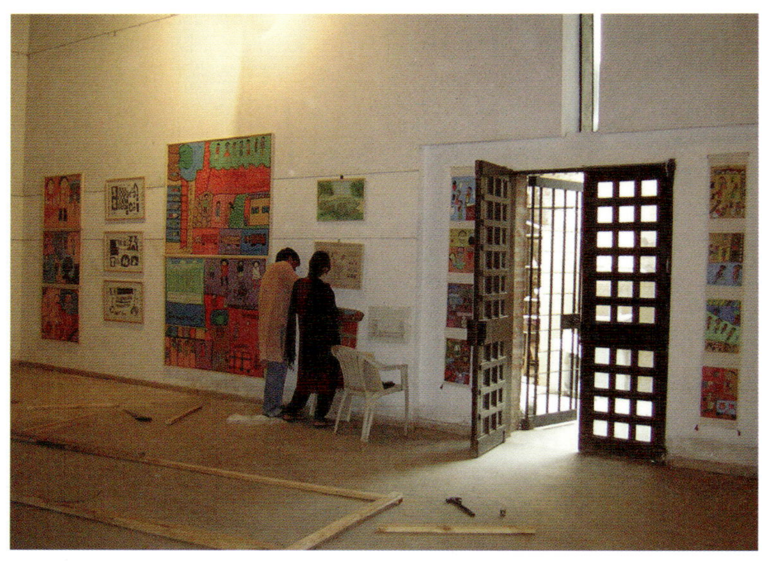

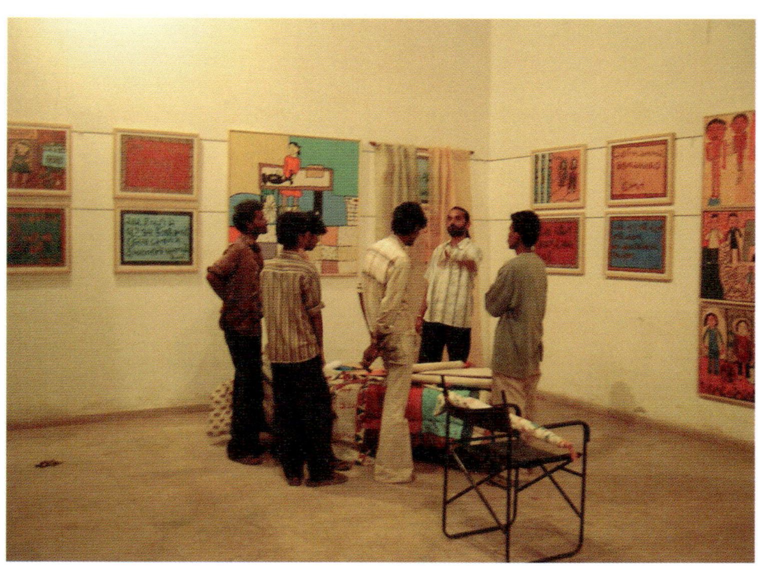

Mounting the exhibit at the Hutheesing Visual Art Centre,
CEPT, Ahmedabad, 2007

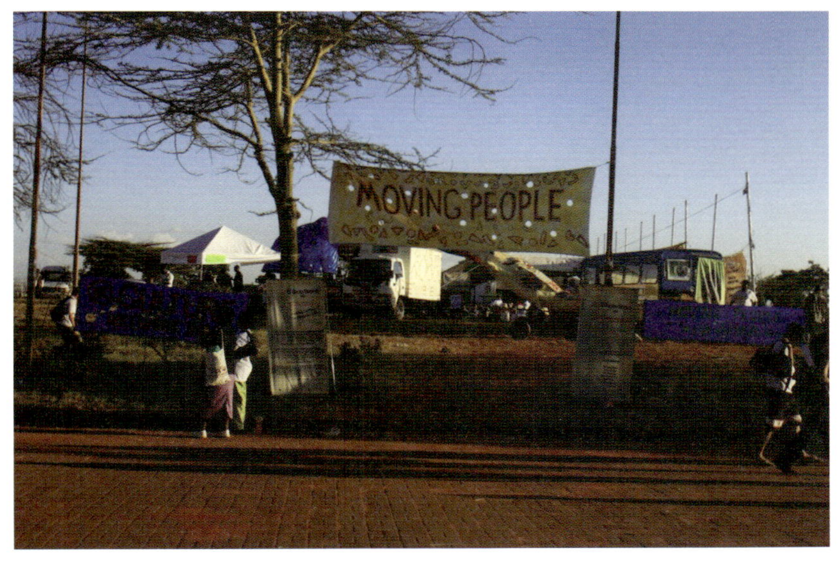

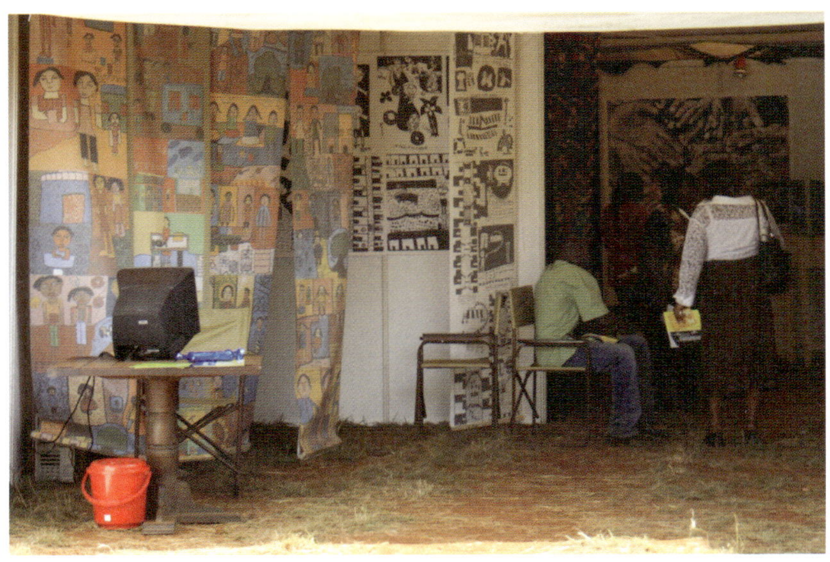

Display at 'Moving People', World Social Forum, Nairobi, Kenya

Experimenta 2007 (Bangalore and Bombay): Screening of *Cutting Chai*, one of the films edited from video footage shot by the participants. Also screened earlier by VIKALP, Bombay.

Reproductions and two of the films were presented at 'Moving People', WSF, Nairobi, in 'Follow the Arrow: Investigating Movement', an event curated by Archana Hande and Mamta Murthy.

Posters from the project, including stills from the films, were compiled into a separate presentation for a seminar organized by Sahiyar at the Fine Art Faculty premises. It was also an attempt to explore the many different kinds of functions that posters can perform.

April/May 2007

Both *Cutting Chai* and the collaborative painting of thirteen panels have been shown in solo exhibitions at Sakshi Gallery, Bombay and at Vadehra Art Gallery, New Delhi. Part of the written narratives are contained in an audio text, as recordings, for *Listening Post*, a voice installation. As an extension of the project, one cubicle at Vadehra was set aside for a free expression of opinions that could be written or painted on the walls – a group of children from Aarohan, a Delhi-based NGO, covered 20 feet of canvas with graffiti, which I will work on to complete.

October 2007

An exhibition curated by Ranjit Contractor, entitled 'After-Images', was held in the wake of the arrest of Chandra Mohan, a student of the MSU. A four-day workshop was conducted at the centre, and the output, three paintings made by Rabia, Tahera and Tasleem, were exhibited at the show. Two were bought by Sakshi Gallery. A small percentage goes to ACUA, an organization of teachers of the MSU, a small percentage to Himmat, and the major part of the proceeds to the girls.

Tahera and Rabia are now enrolled in an open schooling programme, and the funds will probably support their education.

Selected images of paintings/drawings/posters have been printed as cards by Himmat. The girls periodically paint the walls of the centre, and also work with volunteers who regularly visit. Tahera attends community workshops as a representative of Himmat, which we are proud of. She is vocal, articulate and has strong, individual views on most things.

I will continue to work with them on collaborative paintings, as these are a significant source of funding.

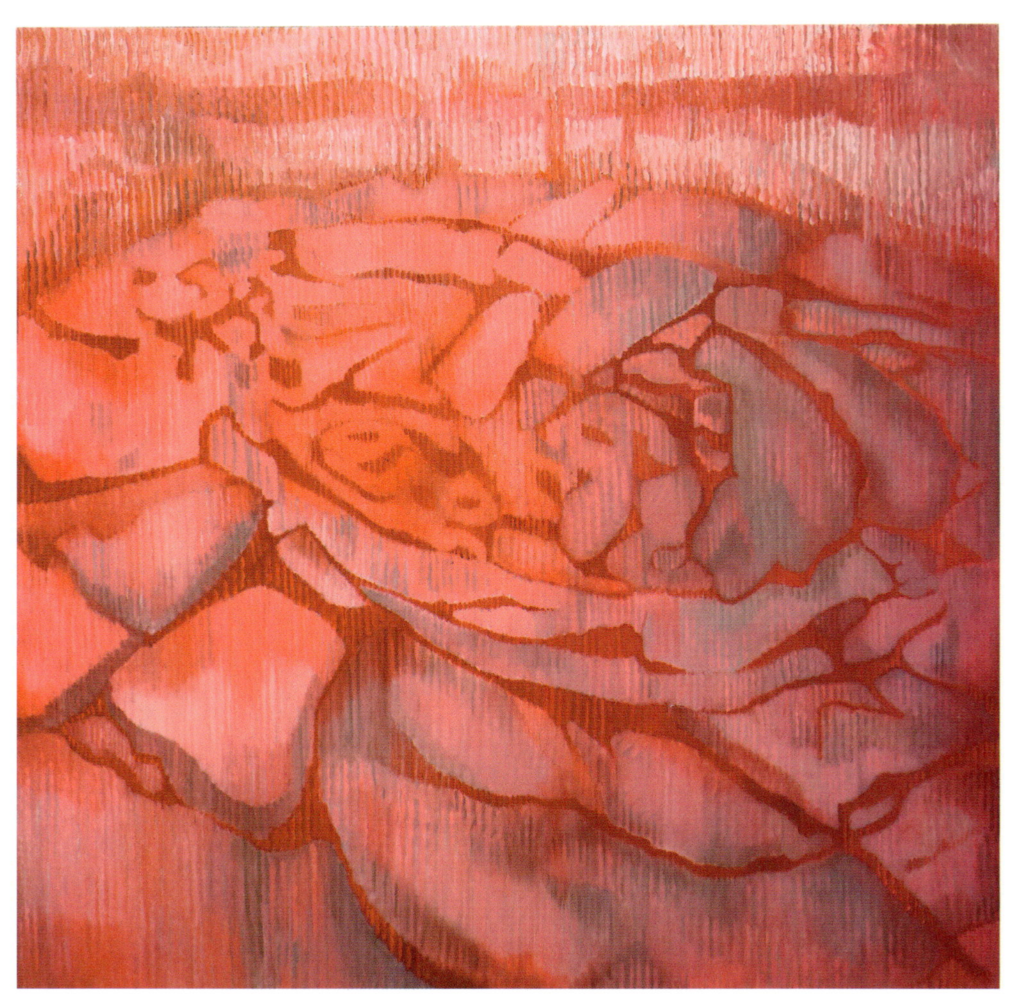

Beyond Pain (detail), 2012–13

BEYOND PAIN: AN AFTERLIFE

While presenting the Himmat project, I have often encountered the question – What about your own work? And this is a question most often asked by members of the art community, to whom the work has not been shown in all its implications. In my mind, the connection is obvious, but it would be a challenge to be able to communicate it visually, apart from making a point – activating a certain space from the outside is as important as performing within it, one supports the other. It is a neglect of one in favour of the other that has created the kind of gap that exists between the two, where the market takes over in place of a functional, and a functioning, relationship between art and the community.

The message, at its most basic, is about friendship. It could also be considered as a working-model through which a range of skills are acquired along with political awareness and the possibility of intervention through visual means, and through just working together, as a group.

There is also a certain virtue in acceding space to those rendered invisible through force of circumstance, and in making this virtue visible – not merely in the moral sense of the word, but even in purely aesthetic/philosophic terms, placing the whole experience within the realm of the abstract, if one indeed wishes to distance oneself from affect.

As a society, a collective predicament calls for a particular kind of response where individual needs become secondary. Appropriate action can restore the situation to the extent where these needs can again be addressed – they are equally relevant to the health of the whole. One is in constant search of the fine line which demarcates the two areas, in time and physical location, especially in our country, a country in ferment. The external world impinges upon the internal to the extent that addressing the issues thus raised is not merely philanthropic but involuntary, apart from being a necessity in the face of continuing threat.

Through the years that I spent researching and implementing the project, much of the time that would normally have been spent in the studio was given to thinking this through. Late in 2006, I was able to actually compose some of the work into a kind of trial exhibit at the invitation of Khoj. The exercise finally gave me the opportunity to experience how the role as facilitator and editor – that I had played till then, shifted to that of a curator of sorts. The idea of working with display as a narrative mode was for me a new one, and opened up further areas of thought. What had hitherto functioned actively within the community as a locus for mobilization and creative process was now transformed into several formations – an artwork, archival material that testified to this process and in addition a kind of working-model that could be referred to when needed. The performance piece that had evolved through the Drishti fellowship was mounted as an installation in one of the rooms, with a short video clip playing on a monitor set within the space. Quilts had been made with pieces of fabric on which the girls had practised their sewing skills, these were placed on the ground, so people could sit on them to watch it.

A clip of the performance was projected on the landing of the staircase that led to this room, creating a passage through the actual event to the artifacts that now represented it.

With much of the fieldwork completed, there still remained something that was unexpressed – which was my own journey through unfamiliar regions. The community at Vatva had also stabilized financially through Himmat's initiatives.

It also became apparent that one could not romanticize tragedy, nor those that were affected by it – in spite of the kind of perspective that they could have gained by living through 2002, the conflicts and petty quarrels persist and multiply as the community grows in economic strength. One's own needs as an artist begin to come to the forefront again, especially the need to be able to act independently, unhampered by factors that arise from acting as a group. The outcome of the interaction however still remains amongst the community in terms of confidence and skills.

Reaching back again to 2002 sometimes seems regressive – but that was the beginning of the story, and can be represented as such, a memory set in stone: hence the painting *Interior: 2002*. Moreover, subsequent events, including 26/11, reinforce the need to reflect on it. Gujarat is a specific context, but in turn, represents the world as it is today. Indeed, considering the series of misfortunes that have plagued the state since the earthquake of 2001, it presents an apocalypse in a nutshell – which is, in fact, the subject of my paintings. The ethics of representation is also uppermost in my mind, as is the need to represent in different ways at different times, impelled by real reasons for doing so. How does one speak the truth through images? Is it possible to detect falsehood? Is it possible for the image to speak in a manner that does not feed upon the dark drama of horror, therefore impelling its creation? Is it possible to create an aesthetic that is not dependent upon surplus, that could still function in the absence of that surplus? One that cannot be appropriated and misused to create conditions that are in direct conflict with its aims, as frequently happens in the political arena, for instance?

Some of the questions that came up vis-à-vis the project when it was first proposed would in fact be answered through the process of showing it. It was impossible at the time to actually predict the exact nature of the outcome, or plan how it would be disseminated. The form of one depends on the form of the other, and the act of display will create yet another framework for demonstrating inter-relationships and functions that mutate and thereby survive through time. Two more paintings are complete, one of them based on a full-length portrait of Shahjehan, one of the girls in the group that I had worked with. Within the present context, one functions as a chronicler of events – maintaining a distance appropriate to one's own position in relationship to these events and to the temporal distance of six years that separates the two. One also traverses the distance between the pressing need to act in the public sphere and the need to process the experience into material that one could refer to in future for answers, or in search of some extra-verbal/extra-lingual? trace of the experience itself.

To present visually all that I have written above would perhaps be central to the exhibit. One would need to weave together the strands of the self and the other into a symbiotic entity, at the human level as well as artistically, besides placing each segment, or segment of segments, within an appropriate framework, taking into consideration the available space and resources as yet another factor that qualifies the present moment.

During the course of the last year, I have concentrated largely on the paintings, as they would take the longest to complete. I am working on several simultaneously, I tend to complete them together in a kind of final, unified movement. The two photo-essays, *Mahakali versus Mega-city* and *Gandhi Ashram to Vatva*, are ready for print.

The paintings have become more ambitious in scale and number than originally intended, but should in all likelihood be completed, along with all the other work, mainly printing – by the end of the year or at the very latest by March 2011.

Apart from considerations of time, the paintings are prioritized for the reason that they represent a completely new body of project-related work, one that also underpins the project in relationship to private practice – or even, to widen the implications further, the public project within the context of art practice, how it could give it a real direction, and a much-needed infusion of fresh blood. I think it is important to underline this relationship to prevent an unhealthy binary from developing any further – that of an ineffective and indulgent art practice versus more public-minded art projects. Often the result of this binary is neither art nor community. The best aspects of both are sacrificed – the lifelong devotion (with its own set of challenges and socio-economic issues) that craft entails, as well as any real or lasting possibilities for social change. What then are we left with?

The Paintings

Interior: 1997/2002

A group of four panels, the first one dates back to 1997 when I moved to Baroda from Madras – the chronicle begins here. There are formal differences in the way the painting is handled which indicate that it belongs to another time frame – the inclusion of this panel within that context is deliberate – as it marks that moment as the beginning.

The red panel: the image in the centre is that of the burning autorickshaw that appeared in several newspapers and magazines during the riots. It is intended that it should be a recognizable image, it refers to that particular moment in history, within the context of communalization and the accompanying violence. It is set in a ruby – a memory set in blood/stone.

But it recedes behind the reflections that partially obscure it – because to invoke that moment in all its horror would be equal to re-creating it. It is after all a memory now, and this is clearly stated, visibly translated, through painting. The ruby is associated with blood, but is also a precious stone – as every crisis denotes a moment of clarity that is also an opportunity for change.

The panels on either side are based on studies of my earlier studio in Nizampura – where I worked at the time. They reflect another, more personal perspective – the simultaneity of experiencing a particularly traumatic moment which manifests itself physically, within and without – and the studio spaces where it is processed, by necessity, in order to survive that moment.

Terminus Erraeus

The monkey in the painting belongs to a species known as the Hanuman Langur – common in Gujarat – we see them all over the city. We have, in fact taken over their habitat.

The burning tail is of course an obvious reference to our mythological past. The animal is however female.

The words *Terminus Erraeus* – 'terminus' of course means a terminal point in space or time, and 'erraeus' is a fragment of a word from a torn piece of packaging paper that further lost its original meaning when I worked it into a sketch for the painting. In my mind, it bears a resemblance to the word 'error' – the title therefore signifies a fatal error.

It could also be read as a reference to the Bajrang Dal – or its Nemesis. The three monkeys in gold represent Gandhi's utopic principles – the reality of course threatens to consume us all.

The painting also speaks of the danger of combining religion with politics – Gandhi's moral fibre could sustain that particular combination and still remain uncorrupted – but set afloat in our world, misappropriated – what does it unleash? An open question, poised, to destroy or to re-generate, as the monkey is.

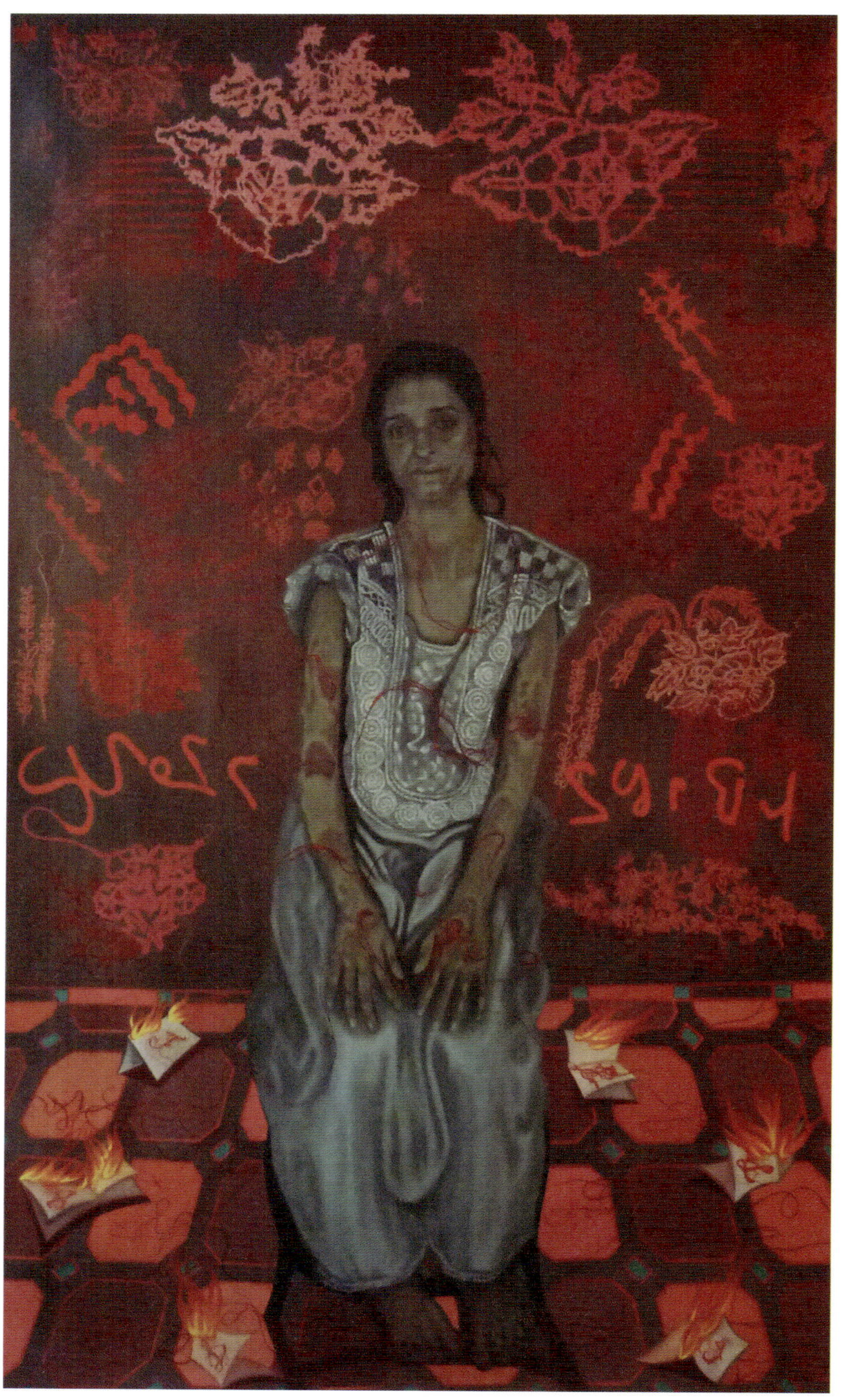

2002: A Portrait

In 2002, Monica gave me a photograph of Shahjehan, a survivor of the massacre at Naroda Patiya. It was taken while she was undergoing a series of surgeries to re-construct her jaw and minimize the visibly burnt areas of her skin. The portrait is based on this photograph.

In one of our conversations while working together in the field, Monica and I discussed the many small cruelties that mark human interaction, no matter what people might have experienced together. Some of the women at the centre would address Shahjehan as *Jaleli*, The Burnt One. The letters that constitute the word are on pieces of folded paper which are ablaze, and scattered at her feet. Not legible or close enough to one another for people to be able to string them together into one word, decipher what it spells out, or its meaning.

Around her are motifs from the samplers, the threads weave into the scars that mark the central figure – the history of the struggle to overcome, through sewing and embroidery – traditionally feminine but also surgical skills.

The group of ten prints on her left, entitled *An Autobiography in Fragments*, is a collection of sections from my paintings over several years, coinciding with the period during which I was involved with Himmat. The first set of prints that were taken were unsuccessful. I painted lace-like motifs over them to repair the damage, these panels are to her right.

In January 2005, I had found two pieces of embroidered fabric in the storeroom at the centre where we held our workshops for six young girls from the community, Shahjehan among them. They were samplers from the early days of Himmat, artefacts from when the older women, mostly widows, were being trained to work on the sewing machines that would soon represent their livelihood. They flank the group on either side. There is an overlapping of personal histories, and an attempt to heal ruptures through painting and embroidery. The motifs in the three central panels are borrowed from the samplers and animated through a temporal movement that takes you from 2002, situated in the outer reaches, towards a centre where a conflation of the self and the other occurs, in visible progression.

Portrait of Shahjehan (detail), 2008–12

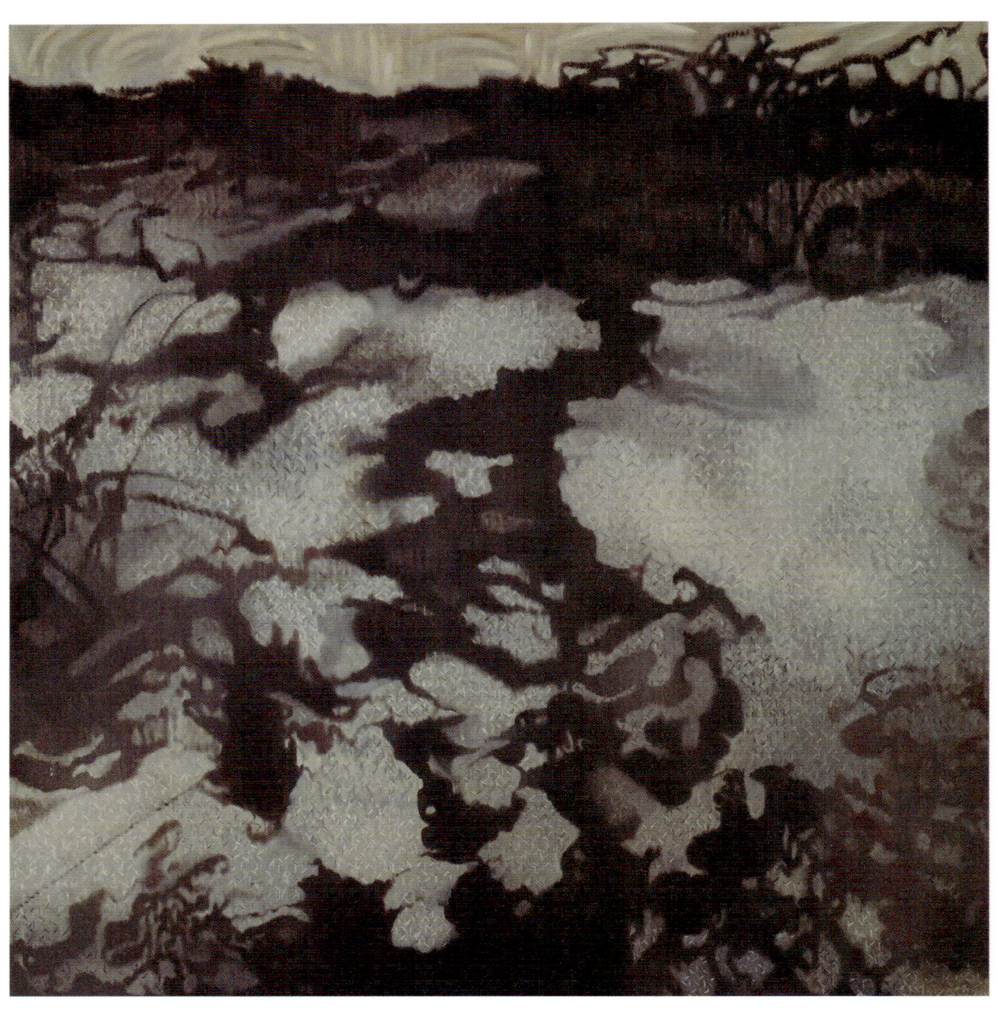

Landscape II, 2008

The paintings are based on photographs from 2001 that Ilesh Vyas (who owns Lalita, the digital studio where I work) had taken on trips to Kutch soon after the earthquake. One of them is sourced from a very grainy newspaper photograph of the site of a bomb blast. The fissures are circular in formation, with a devastated core. It resembles a gigantic flower – in fact very close to the kind of motifs that are on the samplers from Himmat, and in the background of the painting of Shahjehan. The painting explores this relationship – in corresponding colours.

When I began, it was with a sense of wanting to make large drawings in paint, in black and white – I was tired with the degree to which my painting process had slowed down. But in creating a scarred landscape, I was caught again, in a different way, by the nature of the strokes that I used – layer upon layer, time upon time of these till a certain fluency came into being, and a realization – of the Skeleton of Space. The fact that there are also recognizable traces of bones in the painting strengthens this vision of space – and of mass graves, some forever undisturbed by the light of discovery and questioning.

Often, thinking about what I am working on at the moment, the phrase 're-writing genres' (in terms of the portrait, the interior, the landscape, the still life, against the political climate that we are dealing with) comes to mind. Things change at the level of the foundation, formally as well – and considering that the formal has evolved over decades and sometimes centuries – this change is far more significant than overt depictions of specific events. In the light of the magnitude of what was unleashed on people who were least equipped to withstand it, a tectonic shift occurred in the way one understood the world.

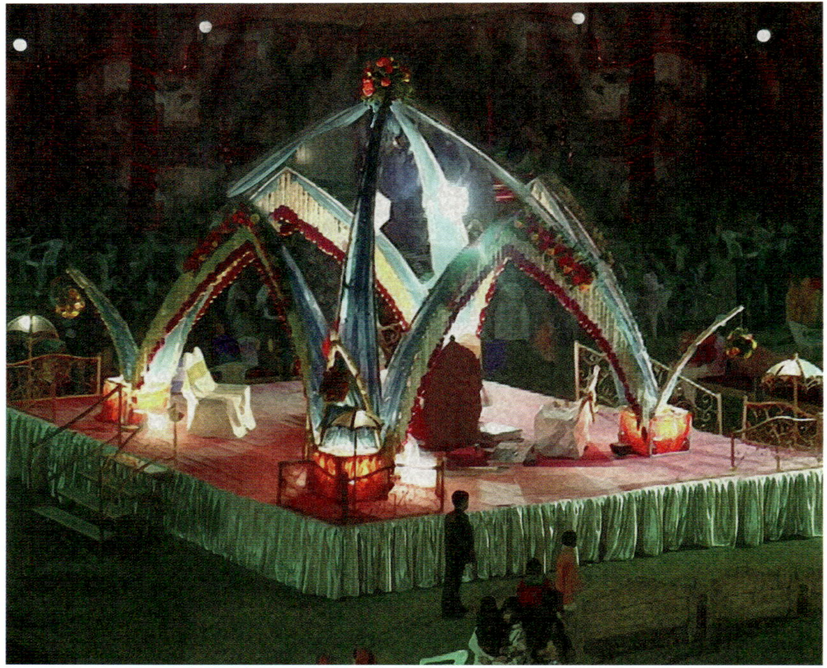

The Party Plot
(photographic micro-narratives)

The Party Plot is a new genre in terms of public spaces that host weddings, functions and parties in Gujarat. I live right next to one, and there are ten or more in the vicinity. They represent a lucrative enterprise: agricultural land grapples with the encroachment of urban development to produce instant, temporary financial benefit before being absorbed into the frenzy of residential construction sites.

The temporary 'sets' that are erected are more and more elaborate and spectacular as the years pass, and create yet another architectural genre.

The decibel levels are unimaginable – several such events happen simultaneously in the same locality, giving rise to a new genre of music, one best described as phantasmagorical – and sometimes death-inducing, as a few persons are reported to have died of cardiac arrest at the intersections of such celebrations. There are certain sounds that one will never hear again; the receding whine of some of the louder firecrackers is, in actual fact, the sound of a dying frequency; we are rendered progressively deafer as yet another, perhaps less dire consequence.

Music mimics music, to an audience that mimics enjoyment and can no longer appreciate the difference. Both have evolved through a series of simulations and estrangements that have long since obliterated their origins in experience, and are reduced to incoherent abstractions.

All this, against the background of an otherwise troubled political climate and the stringent moral policing that has become a part of the nightlife of Baroda and Ahmedabad, makes it even more inexplicable.

Still, it is a visual experience – with a darker edge. I shot some very shaky video footage from my terrace, and during a walk along the highway at night. The digital media are an unavoidable part of our lives, and therefore incidental as opposed to an artistic choice, at least in this case. I wondered what I could do with the footage. The content seemed more like weird wonderlands in haphazard sequence, with no discernable narrative; the handling of the camera was hopelessly inept. There emerged, however, from this set of dysfunctional relationships, the undeniable fascination of glowing nocturnal dreamscapes shot through with dazzling displays of light – panoramic artworks that performed a significant function in mediating the events that were staged in their midst, on a scale and with a conviction that is not often achieved in the 'real' world of art. Addicted as we are to pondering on the function and meaning of art as opposed to so-called 'reality', it was intriguing to see how interchangeable the two were.

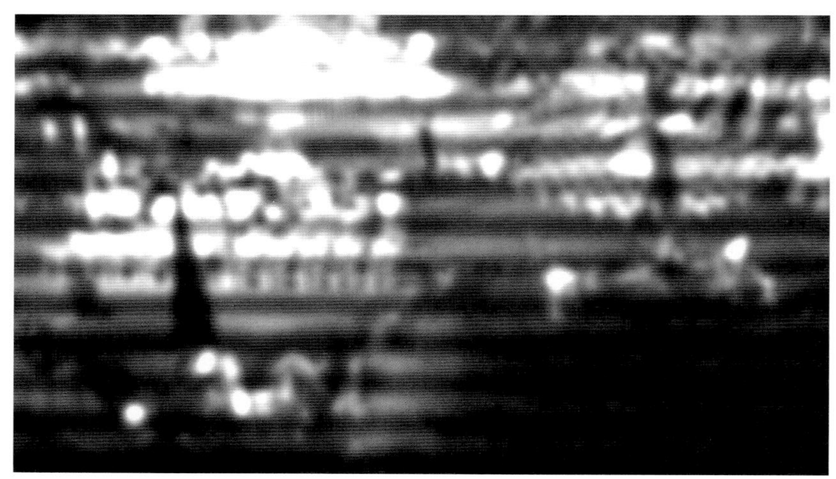

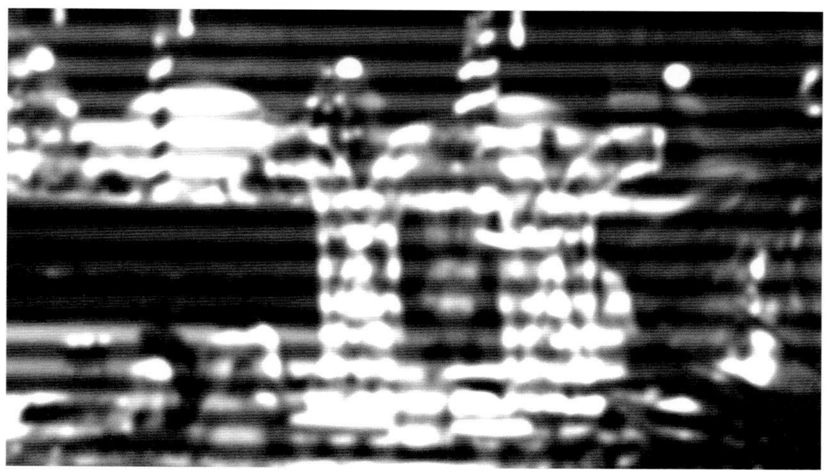

The Anatomy of Celebration, 2010

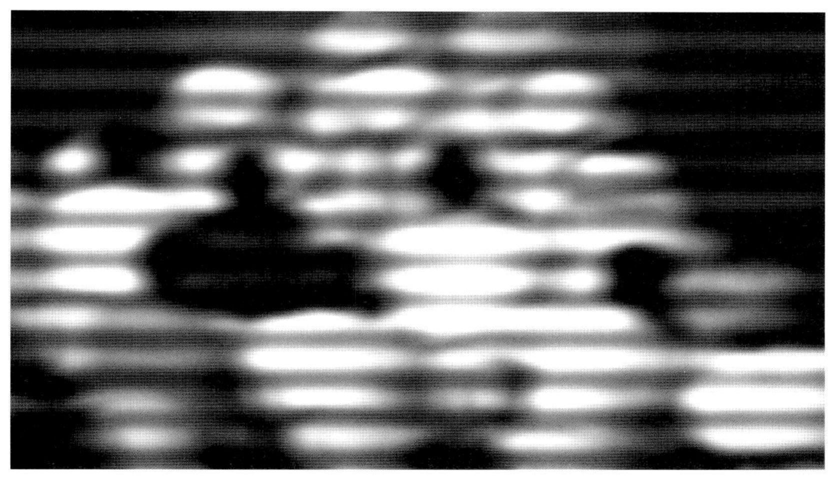

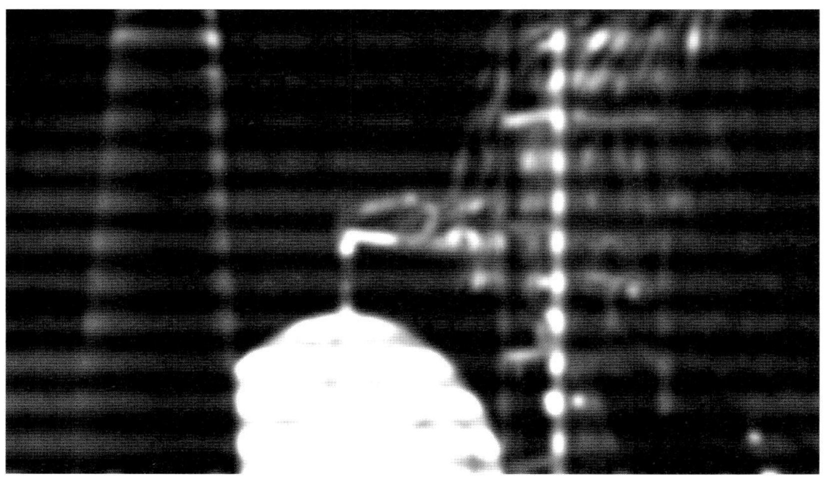

The Anatomy of Celebration, 2010

The attempt to process the material was deferred, till some of us were invited to a media workshop at the Uttarayan Art Centre, Baroda, in October 2008. Given the necessary time to examine the contents, the act of looking, as a starting point, involved isolating the frames that interested me and breaking down the footage into a series of stills. They were then recomposed digitally into a set of panoramic landscapes: the moving image is temporarily stilled, and again set in motion by virtue of a slower and more controlled process, at a painter's pace.

The struggle to understand is therefore the discipline, the method and the form; the stable factor that enables this struggle to be staged is the specific orientation peculiar to one or the other medium. Two very different kinds of sensibilities interact to create a third set of possibilities.

These photo-panoramas are in miniature format, to use a contradiction in terms; printed like running text in a notebook, impelling a closer scrutiny, a reading, an excavation that leads to strange discoveries. The original prints are ten feet long. As a variation, they were sized to fit into two pages set in a notebook format; hence *Notes and Investigations*, at the formal and conceptual level, by a natural and mutual convergence.

Other mutations subsequently emerged, and the temptation to retrieve, from a position of technical disadvantage and cultural displacement, the source – the moving image, and the impulse that created it. Some of the stills and bits of footage were organized into four groups, and four short videos were composed. The challenge of finding a form that could accommodate the discrepancies in a coherent manner was a collaborative process that involved working with a film-maker, Achint Jain.

We decided to keep as close to what was recorded as possible, to excavate the drama that is embedded in the seemingly non-dramatic. As an artist, one has come full circle in that one finds the 'real' more fantastic than anything that the imagination can conjure: that intriguing, recurring inversion here sets the stage for aesthetic discourse. It begins to seem like art could be far closer to truth, or shed light on it in a way that exposes the mirage that stands in for reality.

The central motif in the videos is the nuptial pandal/canopy, or variations of it. Earlier, the entertainment involved semi-cabarets that carried the celebrations to a pitch of hysteria, regardless of the presence of children: a breakdown of conventional morality, in the garb of a social institution designed, paradoxically, to propagate it.

Adrift in a world more fantastic than Disney could have ever envisioned, Donald Duck's meandering passage through the landscape, with a wraith-like Santa Claus trailing in his wake, is telling in more ways than one. These earlier, deceptively benevolent icons of so-called 'western culture' are now mere ghosts, pale in comparison to a layered carnival of cross-referential simulations and covert sexuality that they cannot participate in.

Frenzied male dancers near the pandal stuff currency notes into the mouth of the accompanying drummer in an anticipatory pre-nuptial climax – a grotesque, indeed inhuman parody of the earlier, perhaps equally questionable but marginally more gracious custom of showering the performing artist with gold coins as a mark of appreciation.

The white plastic chair, in multiplicities or as a singular motif, stands mute in more ways than one, a complicit witness to the proceedings.

The term 'micro-narrative' carries implications that extend beyond this particular body of work. Among other things, it is an appendix to the broader, more overt context of a project which I worked on for many years in post-2002 Ahmedabad.

The two however are closely related.

As a painter whose affinities lie with the fragility and power of the brush mark, the experiments and excavations that this body of work represents is one more reflection of the continuing location and interrogation within artistic practice, of media that answer other needs and occasions. The slow, painful imparting of bone, flesh and spirit that marks handcraft, the flash that captures the instant: they give rise to differing perceptions of time, and therefore belie a connective temporal and spatial matrix which is all-pervading, and omnipresent. The micro-narratives embedded within it, in terms of stories as well as the sequence and history of evolving methodologies that tell these stories, are deceptive in that they seem tinged with the tantalizing aura of transience and detachment, novelty and precedence. What is unique, however, is not the medium but the re-configuration that marks every deviation or inclusion – the path that one chooses in finding one's way through new spatial and temporal maps, with the continuing awareness of the distance and closeness between oneself and an ever-receding horizon.

The use of cosmetic devices such as Photoshop and aluminium composite board (which is used to clad the outer surfaces of buildings and is the true architect's nightmare) assumes a special significance, one of equivalence with the artifice that is being investigated.

One arrives at these choices through a process of research, creating thereby an ongoing commentary – there is an aesthetic investment, and also a discourse.

The reflective surface of aluminium echoes and re-creates the fascination that was the original and ruling impulse in creating this body of work. Photoshop dissolves and fuses random prose to create poetry in its place. As the old proverb goes, set a thief to catch a thief. By consuming, and allowing oneself to be consumed, one uncovers a certain lost agency, *feeling* – desire, longing, yearning, consummation and thereby a return to a place of origin through the swirling, bewildering eddies of collective, orgiastic ritual. Something has happened after all, within the heart of that bejewelled, carnivorous bloom set in an emerald field.

Could one argue therefore that at least one very clear, if not primary function begins to emerge for the artist in the present time?

July 2011

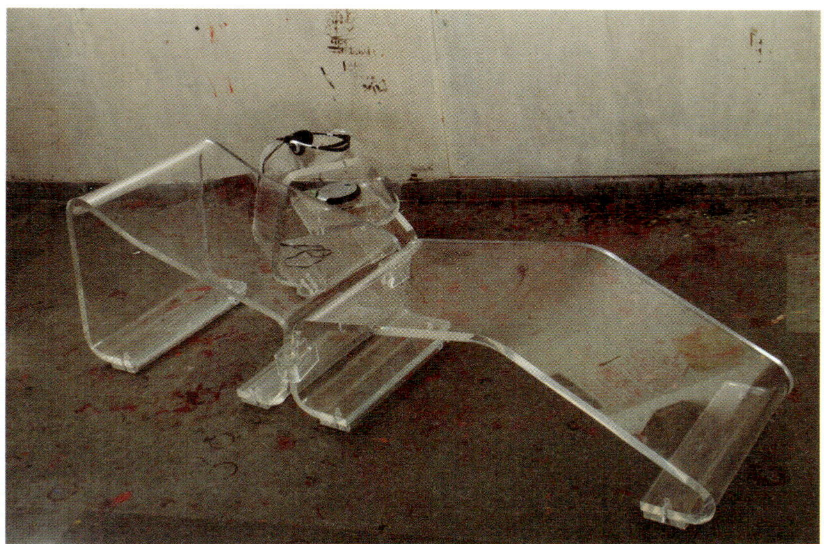

Listening Post is an installation of eight sets of listening and reading stations. The former were conceived in 2006 to support a set of voice recordings of the inner impulses of painting, living and related art forms – an oral psychobiography.

By the time they were fabricated and shown in 2007, they included vital aspects of the prevailing political climate – more specifically references to a public project, The Himmat Workshops, which developed organically post-2002 in Gujarat.

The stations are fabricated from clear sheet acrylic, so as to be almost invisible. Transparency is an important requirement both formally and conceptually, in terms of revealing (process) as opposed to the opacity of conclusion. With *Listening Post*, it becomes a physical reality, along with the play of light, reflection and refraction that it creates.

They were designed in close association with two architects, initially Sarosh Anklesaria and later Vishnu Thozhur Kolleri. The forms are derived from the pictograms and hieroglyphs that I often use in painting – between written script and painted image, caught/frozen in the process of working towards a recognizable logic. Painting as translated into text/into form/into sound, in a sort of trans-mediatic migration. The stations themselves serve as a medium that enables this fluidity, and are configured as a tableau, a set of four whose dimensions are dictated by ergonomic considerations. They support the body in four postures which dramatize and perform the stillness of listening without shattering it. Participants are therefore not just late or incidental entrants into the performative space, but are placed within the alphabets that comprise the work, in an integration that was conceived at its very inception.

The term 'listening post' is generally applicable to military surveillance systems that pick up electronically transmitted messages of imagined or potential 'others' if not enemies, based on key words that are identified as suspicious. In this instance however, it performs an opposite function in that it engenders an intimate sharing of unspoken and unspeakable (!) thoughts in a willing exchange of 'secrets', thereby rendering surveillance redundant.

In 2013, a set of nine books were made as part of the Himmat project 'documentation' for want of a better word – one was looking at documentation as a form of truth-telling as opposed to a set of empirical facts. Four reading stations were made to provide four kinds of spaces for reading the books. Between 2013 and 2015, they were installed at two venues as part of *Beyond Pain: An Afterlife*, a compilation of the work that emerged from a ten-year involvement with a rehabilitated community from Naroda Patiya.

In its current phase, and at the IGNCA, where *Listening Post* was installed in January 2019 as part of FICA's 'Critical Constellations', both sets of stations together underscore an inquiry that has since the year 2000 traversed or rather criss-crossed the space between self-reflection and sustained involvement with notions of community. Certain memorable intersections and conversations with students, who currently 'occupy' a significant part of my life, were included, based on prior association or an expression of interest on their part. It is also an alternative to 'curation' as it is normally understood, and an attempt to create a mutually engaged 'milieu' as the work travels in time and space, in a growing network of friendship and exchange.

It not only occupies but expands time – which otherwise tends to be reduced to a flat line of pure function, representing efficiency and professionalism no doubt, but entirely devoid of the joy of life.

As an artwork, it gathers different kinds of histories and continually morphs by virtue of the fluidity of its function.

As an eclectic sort of library, with artists' books, videos, prints, etc., the seating and reclining stations invite visitors to browse at leisure, and attempt to create conditions that facilitate spending extended time within the space. The notion of hospitality is central to these conditions: the stations are designed with a view to comfort, while at the same time providing an active role for the visitor – to engage at a sensorial and intellectual level, to become part of a larger tableau or installation which therefore remains in a constant state of flux. On the one hand, the flux is visible/physical and on the other, it translates into a morphing of identity as an installation or a library, an affective, interactive, performative or educational space depending on the prevailing conditions at any given point.

The tableau is designed according to the floor plan and other elements within a given space. The stations are angled in a manner conducive to a polylogue – and do not directly confront one another. On occasion, depending on feasibility, recording equipment has also been provided for responses and contributions.

Apart from interested viewers, it accommodates 'other' artworks and practitioners, and thereby raises the question of territory – which is at the heart of most disputes, eventually culminating in war. Is it possible at the individual level to accede rather than claim or retain territory, without experiencing a sense of loss? If not, is it even realistic to expect a world order that offers an alternative to the apocalyptic conditions that surround us?

(2002–)

INSTITUTIONALIZING PRACTICE AND PRACTISING THE INSTITUTION

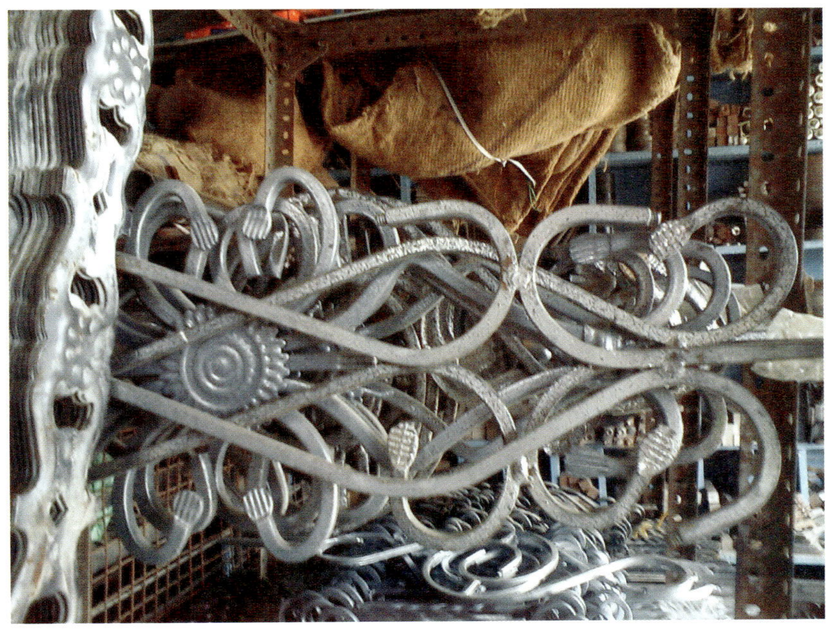

It has been my experience, through four decades of practice, that the need to push frontiers in art finds its counterweight in the turbidity and slowness of the materials that are handled. One works with the systems and people that make up the world – and fashioning or re-fashioning these into any given form involves a shift in the overall composition. It extends beyond the contemplative individual frame into the world within which this frame is located, while still retaining the capacity to communicate uncharted realms of the private – of emotion and experience that are left unsaid or considered inappropriate in the normal course of social interaction. Further, in addition to the pursuit of quality and excellence through the act of making, creative practice increasingly involves critique, resistance, retrieval and a hope that other realities or futures are possible; one could go so far as to call it a responsibility and an ethic.

Art education therefore faces challenges which go beyond classroom instruction. In response, it has passed through several phases, from stringent academicism to open-ended propositions, and at periodic junctures sought to repudiate what preceded it – to its detriment. It would be far more productive to see existing bodies of knowledge for what they are, to be selective in awareness of what there is to choose from without effacing the past and with it, a collective cultural memory.

Pedagogy alone cannot effect the desired result; perhaps, we need to look at the larger framework within which it functions. We are part of a strange federation of institutions, not all of them with the same goal in mind. Unlike the earlier guilds and gurukuls, institutions are mere moments in the flow of an artist's life. They provide temporary support and for a period of time, a sharper definition of one's role and where one plays it. In their current form, do they represent an uneasy conflation of irreconcilable ways of being? And to what extent do they remain mired in bureaucracy, that behemoth which resists change?

Artists increasingly see themselves as active agents of social and cultural change as opposed to an earlier state of servitude to royalty or organized religion. Whether with this in mind or with the notion of a unique creative authorship, we teach or guide students to evolve through a series of difficult decisions that are driven by artistic integrity as a primary value, but this is put to test in the extended network where other forces, including global and political economy play no mean part. Indeed, the all-encompassing force of the latter is astounding. One has participated in its formation. Curricula are as much shaped by it as by internal debates. To have a life outside of it would be almost impossible; it is imperative to recognize its omnipresence and our own involuntary participation in order to reiterate or negate aspects of it.

If we were instead, to think in terms of a sustainable ecology for the arts, what are the means at our students' disposal? Do they provide sufficient opportunity for exploring a range of practices that would actually find their logical ground for dissemination? Livelihood outside of a fickle market continues to remain a question despite the fact that there are many more private foundations, experimental initiatives and grant-awarding bodies than before. In any case, the market, in isolation, is incapable of supporting the increasing numbers of students who pass through art institutions. More important, its tenets are inappropriate to some practices – and those need to find ways to fulfill their potential.

Unless these opportunities occur in sufficient and in various numbers, what are we preparing our students for? The element of risk and uncertainty that exists in creative fields is no doubt invaluable because it tests and strengthens conviction, but should it be so acute as to deter all but the most tenacious? If tenacity is valued to the exclusion of more fragile forms of creative sensibility – would that not be a lamentable loss?

In our case, the problem is compounded by a homogenous system of art education that has been conceived under circumstances very different from our ground realities. Is it at all possible to truly absorb students from varied sociocultural backgrounds into this system? We provide them with a common ground, but in the metropolis, with its own established patterns of exclusion. The problem is not merely one of language as a medium of instruction. If language could be seen as a carrier of culture, verbal or even visual tutelage, while performing a limited function, would only address the tip of the iceberg. Indeed, it contributes to a questionable naturalization of the outsider within a foreign system. If the student chooses to return to the village or town, would she or he at all be able to continue to practise? Apart from a few artists, like Santosh Kumar Das who successfully established the Mithila Art Institute in his native Madhubani – I have known students, present and past, who resort to self-destructive modes of reconciliation, or rather its impossibility. Could a creative individual respond to the needs of the immediate environment, away from a place of centralized approval and governance, and still feel a sense of accomplishment?

In this context, the fact of being located, as an art school, within a landscape and among communities, is rich with possibilities. There are opportunities for building networks through investigations, collaborations and friendships, providing a kind of neutral ground for students to work from, one which looks beneath the surface. Apart from exposing the unevenness and contradictions that surround us, this could create practices and opportunities to permeate through the limits of a hermetically sealed, self-reflexive and, therefore, fragile art world. It further calls for a genuinely engaged participation as opposed to a passive audience.

The shift from a discipline-based to a composite practice has caused a fair degree of confusion, and additional complexities in the history of fluctuating hierarchies within pedagogy. It might be more constructive to acknowledge that each medium or discipline has its own inherent and unique potential, exerting its agency in different ways, in response to where it is situated in time, and what we require it to do for us as a society. This does not preclude or exclude its relationship with other disciplines. There are different paths in space and time to reach the point where something is better said through another medium, paths which allow us to measure distances and speed in ways that clarify our own position while still making visible the spaces between the doors of perception. They however demand a clear understanding of places of transit, of other destinations, other paths, and the wild winds that blow through these passages. Could we understand inter-disciplinarity along these lines? It is as much to do with recognizing and re-absorbing aspects of one's own discipline from other areas of specialization as it is to do with borrowing from them, further it is opposed to relinquishing the existing knowledge base in an attempt to locate the cutting-edge. Could this represent a form of diversification or democratization that does not occur at the expense of quality or complexity, but creates instead a growing repository that continues to nourish new forms? The critical rigour that has enabled us to deconstruct given norms in society and in the arts helps us to discard forms that have long since lost content. It would be a mistake, however to lose the possibilities of the non-rational, of play, pattern and continuity evident in craft, or the palpable transcendence from the mundane that is embodied in the living bhakti and sufi traditions in music, poetry and dance that surround us.

To return to the question of medium, drawing, an early form of representation and in fact of writing, was in the past largely associated with the mechanical and industrial arts, and has been central to much debate. In Europe, it was centuries before it graduated from the category of the 'illiberal' or 'sordid' to the liberal arts. In the sub-continent, it was introduced into the art and design curriculum in the nineteenth century to develop critical faculties as opposed to an adherence to the rigid guidelines and oral tutelage prevalent in the *karkhanas*; to the British, the traditional systems perpetuated mindless repetition of pattern rather than original design. While it was associated with literacy in terms of the artisanal communities, it was looked down upon within the rest of society as a function of the lower-caste occupations, or, in schools, fit only for female education. After a brief period of enhanced status during the early part of the twentieth century or perhaps because of it, painting, drawing and sculpture were again seen as hegemonies that were spawned by the modernist era, part of the aura surrounding the transcendent artist – and therefore dispensable to the present-day counterpart. These attitudes find their echoes in art schools around the world. We are back again where we started.

Could we instead, make an attempt to compile the different forms and applications that have come into being over time? Drawing supports most forms of research and finds extensive application outside of 'Fine Art', in the disciplines of architecture, cartography, topography, engineering, botany and the digital media (including 3-D printing) – the list is endless. Further, there are forms of drawing within earlier art and craft traditions which would together constitute a valuable resource. If these methods were studied within fine art curricula, students would gain perceptions to do with space, scale and dimension as seen or sometimes not seen – from varying cultural and disciplinary perspectives. Considering that art practice extends into these areas, as installation, land art and so on, this is invaluable knowledge.

It is also true that the impulse to compile and hand down to posterity notwithstanding, art has long since crossed over into the area of active praxis. This brings us to the subject of critical citizenship, as a framework which is currently much discussed in the arts. It represents a way forward and a new function in a transparent world which leaves little room for romanticism. But this again need not preclude discipline, medium or language to the extent that art becomes a form of tokenism or an apology for its inability to address the 'real' world. In my research for teaching material, I came across the work of the experimental architect Lebbeus Woods. Though mostly in the form of drawings, the majority of his plans and designs concern the cultural regeneration of society, through confronting urban landscapes and social and political conditions presently undergoing radical transformations due to war or disasters.

'Subversion' is a word that we as artists and students often use, without realizing its weight. It has criminal connotations in relationship to the state or nation; art, on the other hand, is something we cannot do without. Commercial applications in terms of design and political applications in terms of propaganda cannot come into being without institutionalizing art as an area of study and as producer of cultural and symbolic capital. Therefore, a grudging allocation of legitimacy allows it to function within the state, but crossing the line in terms of overt disobedience produces repercussions, cuts in funding, suspension of offending elements and a stifling of agency. With privatization, one is led to imagine that there might be more enlightened forces at work, but when the stakes are dependent on immediate material gain above other considerations, a similar pattern follows. In any case, true freedom of knowledge or practice finds little support, going against the grain of the norm in every sense of the word. The elaborate mechanisms of administration that we put in place to guard our democracies and our resources work or turn against us. We fail to recognize this as the beginnings of that fundamental conflict of interests, which in extreme situations could result in direct confrontation, torture and death. The bribe, sometimes posing as the market, is the buffer between the two.

In recent recorded global histories of two world wars, we lost some of our greatest thinkers, artists and intellectuals; the Armenian Genocide and the Holocaust figure prominently in this context. More recently, in 2011, we have instances of gruesomely articulated political murders in the Arab world.

Ali Ferzat, the cartoonist and graphic artist, was attacked and his hands were broken in retaliation for criticizing the Assad regime in Syria. The protest songwriter, Ibrahim Qashosush, was tortured and murdered and his vocal chords were ripped out in a symbolic silencing of the people's voice. Juliano Mer Khamis, who ran the Freedom Theatre in Jenin refugee camp in occupied Palestine, was assassinated. In our own country, Safdar Hashmi was killed while performing a street play at Sahibabad; Husain spent his last years in exile in the Middle East against a backdrop of increasing communalization in everyday life.

We recognize this as our history, as much as linguistic changes that have evolved along with the work of specific artists. It would be premature to expect students, at the initial stages of their study, to fully grasp the implications of the above, or to connect what seems like perfectly peaceful labour to the extremes of violence that are used to extinguish it. It is also possible that subversion is not something which can be taught; it represents freedom that is attained at a cost. It pre-supposes an understanding of forms of language, their usage and a knowledge of the limits of their legitimacy in organized society. Could the pursuit or imparting of language – and a commitment to its logic actually pre-empt incoherence, miscomprehension and the resulting violence? Language is couched in different forms of praxis – each with its own dynamics of intelligibility, and a grammar that is engendered along with its communicative power, emerging as it is practised in dialogue with those that it addresses. Is this possible? Could one see skill as an embodiment of this process as opposed to an order imposed from above? Could technique, a word that has increasingly acquired negative connotations, be seen as a valuable set of tools and solutions to problems of articulation, as opposed to a cosmetic option or a standardized notion of perfection? In that case, could we re-incorporate them into our curriculum?

Between the condition of being enabled by a set of skills and the outcome of their use, lies the space of community. The grammar of the transformative act involves a series of interactions and exchanges which are embedded in community, one could even go so far as to say that it constitutes community. The proposition of society as a sustainable set of relationships resides in the same space; what we are addressing is a breakdown of the grammar that would allow it to exercise its communicative power. Far from reaching the outer limits of its relevance, pedagogy in the arts today could function in a state of enhanced awareness, challenge and greater responsibility.

(For a seminar organized by Ambedkar University, L' Ecole des Beaux Arts, Tours, Alliance Francaise and FICA, New Delhi, 2013)

THE POLITICS OF URBAN SPACE

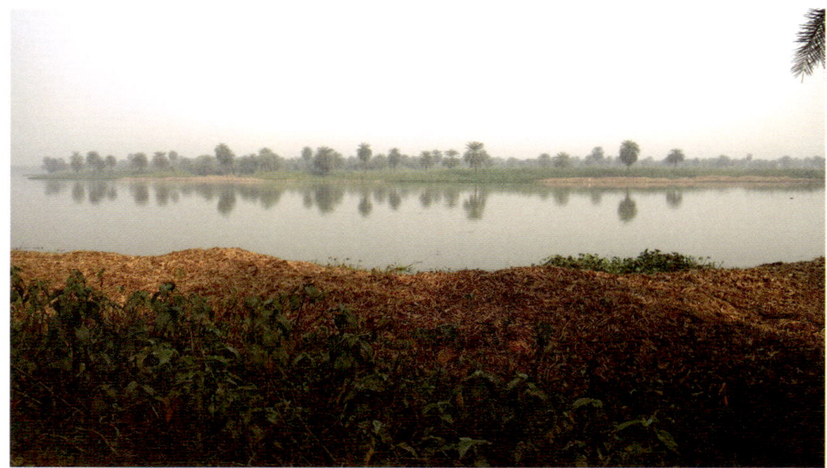

At the risk of reiterating what we already know, I would like to begin with a brief preamble which I hope will address some of the questions that were sent to me.

Our university is situated in an area earlier known as the Doab, between the Ganga and Yamuna rivers. Apart from being fertile agricultural land, it is associated with several mythic and factual histories of turbulence and change. A significant part of it lies along the Grand Trunk Road, which plays a major role in the dynamic nature of its communities and its spaces. Much of the land and the fields around us, however, have been levelled and cleared to make way for malls, golf courses, multi-storey residential complexes and so on – we are therefore in a position to actually witness the rapid erasure of villages, small towns and settlements to make way for the dream of a New India.

In official terms, it is now 'an Industrial Area located at the intersection of the Western and Eastern Dedicated Freight Corridors which is also the

Surajpur Bird Sanctuary

gateway to the Delhi-Mumbai Industrial Corridor (DMIC). It lies within the National Capital Region of New Delhi and is adjacent to Noida, one of the largest industrial townships in Asia'.

Those of us who have recently moved into this area are initially disoriented, as there is no marker of memory or history, no visible temporal dimension. What is apparent, on the other hand, is the regulation of life by a system that is close to militaristic – armed security men who tell you what is allowed or forbidden, barricades, fences, walls where earlier there was free passage.

The colonizer is now embedded deep within our own aspirations. The danger of seeing the enemy as an external agency of 'western' origin is that it stifles self-examination. Business interests, industry, the state in its secession of responsibility to private corporations – have taken over the role, undetected because they seem to represent us. The immunity granted by laws created and legitimized by earlier imperialist powers are still written in stone, and complete the transformation. We see this phenomenon unfold before our eyes – rural, pastoral and other cultures, each with their distinct lifestyle and dialect, moving towards the teeth of the new horizon. The familiar pattern begins with coercive acquisition of ancestral land and loss of the cultural underpinning which enables people to retain their sanity in the face of change. The eventual depletion of compensation money, the resort to firearms and violence on the pretext of communal, ethnic and other issues, are therefore inevitable. Local dons in collusion with the state and other colonizing agencies then begin to wield power for their own personal gain. The religious imagination begins to assume monstrous proportions – as a reaction to the conflict between an inherent incapacity for rapid change, and a greed for short-term gain along with a 'global' lifestyle which is ruthlessly promoted and advertised by the media through monumental hoardings and events, carefully constructed to resemble one's wildest dreams. Its value as propaganda is phenomenal in terms of the mass conversion that it effects – and it is ironic that the power of the image is established through these problematic affirmations.

One begins to have a fair idea of how cities in India have grown, and consequently, how displacement has led to the re-constitution of ethnic or religious groups as objectified entities, devoid of geographical or cultural context and logic. The space of the city is that of a damaged psyche, seething with multitudinous discontents, the broken threads of which weave the fabric of our everyday lives. It requires mutual understanding, caution and compassion to communicate across these wounds. It is also necessary to be continuously alert to the possibility of conflict being created or used as a smokescreen to obscure the relentless siphoning of our resources, and the destruction of our natural environment by those in power at any given point in time, regardless of political affiliations.

In the broadest of terms, this would be the underlying context to the politics of urban spaces in India.

With reference to my fieldwork during and post-2002, we are again looking at a community which is migrant, a religious minority, and poor – factors which send flashing green signals to potential expansionists. We are talking of Naroda Patiya village in Ahmedabad, the site of one of the worst mass murders during the carnage in Gujarat. In Naroda, the population is predominantly Muslim, consisting of labourers from Karnataka and Maharashtra. Around 200 of them were massacred on the 28th of February 2002, by a mob of almost 5,000. In the following year, the Vibrant Gujarat summit proposes '24 projects worth more than a 1,000 crore' to be developed in this part of the city and along the Ahmedabad–Vadodara Expressway. Projects include 'hospitals, clubs, educational institutions, NRI residential colonies, a business park and a 120-room hotel'.

What we had, to begin with, however, was ground zero – the destruction of homes, the extermination of lives and a community that was in no position to speak for itself. Therefore there were protest marches, rallies and demonstrations by concerned groups, who often approached artists for posters that could be used for these events.

Despite varying degrees of emphases, all art is public, in the broadest sense, and subjectivity is the prism that throws light on a world view which is in continuous formation. The studio embodies this position. It is at the threshold to a world whose dimensions are informed by the senses, through which we perceive and interact with what is outside of us. An active use of the streams of language that radiate from this space give rise to different modes of engagement, in quality and quantity, and is a more complex way of envisioning the continuities of our shared space. Within the limitations of each aspect of this space, there is room for an active inter-subjectivity in relationship to those whom we work with or address. There are qualitative differences, but space is always public if we are conscious of the communicative potential of our work.

For example, in pedagogy, through one of the courses that I teach, an attempt is made to study local histories and ecologies, and to re-situate them within an expanded framework which allows subjective interpretations and interventions.

One is also looking at an active public engagement entering the area of visual representation, not necessarily in direct ways, but as assimilated, living vocabularies and forms of language that are consistently and visibly active, not only in rhetoric but also in silence.

A few metres away from our department is a cluster of date palms which are around 3 to 400 years old. In and around the grove are an old well, a small shrine and a dargah. From studies undertaken by our Department of Environmental Sciences, it has been established that armies and travellers along this route, from as far away as Afghanistan or as close as Delhi, stopped by for the abundant water and game available in the area. The

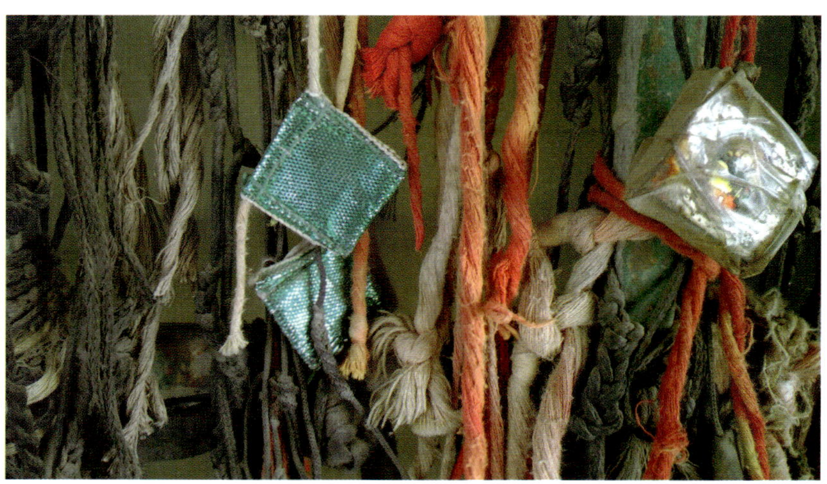

Dargah of Pir Baba Kamaal Shah, Shiv Nadar University Campus

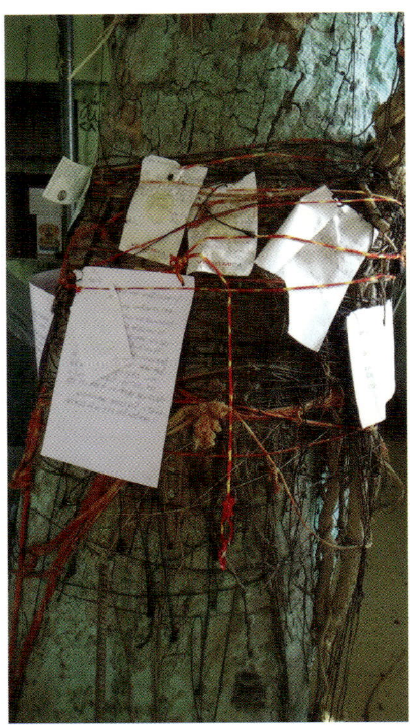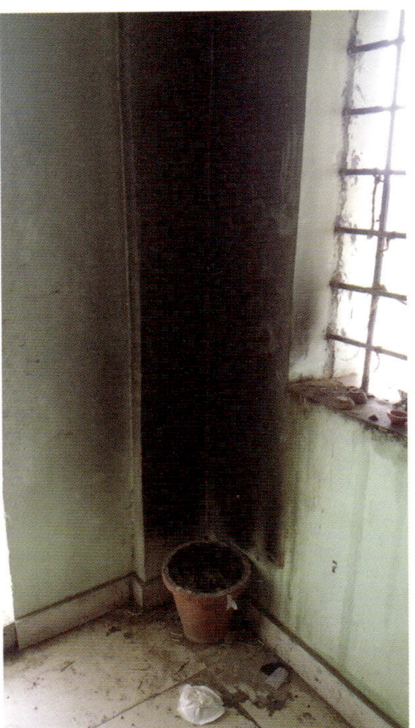

dates that they carried with them created several such clusters of which this is the largest in the vicinity.

There had been plans to clear the area for more construction, but these had been abandoned due to certain mishaps that accompanied the attempt. Interestingly, it turns out that this is a sacred grove, and though it falls within the legal boundaries of the university, it has been mapped and secured – in a different way altogether by the local community. Apart from the two shrines, there is, in keeping with the typology of such spaces, a mythical snake, an *ichchadhari nag*, and a female deity, a *shakti*, who protects it.

Given that sciences such as archaeology, cartography and anthropology gained currency during colonial expansion, and were heavily invested in

Dargah of Pir Baba Kamaal Shah, Shiv Nadar University Campus creating territories and studying communities for reasons other than artistic or academic interest – we are discussing, among other things, counter-mapping, protest and participatory mapping which actually work against erasures.

Ideally, each context is a unique mould which, in interventions of any kind, casts methods and outcomes in a manner specific to its construction. As earlier mentioned, the rapid changes brought about by indiscriminate industrialization exacerbate conflicting ideological positions to the extent of creating an ecology which supports and actively encourages violent confrontation. Generic responses objectify dissent to the extent of participating in the prevailing schizophrenia. We need to take into account specificities, which are various and complex. They challenge our capacities in ways which would intimately impact what we perceive or confront, on the ground, surrounded by the struggles of everyday life and everyday people, brought closer through seeing, feeling, listening and working together.

(Seminar paper for 'Politics of Space and the City', organized by FICA and Noopur Desai, at Max Mueller Bhavan, New Delhi, 2016)

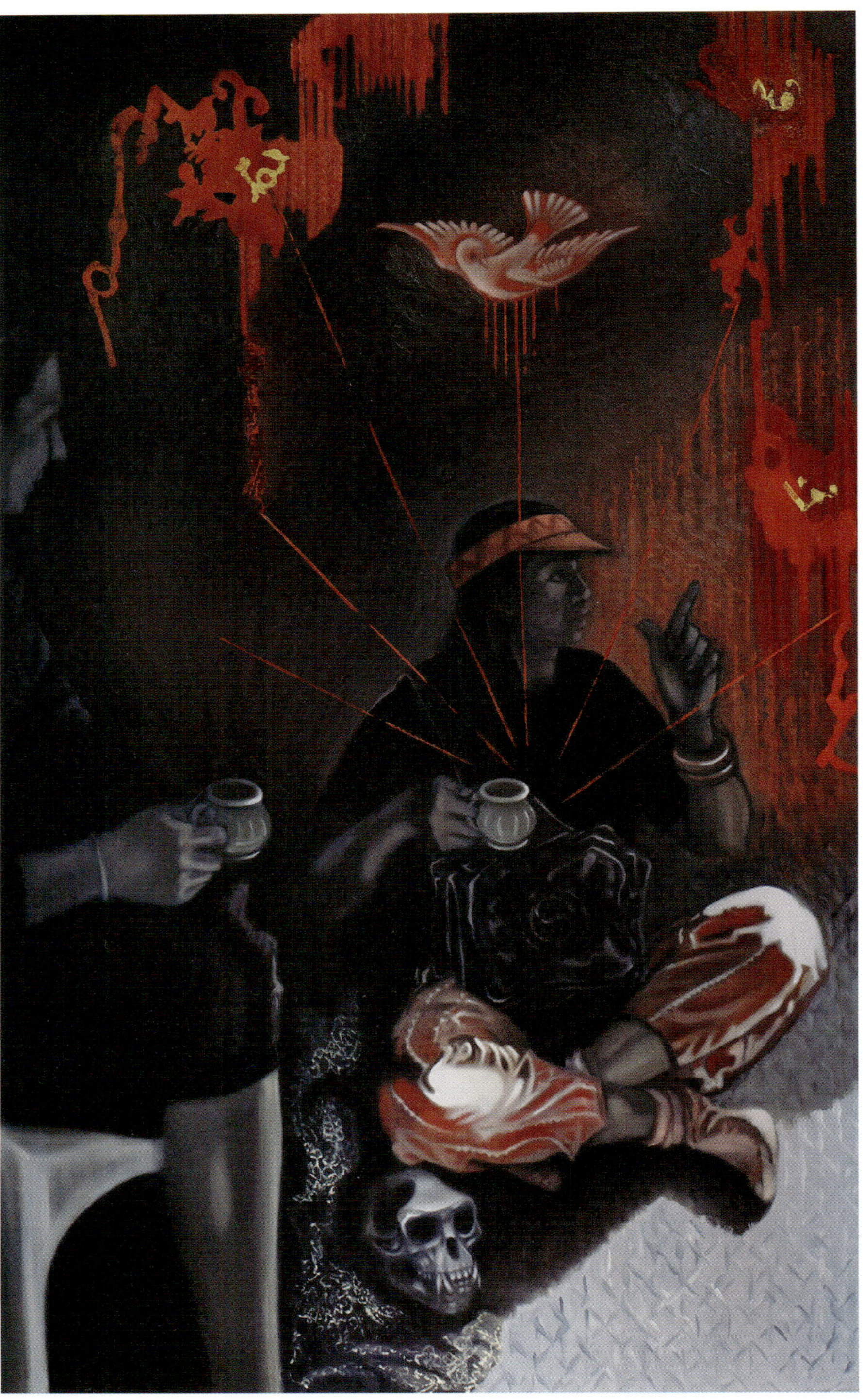

RETROSPECTIVE

What does it mean to show this body of work periodically over several years? It seems to have a continuing relevance in the light of a pervasive sense of implosion. The immediate context (*Beyond Pain: An Afterlife*) is obvious. Apart from that, it is understood to be an 'activist' intervention, which is perhaps one, though limited way of describing it. In actuality, the frame is an infinitely expanding one.

When I present the project in a sequential manner, it appears seamless, whereas in reality every step forward was fraught with challenges and delays. Sometimes I introduce it as a community project, and am guilty of a convenient over-simplification. Perhaps I should take the time to explain that 'community' here is not specific, it is a concept that transcends the notion of grouping people on the basis of commonalities – of geography, ethnicity, religion, profession and so on. Rather, it is based on relationships, both close and distant which seek a deeper understanding and empathy in shared journeys through time, and in the struggle to forge a language which facilitates communication and the possibility of co-existence.

The project itself needs to be seen in sequence, or as a facet of a more complex quest for language, as an ethic and a way of life. Language in this context is seen as a transparent medium which exposes rather than hides; it pre-supposes the fact that truth mutates, thereby escaping definition and sometimes detection. Truth-telling is not a narrative of an absolute and unquestionable state, it is about revealing or unmasking: creating several filters and registers through which to deconstruct and thereby optimize visibility.

Secret Life is a body of work which was made at a time when the aura around creative authorship gave way to a more democratic, sociopolitical premise for art-making. While one was in alignment with this shift, it seemed necessary to link the two – or risk having content degenerate into abstract yet over-defined exercises on issues that exist in isolation of lived experience – thereby attaining a rigidity of meaning and articulation which is at odds with what the shift proposed to achieve.

Beyond Pain (detail), 2012–13

This and the subsequent body of work, *Untouchable*, underline this link
and the self-portrait is metaphoric of this emphasis. Perhaps the mode
of narration could be loosely associated with what is commonly termed
'confessional' – it describes an inner journey which begins at a point closest
to the heart. *Secret Life* revolves around an imaginary home which is central
to the drama that is played out. *Untouchable* ventures from this space towards
certain generic narratives of power, marginalization and othering by touching
upon specific events which bring these narratives into sharper focus, while
still remaining rooted in painting as a chosen medium for living and working.

The multiple panels however are a way of de-constructing the 'absoluteness'
of an artwork – and of authorship – in order to regain an objective distance,
and to create spaces which allow free interpretation and conversations
which touch upon areas of common concern, within and without the chosen
medium or language. They also allow for inclusions of various kinds, binaries
and polarities which would not fit within a single frame. Juxtaposed, they
attain optimum resonance, as in colour complementarities which attain
maximum saturation only in close relationship, without which neither
survives. An aesthetic can emerge that is as much shaped by political belief
as by formal considerations or personal inclination, as a grammar that could
unify thought and action at the individual level with a societal ethic.

But what are all these discourses amounting to? Do they play an active role
in reaching beyond the polemical, in addressing escalating and widespread
violence? In an economic climate dominated by profiteering of different
kinds, along with the secrecy and surveillance which protects it, creative
research, including art practice – that works against the speed and efficiency
of the ensuing devastation is seen to have no real value – worse, it is
condemned as a deterrent – and is relegated to the realm of entertainment
to render it toothless. As is the devastation, presented in the manner of a
performance, within the same category. Escape from such categorization
into reality is a state fraught with danger.

Therefore, the project was undertaken in an hour of mutual need as a way
out in a situation which offered few or no options. The time for discourse
or entertainment was past, because the space for conversation no longer
existed. It had to be re-created at ground zero, a place that articulated
this absence with a clarity that threw light on the architecture required to

reconstruct such a space. The foundation had been laid, and a collective set up by Monica Wahi, Zaid Ahmed Sheikh and a group of women and children, who had survived the massacre at Naroda Patiya. They had established a small sewing unit at Vatva, Ahmedabad, where they now lived. I worked with six girls between ages 12 and 17 – we started work on the terrace, in January 2005. As four of the six girls were illiterate, visual expression was far easier to work with, and its scope phenomenal, as we discovered.

By April, we had put up a bamboo shelter – the much debated 'studio' is re-built, and it remained to be seen if it could generate systems of communication which otherwise might not be possible, and in doing so play a vital role in supporting the community as it struggled to regain some semblance of normal life – including education and recreation for the children. How it came about is a long story, as every module of the workshops turned out to be – with random elements and exceptional people coming together at opportune moments. Riyaz Tyebji and Sarosh Anklesaria are two very good architect friends, Binu from the Gandhi Ashram in Verchi was an expert with bamboo construction, the landlord who owned the building needed to be convinced that a covered terrace would enhance the value of his property.

Of course, it was more than merely creating a space for conversations – time was costly, and there were urgent considerations of economic support and the need for basic living infrastructure. As a cultural centre, and in the activities that it engendered, it became pivotal to facilitating other initiatives, and the possibility of a symbiotic relationship between language/culture and socio-economic health, art and community, became increasingly obvious.

So, post the project, through extended periods of trying to work with existing systems, what one had earlier trusted as logical, however disparate or various, began to seem increasingly dystopic, and perfect material for investigation, which in turn led to the realization of any given reality as a collaborative work of art with imagination at its core. Art as a primary calling began to seem less whimsical and more centrally located than I had ever believed.

The next body of work, entitled *The Anatomy of Celebration* was an investigative process which revolved around this realization. It involved de-coding the visual to arrive at an understanding of the circumstances

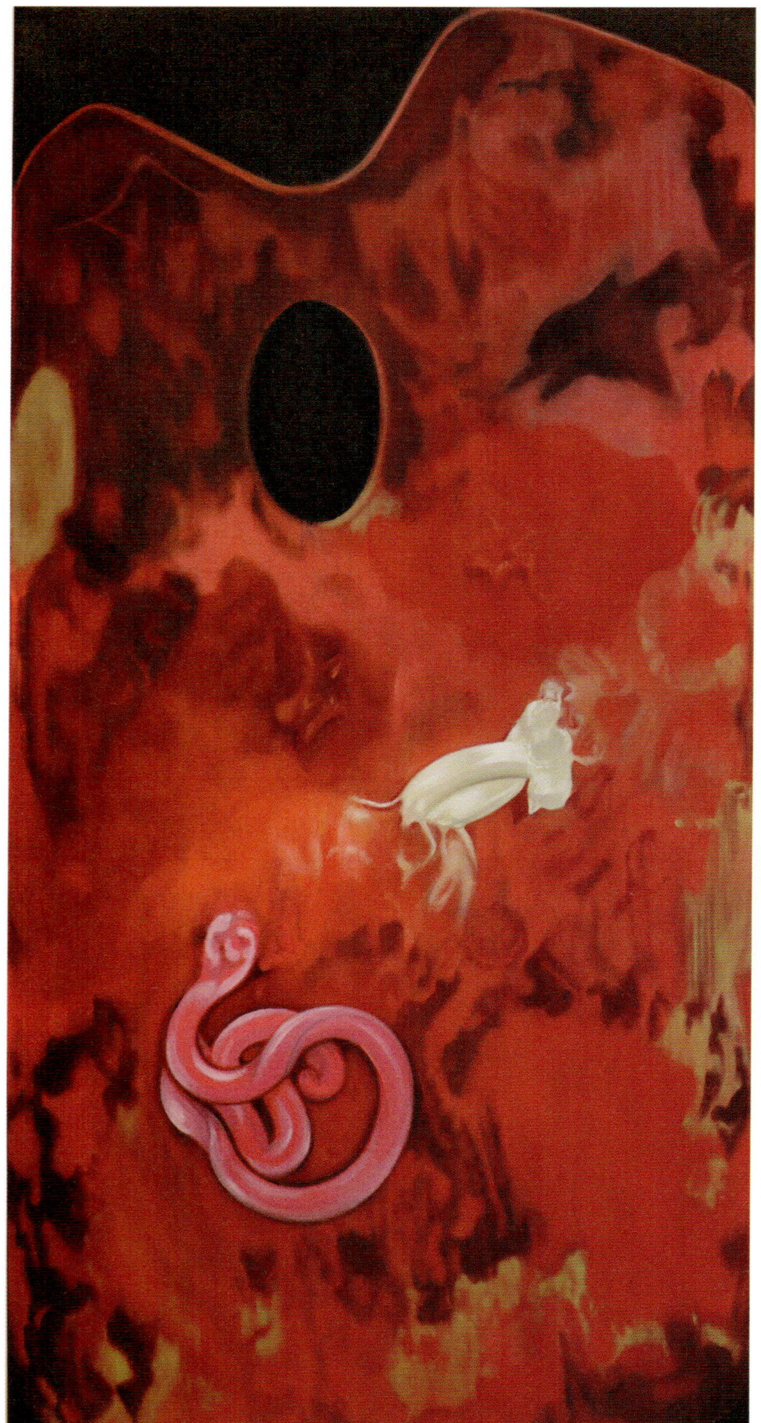

and motives which created it, what seems innocuous on the surface begins
to give rise to increasing disquiet. Well-being in its infinite sense finds a
substitute in mass enactments laced with entertainment, in a prescribed
form to be adhered to at all costs, including the possibility of a real or
sustainable sense of community. The perpetuation and elaboration of
this form, no matter how destructive, becomes a matter of continuous
engagement dissociated from the original impulse. Virtuality and reality
become interchangeable commodities, life becomes inconsequential in
a frenzy of transactions that produce dangerously seductive images as
opposed to living, functioning formations.

Sometimes, I feel that I paint in order to preserve the shrinking space
and time required to actually think, to pull the brakes on the kind of
speed which morphs into violence. Aggressive confrontation occurs at an
irretrievable point beyond real solutions, and signals neglect at the root. Its
strategies are of short duration, with limited scope: it is pointless to locate
one's work entirely on that edge, as there is nothing beyond but apocalypse,
the seeds of which are embedded in everyday interactions and concerns,
including education – and its potential as a major factor in steering the
course of future events.

As much as art practice responds to the need of the hour, with a
corresponding effect on its outward manifestations, its core is built upon
the grammar which our convictions and beliefs lend to it. It is consistently
active and adaptive at the same time; and its importance within the
educational system is enormous. The dangers of conflating it with business
or political interests cannot be undermined, and this is a further challenge
that we face as a community: to set up a network of informal and flexible
systems which by their amorphous nature resist being subsumed by either.

Every movement in art practice finds its echo in the public life of the image,
but it is something that we pay scant heed to. The 'popular' is of course
the most obvious example, and its origins the most difficult to trace – is it
the myth, or visualizations of the myth by artists and film-makers through
the years, which produce current versions of the Rath Yatra as the triumph
of right over evil? The artistic possibilities of state-of-the-art technology,
used to project holograms of demagogues in several cities all at once are
precisely those which we contain within the walls of museums – while

seeking to release their scope into the public domain, we are still hampered by an unwitting adherence to the language of the enclosed space. Have we seceded our communicative skills to those who use it with devastating effect, while we are left with abstractions that speak to no one?

So, we have a world which is in a continuous state of war. The distances that separate us from areas of active conflict are shrinking, and are permeated with still and moving images which flow unimpeded across blurring lines and grey zones like phantoms which haunt our emotional and intellectual space.

It comes as a shock to realize that even within the parameters of our professional lives, they dominate our visual memory to the extent of obliterating those canonical artworks which earlier filled us with hope.

(On the occasion of staging **Beyond Pain: An Afterlife** *at the School of Arts and Aesthetics, JNU, 2015)*

p. 172
Sanctum (detail), 2006,
207.3 cm (approx. ht),
oil on canvas

p. 176
At the Kanoria Centre for
Arts, Ahmedabad, 2005

p. 178
Tasleem (above), Rehana
and Shahjehan (below),
at the Himmat Centre,
Mayur Park, Vatva

p. 182
Ahmedabad Hamara, by
Shahjehan Sheikh, 2006,
72.7 x 48 cm,
silk-screen print

p. 183
(Above) Faizal Park
during the floods, 2005,
artist not known,
56.5 x 39 cm,
pen and ink drawing
(Below) Faizal Park
during the floods,
2005, by Shahjehan
Sheikh, 56.5 x 39 cm,
pen and ink drawing

p. 188
Mounting the exhibit at
the Hutheesing Visual Art
Centre, CEPT, Ahmedabad,
2007

p. 189
Display at *Moving People*,
World Social Forum,
Nairobi, Kenya

p. 192
Beyond Pain (detail),
2012–13, 243.8 cm (ht),
oil on canvas

p. 198
Portrait of Shahjehan
(detail), 2008–12,
243.8 cm (ht),
oil on canvas

p. 200
Landscape II, 2008,
243.8 x 243.8 cm,
oil on canvas

p. 202
*The Anatomy of
Celebration*, 2010,
99 x 122 cm,
inkjet print on aluminium
composite board

p. 204
*The Anatomy of
Celebration*, 2010,
50.8 x 87.6 cm, inkjet
print on aluminium
composite board

p. 205
*The Anatomy of
Celebration*, 2010,
50.8 x 87.6 cm,
inkjet print on aluminium
composite board

p. 209
Listening Post, 2007,
48.3 cm (approx.
maximum ht),
sheet acrylic

p. 213
Wrought iron in Dadri,
2014

p. 220
Surajpur Bird Sanctuary,
Greater Noida, Uttar
Pradesh

p. 223
Dargah of Pir Baba
Kamaal Shah, Shiv Nadar
University Campus,
Greater Noida, Uttar
Pradesh

p. 224
Dargah of Pir Baba
Kamaal Shah, Shiv Nadar
University Campus,
Greater Noida, Uttar
Pradesh

p. 226
Beyond Pain (detail),
2012–13,
243.8 cm (ht),
oil on canvas

p. 230
Still Life (detail),
2010–12,
243.8 cm (ht),
oil on canvas

Vasudha Thozhur would like to thank:
Geeta Kapur, Vivan Sundaram, Suhani Arora Sen,
Sher-Gil Sundaram Arts Foundation, Tulika Books,
and Azra Khan, Lalita (Designers), Vadodara.

First published in India in 2021 by
SSAF–Tulika Books

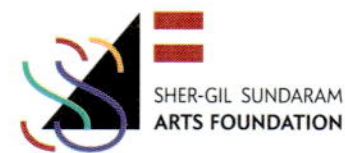

Sher-Gil Sundaram Arts Foundation (SSAF)
3/9 (first floor), Shanti Niketan, New Delhi 110 021, India | ssaf.in

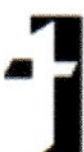

Tulika Books
44 (first floor), Shahpur Jat, New Delhi 110 049, India | tulikabooks.in

© Vasudha Thozhur 2021
ISBN: 978-81-945348-3-9

Design: Suhani Arora Sen
Printed at Lustra Print Process Pvt. Ltd., New Delhi